The Routledge Course in Modern Mandarin Chinese is a two-yea[r] students with no prior background in Chinese study. Designed t[o build a strong] in both the spoken and written language it develops all the basic skills such as pronunciation, character writing, word use, and structures, while placing strong emphasis on the development of communication skills.

The complete course consists of Textbook Level 1, Workbook Level 1—including free CDs, and Textbook Level 2 and Workbook Level 2—including free CDs. All books are available separately in simplified as well as traditional characters and take the students from complete beginner to post-intermediate level.

Workbook Level 2 is designed to accompany *Textbook Level 2* lesson by lesson, and offers exercises for homework, independent study, and classroom use. Each lesson focuses on the skills of listening and speaking, as well as reading and writing.

The course is also fully supported by an interactive companion website which contains a wealth of additional resources for both teachers and students.

- Teachers will find lesson plans in both English and Mandarin, providing a weekly schedule and overall syllabus for fall and spring, as well as activities for each lesson, and answer keys for all workbook exercises.
- Students will be able to access downloadable character practice worksheets, along with interactive vocabulary and character practice exercises. All the audio material necessary for the course is also available online and conveniently linked on screen to the relevant exercises for ease of use.

For more information about the course and to access these additional resources, please visit the companion website at http://www.routledge.com/textbooks/9780415472500.

Claudia Ross is Professor of Chinese at the College of the Holy Cross, Massachusetts. She has served as President of the Chinese Language Teachers Association and as Director of the CET Chinese Program in Beijing. Her publications include *Chinese Demystified* (2010); *The Lady in the Painting, Expanded Edition* (2008); *Modern Mandarin Chinese Grammar: A Practical Guide*, co-authored with Jing-heng Sheng Ma; *Modern Mandarin Chinese Grammar Workbook*, co-authored with Jing-heng Sheng Ma and Baozhang He (both Routledge, 2006); *Outline of Chinese Grammar* (2004); and *Traditional Chinese Tales: A Course in Intermediate Chinese* (2001).

Baozhang He is Associate Professor of Chinese at the College of the Holy Cross, Massachusetts. He has served as Director of the Chinese Language Program at Harvard University and as Head Instructor in the "Princeton in Beijing" language program. His publications include *Modern Mandarin Chinese Grammar Workbook* (Routledge, 2006), co-authored with Claudia Ross and Jing-heng Sheng Ma, and *Elementary Chinese* (2006), co-authored with Pei-Chia Chen.

Pei-Chia Chen is Lecturer in Chinese at UC San Diego and has previously taught at Harvard University. Her publications include *Elementary Chinese* (2006), co-authored with Baozhang He.

Meng Yeh is Senior Lecturer in Chinese at Rice University, Texas. She has served as a Board Member of the Chinese Language Teachers Association and is a founding member of CLTA-TX. She is an AP Chinese consultant for the College Board and a certified Oral Proficiency Interviewer in Chinese for Language Testing International, ACTFL. Her publications include *Advancing in Chinese* (2010) and *Task-based Listening Workbook: Communicating in Chinese Series* (1999).

"*The Routledge Course in Modern Mandarin*, Level 2, offers a step-by-step introduction to the Chinese language for real-life scenarios. It is a fantastic resource which effectively assists both autonomous learning while offering practical guidance for teachers."

Wei Jin, *The School of Oriental and African Studies, University of London, UK*

"*The Routledge Course in Modern Mandarin Chinese* is a valuable addition to the field of Chinese language textbooks. Thorough and careful pedagogical considerations continue to be evident throughout the second volume of this two-year series. Students using this series will be provided with strong and clear guidance for their learning, both in terms of form and function connection and in developing their four skills in a spiraling fashion that has been meticulously designed to reflect the most up-to-date knowledge in second language acquisition. I highly recommend this series."

Cecilia Chang, *Williams College, USA*

THE ROUTLEDGE COURSE IN

Modern Mandarin Chinese

現代漢語課程

Workbook Level 2: Traditional Characters

練習本　　第二冊

繁體版

Claudia Ross
Baozhang He
Pei-Chia Chen
Meng Yeh

Routledge
Taylor & Francis Group

LONDON AND NEW YORK

First published 2012
by Routledge
711 Third Avenue, New York, NY 10017

Simultaneously published in the UK
by Routledge
2 Park Square, Milton Park, Abingdon, Oxon OX14 4RN

Routledge is an imprint of the Taylor & Francis Group, an informa business

Library of Congress Cataloging in Publication Data
Ross, Claudia.
  The Routledge course in modern Mandarin Chinese. Textbook level 2 : Simplified
characters / Claudia Ross . . . [et al.]. — 1st ed.
     p. cm.
   1. Chinese language—Textbook for foreign speakers—English.   2. Mandarin dialects.
I. Title.   II. Title: Modern Mandarin Chinese.
   PL1129.E5R678 2011
   495.1'82421—dc22

                                                           2010052079

British Library Cataloguing in Publication Data
A catalogue record for this book is available from the British Library

ISBN: 978-0-415-47246-3 (Textbook Level 2, Traditional characters)
ISBN: 978-0-415-47250-0 (Textbook Level 2, Simplified characters)
ISBN: 978-0-415-47253-1 (Workbook Level 2, Traditional characters)
ISBN: 978-0-415-47247-0 (Workbook Level 2, Simplified characters)

Typeset in 12/15pt Scala
by Graphicraft Limited, Hong Kong

Printed and bound by Sheridan Books, Inc. in the United States of America on acid-free paper.

Contents

Acknowledgments

We thank all of the people who have been involved in the development of this course. We give a special thanks to Jessica Lee, who provided the illustrations for the textbooks and workbooks for Levels 1 and 2. The photographs in the textbook are originals supplied by the photographers Wenze Hu, Jin Lu, and Claudia Ross, and are used with their permission. We thank Wenze Hu and Jin Lu for their contributions. Thanks also to the students in the intermediate Chinese classes at the College of the Holy Cross 2008–2010 for their patience and feedback as we field-tested and revised each lesson, and to Sun Shao-Hui, Yao Shu-Ting, Ho Chia-Jung, and Chang Yu-Lun, foreign language assistants in Chinese at Holy Cross during those years, for their help on many aspects of the project. We are grateful to the College of the Holy Cross for its generous support in the way of released time and resources, and to the members of the Audio-Visual Department at the College for their help in producing audio recordings that enabled field-testing. We thank our editors for their guidance and for their help in keeping us on track. Last but not least, we thank our families for their ongoing support and their confidence in our work.

The stroke order flow charts in this book were produced with eStroke software and are included with the permission of EON Media Limited:

http://www.eon.com.hk/estroke

Introduction

The Routledge Course in Modern Mandarin Chinese is an innovative two-year course for English-speaking learners of Chinese as a foreign language that guides students to build a strong foundation in Mandarin and prepares them for continued success in the language. The course is designed to address the five goals (the 5 *C's*) of foreign language learning highlighted by the American Council on the Teaching of Foreign Languages (ACTFL). Each *communication*-focused lesson is grounded in the *cultural* context of China, guiding students to make *comparisons* between language and social customs in the United States and the Chinese-speaking world, and providing activities that *connect* their language study to other disciplines and lead them to use Chinese in the wider *community*.

Set in China, the course introduces themes that students encounter in their first experience abroad and prepares them to converse, read, and write in Chinese on everyday topics. The themes in Level 2 include *courses and majors, getting sick and seeing a doctor, weather, sports and exercise, shopping and bargaining, celebrating the Chinese New Year, cooking and eating out, travel, job hunting,* and *talking about the Chinese language.*

The Routledge Course in Modern Mandarin Chinese is available in Simplified or Traditional characters and includes:

- A textbook with narratives, dialogues, vocabulary and character lists, stroke order tables, jargon-free explanations of use and structure, *Sentence Pyramids* to illustrate phrase and sentence structure, and notes on Chinese culture and language use.
- A comprehensive workbook with extensive information-focused and skill-focused exercises that target all aspects of each lesson.
- Alphabetically arranged indices for vocabulary, characters, and structures.
- A student website with character and vocabulary flashcards, downloadable character practice sheets, and easily accessible audio files for the *Structure Drills* and *Listening for Information* exercises provided in the Workbook.
- A *Teacher Resources* section of the website containing a wealth of communication-based classroom activities, project suggestions, lesson plans, and teaching tips.

Innovative features of *The Routledge Course in Modern Mandarin*

- Separate introduction of *words* and *characters*. Vocabulary items are presented in Pinyin in the lesson in which they are introduced so that students learn the pronunciation and meaning of new words before they learn to read and write them in characters. Character introduction is staggered and selective. Characters are introduced at the second or later occurrence of a vocabulary item in the text, with a focus on the introduction of high-frequency characters. Level 1 introduces approximately 575 words and 180 characters. Level 2 introduces an additional 800 vocabulary items and 330 characters. Since a single character often serves as a component in many different words, by the end of Level 2, the gap between written and spoken vocabulary is small.

- Complete replacement of Pinyin by characters. When a character is introduced, it replaces the Pinyin form in all subsequent occurrences without additional Pinyin support. Students must focus on the character as the primary written form of the Chinese word or syllable.
- Character literacy instruction. Once characters are introduced, workbook exercises guide students to understand the structure of characters and to develop reading and writing strategies.
- Integration of form and function. Structures are introduced to support communication.
- "Basic to complex" introduction of grammatical structures. Students build a solid foundation in basic structures before learning more complex variations.
- Recycling. Vocabulary and structures are recycled in successive lessons to facilitate mastery.

Features of Level 2

Level 2 begins the transition from the study of colloquial Chinese to that of the formal written and spoken language. Features include:

- Presentation of themes in *colloquial* and *formal* contexts. Each lesson includes a dialogue that develops a theme in conversational format, and a narrative that develops the same theme in a more formal written style. This presentation facilitates the *introduction of features of formal literary language*, including vocabulary, sentence structures, and narrative conventions, and serves as a *transition* to the reading and discussion of formal written texts in subsequent levels of Chinese language study.
- Development of written narrative skills in a variety of rhetorical modes: description, narrative, explanation, and persuasion. Lessons introduce features of written narrative, including the development of a topic, text cohesion, and parallel structure, and use a variety of exercises to guide students to write progressively longer and more complex narratives in a variety of rhetorical modes.
- Continued focus on an understanding of the structure of characters including the recognition of radicals, and the development of dictionary skills.
- Continued focus on strengthening listening comprehension skills through longer and more complex narratives in the form of speeches, reports, and instructions.
- Continued focus on the strengthening of oral presentation skills through tasks involving responses to oral messages, and summarizing explanations, arguments and descriptions.
- Continued focus on the strengthening of interpersonal speaking skills through tasks involving interviews, negotiations, and shared responsibilities.

引言

《Routledge 现代汉语课程》是针对母语为英语的学习者编写的一套创新汉语教材。本教材为两年的课程，帮助学生打下坚实的汉语基础并为他们继续在语言学习的成功上做好准备。教材的设计上力求全面反映全美外语教学学会 (ACTFL) 倡导的外语学习的五项目标(5 C's)。每一课以语言交际为中心，以中国文化为背景，引导学生做中美语言及社会习俗方面的对比，并提供大量的教学活动使学生把语言学习与其他专业知识的学习贯穿起来，以使他们能在更广的范围内使用汉语。

教材的背景是在中国，给学生介绍第一次到中国通常会遇到的情景。第二册教材的情景包括课程与专业、看病、天气、运动与健身、购物与讨价还价、欢度春节、做饭、去饭馆、旅游、找工作及中国语言。

《Routledge 现代汉语课程》有简繁体两种版本，内容包括：

- 课本中每一课有叙述、对话、生词、所学的汉字及汉字笔顺表、通俗易懂的用法和结构的介绍、句型扩展、语言常识及中国文化点滴。
- 综合练习本内有大量的针对每课所学内容的信息交际及语言技能的练习。
- 以字母顺序安排的生词、汉字及语法点的索引。
- 学生学习网页：汉字和生词学习卡、可以下载的汉字练习表格、及练习本中的句型操练和听力练习等语音档案。
- 教师资源网页：大量的语言交际的课堂活动、教学建议、课程安排及教学技巧。

《现代汉语课程》的创意性特点：

- "词"、"字"分开介绍。生词在第一次出现的时候，只以拼音的形式介绍。这样，学生可以先把精力集中在发音、意思及用法上，然后再学汉字。介绍哪些汉字是有步骤有选择的。所介绍的汉字一定在课文的词汇中出现过两次以上，重点介绍使用频率高的汉字。第一册介绍了575个生词，180个汉字。第二册介绍800个生词330个汉字。因为一个汉字往往在不同的生词中出现，到第二册结束的时候，学生所能说的词汇和能写的词汇（汉字）差距是很小的。

- 汉字全部代替拼音。某一汉字一经介绍，该字的拼音形式就不再出现。学生必须学着把注意力集中在汉字上，因为只有汉字才是汉语的词或音节的真正书写形式。
- 识字教学：针对每课所介绍的汉字，课本和练习本都有相应的练习帮助学生了解汉字的结构，并培养学生阅读和书写的策略。
- 形式和功能结合：句型结构的介绍是为了便于交际。
- "由简到难"引进语法结构。学生在充分掌握了简单的语法结构后，再逐步学习较为复杂的结构。
- 重复。为帮助学生掌握运用，句型和生词在后续几课的课文和练习中尽量重复。

第二册的特点

第二册开始从学习白话的口语过渡到正式的口语和书面语。其特点包括：

- 在正式和非正式的语境中介绍主题。每课都有对话，以对话的形式发展情景，及一段叙述，同样的情境但以正式的书写的形式呈现。这样的安排易于引进正式的书面语的特征，其中包括词汇、句型、叙述的格式，为学生以后阅读讨论正式书面语起一个过渡的作用。
- 培养学生叙述不同的情景的语言能力：描写、叙述、解释及说服。课中介绍书写体的特征，包括发挥主题、起承转合、对称结构等，并通过不同的练习引导学生逐步以更长更复杂的段落书写不同情境。
- 继续强调了解汉字的结构，包括识别偏旁部首、学习使用字典等。
- 通过更长的，更复杂的讲话、报告及指令等不同的听力材料继续加强听力理解的能力。
- 通过对口头信息的回答、对解释性文字的总结、辩论及描述继续增强学生的口头表达能力。
- 通过完成提问、面谈、协商及职责等教学任务继续加强学生人际交流的能力。

引言

《Routledge 現代漢語課程》是針對母語為英語的學習者編寫的一套創新漢語教材。本教材為兩年的課程，幫助學生打下堅實的漢語基礎並為他們繼續在語言學習的成功上做好準備。教材的設計上力求全面反映全美外語教學學會 (ACTFL) 倡導的外語學習的五項目標 (5 C's)。每一課以語言交際為中心，以中國文化為背景，引導學生做中美語言及社會習俗方面的對比，並提供大量的教學活動使學生把語言學習與其他專業知識的學習貫穿起來，以使他們能在更廣的範圍內使用漢語。

教材的背景是在中國，給學生介紹第一次到中國通常會遇到的情景。第二冊教材的情景包括課程與專業、看病、天氣、運動與健身、購物與討價還價、歡度春節、做飯、去飯館、旅遊、找工作及中國語言。

《Routledge 現代漢語課程》有簡繁體兩種版本，內容包括：

- 課本中每一課有敘述、對話、生詞、所學的漢字及漢字筆順表、通俗易懂的用法和結構的介紹、句型擴展、語言常識及中國文化點滴。
- 綜合練習本內有大量的針對每課所學內容的信息交際及語言技能的練習。
- 以字母順序安排的生詞、漢字及語法點的索引。
- 學生學習網頁：漢字和生詞學習卡、可以下載的漢字練習表格、及練習本中的句型操練和聽力練習等語音檔案。
- 教師資源網頁：大量的語言交際的課堂活動、教學建議、課程安排及教學技巧。

《現代漢語課程》的創意性特點：

- "詞"、"字"分開介紹。生詞在第一次出現的時候，只以拼音的形式介紹。這樣，學生可以先把精力集中在發音、意思及用法上，然後再學漢字。介紹哪些漢字是有步驟有選擇的。所介紹的漢字一定在課文的詞彙中出現過兩次以上，重點介紹使用頻率高的漢字。第一冊介紹了575個生詞，180個漢字。第二冊介紹800個生詞330個漢字。因為一個漢字往往在不同的生詞中出現，到第二冊結束的時候，學生所能說的詞彙和能寫的詞彙（漢字）差距是很小的。

- 漢字全部代替拼音。某一漢字一經介紹，該字的拼音形式就不再出現。學生必須學著把注意力集中在漢字上，因為只有漢字才是漢語的詞或音節的真正書寫形式。
- 識字教學：針對每課所介紹的漢字，課本和練習本都有相應的練習幫助學生瞭解漢字的結構，並培養學生閱讀和書寫的策略。
- 形式和功能結合：句型結構的介紹是為了便於交際。
- "由簡到難"引進語法結構。學生在充分掌握了簡單的語法結構後，再逐步學習較為複雜的結構。
- 重復。為幫助學生掌握運用，句型和生詞在後續幾課的課文和練習中盡量重復。

第二冊的特點

第二冊開始從學習白話的口語過渡到正式的口語和書面語。其特點包括：

- 在正式和非正式的語境中介紹主題。每課都有對話，以對話的形式發展情景，及一段敘述，同樣的情境但以正式的書寫的形式呈現。這樣的安排易於引進正式的書面語的特徵，其中包括詞彙、句型、敘述的格式，為學生以後閱讀討論正式書面語起一個過渡的作用。
- 培養學生敘述不同的情景的語言能力：描寫、敘述、解釋及說服。課中介紹書寫體的特徵，包括發揮主題、起承轉合、對稱結構等，並通過不同的練習引導學生逐步以更長更複雜的段落書寫不同情境。
- 繼續強調瞭解漢字的結構，包括識別偏旁部首、學習使用字典等。
- 通過更長的，更複雜的講話、報告及指令等不同的聽力材料繼續加強聽力理解的能力。
- 通過對口頭信息的回答、對解釋性文字的總結、辯論及描述繼續增強學生的口頭表達能力。
- 通過完成提問、面談、協商及職責等教學任務繼續加強學生人際交流的能力。

How to use the resources in this course to learn Chinese

This course consists of a textbook, workbook, and website with a wealth of material designed to help you to learn to speak Mandarin and read and write in Chinese. Here is an overview of the resources, with suggestions to help you to do your best work.

Textbook

The textbook presents new material and explanations.

- *Narratives* and *Dialogues* illustrate the use of words and structures, and also the cultural conventions of communication associated with each topic.
- *Stroke Order Flow Charts* show you how to write each new character, stroke by stroke.
- *Use and Structure* notes explain how new structures function, and how structures and phrases are used.
- *Sentence Pyramids* show you how words and phrases are grouped into sentences, and help you to understand Chinese word order.
- *Narrative Structure* explanations show you how to organize information into cohesive essays for different communicative functions.
- *Language FAQs* and *Notes on Chinese Culture* provide additional information about language use and Chinese culture related to the topic of the lesson.

Workbook

The workbook provides exercises that you can do as homework or in class to practice the words, structures, and themes introduced in each lesson. These include:

- *Structure Drills*
- *Listening for Information*
- *Focus on Chinese Characters*
- *Focus on Structure*
- *Focus on Communication*

Website

The website includes listening files that you need in order to complete workbook exercises and additional resources that help you practice and review. Resources include:

- Character and vocabulary flash cards
- Character practice sheets
- Listening files for *Structure Drills*
- Listening files for *Listening for Information*

Study tips

- Learn vocabulary and characters. If you don't know the words in a lesson, you can't participate in class and you cannot do the homework. You need to begin each lesson by learning the new vocabulary and characters. *Regularly review* vocabulary and characters from earlier lessons. Use the resources provided with this course to help you study. Download the character practice sheets from the course website to practice writing characters. Pay attention to the stroke order presented on the practice sheets so that you learn to write characters correctly. Using the same stroke order each time you write a character helps you to remember the character. Conversely, if you write a character differently each time you write it, your brain will have a hard time remembering it. Use the vocabulary and character flash cards on the website to help you review vocabulary and characters, but be sure to write down your responses in Chinese to make sure that you really know the tones in each vocabulary item, or the correct way to write each character.
- Learn the structures. Notice that most of the *Focus on Structure* exercises refer to a specific *Use and Structure* note. Read the *Use and Structure* note before you do the exercise, and follow the model sentences in the note as you complete your work. Work through the *Sentence Pyramids* in the textbook to see how phrases are built up into sentences in Chinese. Use the *Sentence Pyramids* to test yourself, translating the Chinese column into English and checking your answers, and then translating the English column into Chinese. Work through the *Structure Drills* on the website to practice new structures on your own.
- Use the listening resources. If you could understand a sentence or narrative in Chinese the first time you heard it, you wouldn't need to study Chinese. Do not expect to understand listening files on your first try. Instead, listen to the same texts over and over again in order to train your brain to understand what it hears. When you work on the *Listening for Information* exercises, expect to listen to each 'clip' multiple times until you are sure that you understand it. Help your brain to focus on information by reading the instructions and the answer choices before you listen. The *Structure Drills* provided on the website will exercise your listening skills as they increase your control of new structures and vocabulary.
- Focus on communication. Many of the exercises in this section require you to read or write longer passages in Chinese. Before you read, identify the sentence structures so that you know how words and phrases in the text are related. Identify word boundaries

so that you group characters correctly, and look for connecting words that tell you if the text is presenting a sequence, or a description, or an explanation, etc. Before you write, think of what you want to say, and jot down the Chinese structures that you can use to express your meaning. Think of how you want to organize your ideas, and make a list of the connecting words or structures you need for the organization you are planning. After you write, proofread your work. Be sure to write characters where you have learned them, and be sure that the characters you write are correct. When reading or writing, if you cannot remember a character or a vocabulary item, use this as an opportunity to review.

If you spend the time you need to prepare and review, you will have a successful and satisfying Chinese-learning experience. Good luck in your studies!

How to use the resources in this course to teach Chinese

The textbook, workbook, and website material in this course are designed to be used together to help students learn to communicate in Mandarin Chinese in speech and writing. We suggest the following approach to maximize your students' success in learning Chinese. (More detailed suggestions are provided in the lesson plans that are included on the course website.)

Coordinating the textbook with workbook assignments

- *Focus on Chinese Characters.* Require students to learn the new characters in each lesson at the start of the lesson. The exercises in the *Focus on Chinese Characters* section of the workbook rely on grammar introduced in previous lessons, so students can do these exercises before new grammar is presented in class.
- *Focus on Structure.* The text in each lesson is presented in modules: a *Narrative*, and a *Dialogue* divided into several parts. Each module has its own list of new vocabulary, and modules are sequentially linked to *Use and Structure* notes. Present each lesson module by module, and assign relevant *Focus on Structure* homework as you complete a module. You can assign a few structure exercises at a time, after the introduction of the targeted structures in each module.
- *Listening for Information.* Assign *Listening for Information* exercises for homework after the relevant structures have been introduced. You can assign a few exercises at a time, after you have introduced and practiced the targeted structures in class.
- *Focus on Communication.* Use *Focus on Communication* exercises as classroom activities or homework after all modules have been covered to help students apply what they have learned in the lesson to new situations.

Classwork or homework?

Distinguish between activities that students can do on their own and activities that are appropriate for the classroom setting. *Do not use valuable class time for activities that students can do on their own.*

Activities that students should do on their own include:

- Memorization of vocabulary and characters. Do not explain vocabulary in class. English definitions and structure notes in the textbook provide the information that students need to understand the meaning and use of vocabulary.
- Reading of narratives and dialogues. Have students read the text at home and discuss the content in class. Discussion can take a question-answer format.
- Exercises involving identification, completion, and stroke count in the *Focus on Chinese Characters* section of the workbook.
- *Listening for Information* exercises. Listening exercises are designed to help students develop listening skills at their own pace, and students should be encouraged to listen to audio files as many times as necessary in order to complete each listening task. In-class listening practice deprives students of the opportunity to listen at their own pace and should not be used as a classroom activity.
- *Focus on Structure* exercises involving the use of targeted structures in individual sentences. These should always be assigned as homework after the structures are introduced in class. Problematic structures can be reviewed in class after homework assignments are complete. In short, follow these steps: presentation (in class), practice (at home), review (in class).
- Essay writing.

Activities that can be done in class include:

- Communication-based activities such as those suggested in the *Dialogue Practice* section of the textbook.
- *Structure Drills.*
- Communication-focused activities that lead students to practice new structures in context. Detailed suggestions are presented on the lesson plans in the *Teacher Resources* section of the course website.
- Discussion of the lesson's *Narrative* and *Dialogue* in Chinese.
- Brainstorming in preparation for essay writing.
- Small-group editing sessions in which students correct essays written by their peers.
- Problem-solving. The *Focus on Chinese Characters* and *Focus on Communication* sections of the workbook include a number of activities that lend themselves to group work. See the lesson plans in the *Teacher Resources* section of the course website.
- Group presentations of projects or skits.

How much homework?

The workbook includes extensive listening, reading, and writing practice, and you may choose to assign all or part of the exercises for homework. Meaningful homework, including preparation and review, expands the time that students work on Chinese outside of the classroom and accelerates the learning process.

Typing or handwriting?

Require students to complete some assignments by hand and some by computer. Writing Chinese by hand makes students focus on the structure of Chinese characters. Typing helps strengthen character recognition and proofreading skills.

练习本教师使用指南

练习本为培养和巩固学生的汉语语言技能及每课所介绍的交际功能提供练习。这些练习是作为课外功课设计的，使学生能在课外有更多的用汉语互动的机会。有的练习也可以在课堂上作为小组活动。

如何使用练习本我们提出如下建议。更加具体的建议在课程网页教案和"教学活动"的栏目中提供。

- 把学生可以自己独立完成的练习和最好在课堂上做的练习分开。不要把课堂上宝贵的时间用来做学生自己可以做的练习。
- 练习均匀分配，让学生在上每一节课之前做不同的活动，同时也使学生一周内每节课课前的预习时间均等。

学生自己可以独立完成的练习包括：

- 生词和汉字的记忆。课堂上用少量的时间"测验"生词和汉字，但不要花很多时间"解释"。
- 聚焦汉字的练习，包括识别、完成、笔画数目。
- 掌握信息的听力练习。听力练习是为帮助学生按照自己的进度提高听的能力而设计的。应鼓励学生在完成某一听力任务时尽量多听。我们建议不要利用课堂时间练习听力。
- 聚焦结构的练习在单句中使用某一特定的结构。这一练习应在课上介绍了该结构后作为课外作业。容易出错的结构可以在学生完成作业后课堂上集体讲评。简言之，遵循如下步骤：介绍（课上），练习（课下），复习（课上）。
- 作文。作文应该是家庭作业。但是，作文也可以在课堂上分小组学生相互修改。

利用课堂时间作学生不能自己作的练习。这些有：

- 以交际为基础的活动，如课本中介绍的对话练习。
- 新结构介绍。句型操练可以在课堂上练习新句型。教师资源网页也介绍很多帮助学生掌握新句型的交际活动练习。
- 课堂上讨论课文。让学生讲课文的内容、回答问题、或让学生针对课文内容准备问题在课堂上问别的同学。

- 集思广益准备作文。在布置家庭作业作文时，课堂上的讨论帮助学生明确思路、观点。
- 解决问题。练习本中<u>聚焦汉字</u>和<u>交际</u>部分都有可以作为课堂活动的练习。在<u>聚焦汉字</u>中有识别和改错字，识别形旁和声旁。在<u>信息交际</u>中有访问同学后做作文、选择词汇或短语完成句子、句子组合成段落等。
- 小组汇报和短剧。

课文的每一组成部分：叙述、对话的每一段可以视为相对独立的部分。每部分的生词和语法点都单独列出。我们建议每一课时完成一小部分。要求学生课前掌握所要学习部分的生词。上课开始时用几分钟生词测验以确保学生课前预习。另外，要求学生课前预习语法点的解释，课后复习。不建议学生在课上做语法解释的笔记，因为做笔记分散学生精力，降低学习效果。学生所需要掌握的每一语法点在<u>用法与结构</u>中均有讲解。

每课的新汉字都有一个汉字表。让学生从认字到发音，再到书写分为不同的步骤在几个课时中学完。

在课堂上介绍语法点时，让学生做学习网页（练习本）上的<u>结构操练</u>，以使学生更好地掌握本课介绍的语法结构。

练习本中有大量的听力、阅读和书写的练习。可以让学生做部分或所有的练习。下面建议布置作业的顺序。

- <u>聚焦汉字</u>练习中所涉及的语法点都是本课前出现的，所以可以在学完全部课文前做。
- 课堂上介绍了语法结构后再布置练习本中的<u>结构练习</u>。
- 在所有的新语法点都介绍以后再布置<u>听力练习</u>。
- 用<u>信息交际</u>练习帮助学生在新情景中使用本课所学的内容。

練習本教師使用指南

練習本為培養和鞏固學生的漢語語言技能及每課所介紹的交際功能提供練習。這些練習是作為課外功課設計的，使學生能在課外有更多的用漢語互動的機會。有的練習也可以在課堂上作為小組活動。

如何使用練習本我們提出如下建議。更加具體的建議在課程網頁教案和"教學活動"的欄目中提供。

- 把學生可以自己獨立完成的練習和最好在課堂上做的練習分開。不要把課堂上寶貴的時間用來做學生自己可以做的練習。
- 練習均勻分配，讓學生在上每一節課之前做不同的活動，同時也使學生一週內每節課課前的預習時間均等。

學生自己可以獨立完成的練習包括：

- 生詞和漢字的記憶。課堂上用少量的時間"測驗"生詞和漢字，但不要花很多時間"解釋"。
- 聚焦漢字的練習，包括識別、完成、筆畫數目。
- 掌握信息的聽力練習。聽力練習是為幫助學生按照自己的進度提高聽的能力而設計的。應鼓勵學生在完成某一聽力任務時盡量多聽。我們建議不要利用課堂時間練習聽力。
- 聚焦結構的練習在單句中使用某一特定的結構。這一練習應在課上介紹了該結構後作為課外作業。容易出錯的結構可以在學生完成作業後課堂上集體講評。簡言之，遵循如下步驟：介紹（課上），練習（課下），復習（課上）。
- 作文。作文應該是家庭作業。但是，作文也可以在課堂上分小組學生相互修改。

利用課堂時間作學生不能自己作的練習。這些有：

- 以交際為基礎的活動，如課本中介紹的對話練習。
- 新結構介紹。句型操練可以在課堂上練習新句型。教師資源網頁也介紹很多幫助學生掌握新句型的交際活動練習。
- 課堂上討論課文。讓學生講課文的內容、回答問題、或讓學生針對課文內容準備問題在課堂上問別的同學。

- 集思廣益準備作文。在佈置家庭作業作文時，課堂上的討論幫助學生明確思路、觀點。
- 解決問題。練習本中聚焦漢字和交際部分都有可以作為課堂活動的練習。在聚焦漢字中有識別和改錯字，識別形旁和聲旁。在信息交際中有訪問同學後做作文、選擇詞彙或短語完成句子、句子組合成段落等。
- 小組彙報和短劇。

課文的每一組成部分：敘述、對話的每一段可以視為相對獨立的部分。每部分的生詞和語法點都單獨列出。我們建議每一課時完成一小部分。要求學生課前掌握所要學習部分的生詞。上課開始時用幾分鐘生詞測驗以確保學生課前預習。另外，要求學生課前預習語法點的解釋，課後復習。不建議學生在課上做語法解釋的筆記，因為做筆記分散學生精力，降低學習效果。學生所需要掌握的每一語法點在用法與結構中均有講解。

每課的新漢字都有一個漢字表。讓學生從認字到發音，再到書寫分為不同的步驟在幾個課時中學完。

在課堂上介紹語法點時，讓學生做學習網頁（練習本）上的結構操練，以使學生更好地掌握本課介紹的語法結構。

練習本中有大量的聽力、閱讀和書寫的練習。可以讓學生做部分或所有的練習。下面建議佈置作業的順序。

- 聚焦漢字練習中所涉及的語法點都是本課前出現的，所以可以在學完全部課文前做。
- 課堂上介紹了語法結構後再佈置練習本中的結構練習。
- 在所有的新語法點都介紹以後再佈置聽力練習。
- 用信息交際練習幫助學生在新情景中使用本課所學的內容。

List of abbreviations

V   verb
AdjV   adjectival verb
ActV   action verb
Adj   adjective
Adv   adverb
VP   verb phrase
N   noun
NP   noun phrase
S   sentence
NEG   negation
PP   prepositional phrase
CL   classifier
QW   question word

Lesson 17 Workbook

 ## Listening and speaking

Structure drills

1. 有的 NP... 有的 NP (Use and Structure note 10.9)

You will hear a question asking about some person or thing. Use 有的... 有的 to say that the description is true for *some* and not others, as in the example.

> **Example:**
> *You will hear:* 課本都很 **guì** 嗎？
> *You will say:* 有的 **guì**，有的不 **guì**。
> *Click "R" to hear the correct response:* 有的 **guì**，有的不 **guì**。

(a)   (b)   (c)   (d)   (e)   (f)   (g)   (h)

2. It hasn't happened in a while (Use and Structure note 17.4)

> **Example:**
> *You will hear:* 這三個月我沒說中文。
> *You will say:* 我有三個月沒有說中文了。
> *Click "R" to hear the correct response:* 我有三個月沒有說中文了。

(a)   (b)   (c)   (d)   (e)   (f)   (g)   (h)

3. **Yīn** 為...**suǒ** 以 *because...therefore* (Use and Structure note 17.5)

You will hear a statement. Rephrase the statement, adding **yīn** 為 and **suǒ** 以 to emphasize cause and effect, as in the example.

> **Example:**
> *You will hear:* 我很忙，沒有給你打電話。
> *You will say:* **Yīn** 為我很忙，**suǒ** 以沒有給你打電話。
> *Click "R" to hear the correct response:* **Yīn** 為我很忙，**suǒ** 以沒有給你打電話。

(a)   (b)   (c)   (d)   (e)   (f)   (g)   (h)   (i)   (j)

4. What did they say? 說 and **gàosu** (Use and Structure note 17.7)

You will hear a statement indicating what someone said to someone. If the verb used is 說, rephrase the statement with **gàosu**; if the verb used is **gàosu**, rephrase the sentence with 說, as in the examples.

Example:
You will hear: 他跟我說明天沒有 **kǎoshì**。
You will say: 他 **gàosu** 我明天沒有 **kǎoshì**。
Click "R" to hear the correct response: 他 **gàosu** 我明天沒有 **kǎoshì**。
Or
You will hear: 他 **gàosu** 我明天沒有 **kǎoshì**。
You will say: 他跟我說明天沒有 **kǎoshì**。
Click "R" to hear the correct response: 他跟我說明天沒有 **kǎoshì**。

(a)　　(b)　　(c)　　(d)　　(e)　　(f)　　(g)　　(h)　　(i)　　(j)

5. What did he say? Asking indirect questions (Use and Structure note 17.9)

Xiao Zhang is asking you some questions. Tell me what he asked you, using an indirect question in each of your reports, as in the example.

Example:
You will hear: 那個老師 **yán** 嗎？
You will say: 他問我那個老師 **yán** 不 **yán**。
Click "R" to hear the correct response: 他問我那個老師 **yán** 不 **yán**。

(a)　　(b)　　(c)　　(d)　　(e)　　(f)　　(g)　　(h)

6. Practice with intensifiers: 有一點 AdjV, **bǐjiào** AdjV (Use and Structure note 17.13)

You will hear a question followed by an intensifier. Reply to the question, adding the intensifier right before the adjectival verb, as in the example.

Example:
You will hear: **Jiāo** 文 **huà** 課的老師 **yán** 嗎？（有一點）
You will say: **Jiāo** 文 **huà** 課的老師有一點 **yán**。
Click "R" to hear the correct response: **Jiāo** 文 **huà** 課的老師有一點 **yán**。

(a)　　(b)　　(c)　　(d)　　(e)　　(f)　　(g)　　(h)　　(i)

7. What are you interested in? (Use and Structure note 17.14)

You will hear a question asking what someone is interested in followed by a noun phrase. You use that noun phrase to answer the question.

Example:
You will hear: 小高對甚麼有 **xìngqu**？（中國文 **huà**）
You will say: 小高對中國文 **huà** 有 **xìngqu**。
Click "R" to hear the correct response: 小高對中國文 **huà** 有 **xìngqu**。

(a)   (b)   (c)   (d)   (e)   (f)   (g)   (h)

8. Not interested (Use and Structure note 17.14)

You will hear a person's name followed by a place, thing, or action. Say that the person is not interested in the place, thing, or action, as in the example.

Example:
You will hear: 小高，**lǚyóu**
You will say: 小高對 **lǚyóu** 沒有 **xìngqu**。
Click "R" to hear the correct response: 小高對 **lǚyóu** 沒有 **xìngqu**。

(a)   (b)   (c)   (d)   (e)   (f)   (g)   (h)

Listening for information

1. Class schedule

He Fang is telling her friends the classes that she is taking this semester. Listen carefully **(CD1: 3)** and present He Fang's class schedule on the following form, indicating the name of each course and its meeting time.

星期一	星期二	星期三	星期四	星期五

2.   What are they busy doing?

(CD1: 4) You will hear five statements stating what five people are busy doing. Write the name of each person underneath the picture of his or her activity. Listen carefully so that you can transcribe the names accurately in pinyin.

3.   Yuan Kai's week

(CD1: 5) The following is Yuan Kai's weekly schedule. You will hear six questions. Based on his schedule, answer the questions in English.

time	星期一	星期二	星期三	星期四	星期五
9:00–10:00 a.m.		Chinese Culture class		Chinese Culture class	
10:00–11:00 a.m.	Math class		Math class		
1:00–2:00 p.m.		Computer class		Computer class	
7:00–9:00 p.m.	Work in the library	German class	German class	Work in the library	

a.

b.

c.

d.

e.

f.

4. Interviewing YOU

You are having a conversation with your classmate, Yu Shi, who is asking about your **(CD1: 6)** semester. Answer each question in Mandarin, based on your real-life situation, using characters where we have learned them.

a.

b.

c.

d.

e.

f.

g.

5. Comparisons

You will hear five questions, one for each picture. Answer each question in Mandarin, **(CD1: 7)** based on the pictures.

a. Xiao Chen's   Lao Wang's

¥65   ¥70

c.

Bob   Eric

e.

Carl   Max

b.

Bao Kang   Shu Wen

Sam

d.

a.

b.

c.

d.

e.

6. Listen and reply

(CD1: 8) This is the first day of the Chinese course and Teacher Wu is describing the basic structure of the class. Listen to her description, and then answer the six questions that follow in English, based on the information that she gives.

a.

b.

c.

d.

e.

f.

7. Dialogue I

(CD1: 9) You will hear a telephone conversation between two students who attend different schools. Answer the questions based on the dialogue.

a. When did/does the woman's school start?
   1) in another three days
   2) three days ago
   3) next week

b. Why is the woman taking Chinese this semester?
   1) She is required to take two years of Chinese.
   2) She has been taking Chinese for two years and wants to continue.
   3) She needs to take five courses this semester.

c. What is the main topic of this conversation?
   1) studying Chinese
   2) starting a new semester
   3) planning a trip to China

8. Dialogue II

You will hear a dialogue between a man and a woman. Answer the questions based on the (CD1: 10) dialogue.

a. What is the main topic of their conversation?
1) where to eat tonight
2) what the new restaurant is like
3) which dish to order in the new restaurant
4) how to get to the new restaurant

b. Based on the information in the dialogue, what do we know about the restaurant?
1) It is far away. They need to take the subway.
2) It is a bit pricey, but the food is excellent.
3) We do not know much, since neither of them has been there.
4) The dumplings in that restaurant are pretty good.

Reading and writing

Focus on Chinese characters

1. Number of strokes

Indicate the number of strokes used in writing each of the following characters.

a. 課 _____   f. 些 _____

b. 思 _____   g. 意 _____

c. 聽 _____   h. 直 _____

d. 為 _____   i. 校 _____

e. 忙 _____   j. 每 _____

2. Which character?

Circle the character in each line that corresponds to the meaning on the left.

a. **zhí** (**yīzhí** *continuously*)   直   真

b. **guān** (**guānxi** *connection*)   關   開

c. **gōng** (**gōngkè** *course work*)   工   功

d. **měi** *every*   每   母

e. **tīng** *listen*   聽   德

f. **xiào** (**xuéxiào** *school*)   餃   校

g. **xiē** *several*   此   些

h. **zhōng** *clock*   鐘   種

i. **kè** *class*   顆   課

j. **sī** (**yìsi** *meaning*)   思   想

k. **cái** (*less than expected*)   才   寸

l. **yòng** *use*   用   月

3.   First strokes

Write the first two strokes of each of the following characters.

a. 思 _____   f. 關 _____

b. 校 _____   g. 意 _____

c. 才 _____   h. 係 _____

d. 些 _____   i. 忙 _____

e. 為 _____   j. 鐘 _____

4.   Missing strokes

Complete each character by writing in the missing strokes.

a.   丁   **gōng** (**gōngkè** *course work*)

b.   耳   **tīng** *listen*

c.   訂   **kè** *class*

d.   ⺈   **měi** *every*

e.   亻   **xì** (**guānxi** *connection*)

f.   ⺊   **yì** (**yìsi** *meaning*)

g.   ⺀   **xiē** *several*

h.   古   **zhí** (**yīzhí** *continuously, straight*)

i.   金   **zhōng** *clock* (**yīdiǎn zhōng** *1 o'clock*)

j.   冂   **yòng** *use*

5. Total strokes

Rewrite this list of characters, arranging the characters in terms of their total number of strokes. Begin your list with the character with the fewest strokes.

為	校	每	意	些	才	課	思	直	用	忙	鐘	聽	功	係	關

6.   Radicals

Here is a list of characters that we have learned through this lesson. Rewrite each character in the row next to its radical.

叫	課	鐘	聽	快	請	思	您
意	校	忙	怎	想	本	錢	慢

心	
木	
金	
口	
忄	
言	

7.   Character sleuth

Group the following characters in terms of a part that they share in common. The shared part need not be the radical in each character. Write the shared part first, and then list the characters that share the part afterward, as in the example. You can use a character more than once.

給	鐘	係	用	朋	意	二	直	道
真	關	些	思	男	星	說	經	半

shared part	characters
人	人，大，太，天
田	
目	
二	
月	
糸	

8.   Find the words and phrases

You won't be able to completely understand the following passage, but it contains many characters that we have learned, including more than twenty words composed of two or more characters.

a. Circle fourteen *words* that we have learned that are *composed of two or more characters each* and write them on the answer sheet below.

"今年" is an example of a word that is composed of two or more characters.

"我也" is composed of two characters in a row that we have learned, but it is *not* a word.

今年夏天放暑假的時候，我從中國回美國看我的父母。我有半年多沒有看見他們
了，很想他們。他們當然也很想我。到了家，我媽媽問我最想吃甚麼，她可以去買
給我做。我說我很想吃的東西，不用去買，家裏一定有很多。我跟他們說我剛到
中國的時候，最不習慣的就是吃北京的早飯。我覺得北京的早飯油很多，不太健康。
我喜歡美國的穀物早餐，加一些牛奶就可以了。又方便，又健康。中國雖然有穀物
早餐，可是很貴。爸爸說：“對。穀物早餐在宿舍吃就可以了。又可以起得很晚，
又可以不去餐廳。”我說：“爸爸，你上大學的時候就這樣吧。”

Words in this paragraph composed of two or more characters:

1. ____   2. ____   3. ____   4. ____   5. ____   6. ____   7. ____

8. ____   9. ____   10. ____   11. ____   12. ____   13. ____   14. ____

b. In one sentence in English, state the general topic of this passage.

9. Dictionary skills

Following the instructions in Lesson 17 of the Textbook, look up these characters in a Chinese dictionary and provide the requested information.

a. 選
pronunciation:
meaning:
one two-character word or phrase in which it occurs:

b. 自
pronunciation:
meaning:
one two-character word or phrase in which it occurs:

c. 最
pronunciation:
meaning:
one two-character word or phrase in which it occurs:

10. Find the incorrect characters

Xiao Zhang has written this email to a friend back home, but he has written thirteen different characters incorrectly (some more than once). Read the passage aloud, circle the mistakes, and correct them on the answer sheet below. If the same mistake occurs twice, count it as a single mistake.

> 學期錢天就開學了。我非常忙。這個學期我上了四們課，一們 **yīnyuè** 科，一們法問課，還有兩們中文課。**Yīnyuè** 課早上八店中就開 **shǐ**，**suǒ** 以我得早一點七 **chuáng**。我七 **chuáng** 的是候我得 **tóngwū** 還再 **shuì** 覺。我美天上課一前現吃一點東西。

a. _____   b. _____   c. _____   d. _____   e. _____   f. _____   g. _____

h. _____   i. _____   j. _____   k. _____   l. _____   m. _____

11. Scrambled sentences

Rewrite these phrases as sentences, putting the words in the correct order to match the English translations.

a. 會 / **kuài** 子 / 很 / 吃 / 喜歡 / 不 / 用 / 吃飯 / 可是 / **suī** 然 / 她 / 她 / 中國飯
Although she likes to eat Chinese food a lot, she can't use chopsticks to eat.

b. 都 / 的時候 / 忙 / 學生 / 非常 / 剛 / 學期 / 開 **shǐ**
When the semester just begins, the students are all extremely busy.

c. **yīnyuè** / 一直 / 我 / 有 **xìngqu** / 對 / 很
I've always been very interested in music.

d. 有意思 / 那本 / 沒 / 聽說 / 書
I have heard that that book is not interesting.

e. 都 / 學校 / 他們 / 在 / 的 / 吃飯 / **cāntīng** / 每天
They eat at the school cafeteria every day.

12.   Translation

Read the following passage and translate it into English.

明天的明天是後天。"後天"的"後"是"後 **biān**"的"後"。中文的後天不是在你的後 **biān**。中文的後天是在你的前 **biān**。後天還沒有到呢。昨天的昨天是前天。"前天"的"前"是"前 **biān**"的"前"。中文的前天不是在你的前 **biān**。中文的前天在你的後**biān**。前天已經過去了。

13.   Pinyin to characters

Rewrite the following sentences in Chinese characters.

a. **Wǒ shì dàxué èr niánjí de xuésheng**。   (Write **jí** in Pinyin.)

b. **Wǒ qiántiān gāng cóng jiā huí xuéxiào**。

c. **Zhè gè xuéqī wǒ yào shàng Zhōngwén kè xué Zhōngwén**。

d. **Wǒ tīngshuō Zhōngwén kè yǒu yīdiǎn nán, kěshì wǒ yīzhí juéde Zhōngwén hěn yǒu yòng**。

e. **Wǒ de xuéxí hěn máng, bùguò wǒ de kè dōu hěn yǒu yìsi**。

Focus on structure

1. Everyone is busy (Use and Structure note 17.2)

It is Sunday evening. Everyone in the house is so busy concentrating on what they are doing that no one hears the doorbell ringing. Describe what everyone is busy doing, using 忙 **zhe**.

(cooking)	(surfing the internet)
a. 媽媽	b. 爸爸
(doing homework)	(talking on the phone)
c. 小明	d. 小明的 **jiějie**

a.

b.

c.

d.

2. 回來，回去 (Use and Structure note 17.3)

Here are the names of some Chinese students studying at our school. Write a sentence in Mandarin for each one, stating what date they went back to their home country last spring and what date they came back to campus this fall.

	went home in the spring	came back this fall
a. Zhái Yàn	June 9	August 14
b. Wáng Jú	May 29	September 1
c. Chén Wén	July 2	August 31

a.

b.

c.

3.   I haven't done that for a long time (Use and Structure note 17.4)

Xiao Yang has been busy working on a school project for two months now. He finally turned it in today and is complaining about all the fun that he missed. Write each of his complaints in Mandarin, using the example as your guide.

Example:

watching movies, two months   →   我有兩個月沒有看電 **yǐng** 了。

a. singing Karaoke, one and a half months   →

b. calling my girlfriend, ten days   →

c. going home, one month   →

d. watching television, three weeks   →

e. taking a shower, two days   →

f. sleeping, twenty-five hours   →

4.   Cause and effect (Use and Structure note 17.5)

Here is a list of people, followed by some information about them. Express each line of information in a complete Mandarin sentence, using **yīn** 為 and **suǒ** 以. Then translate your sentences into English.

a. 小王…用功…學得很好
    your sentence:
    English:

b. 陳明…**cōng** 明…學得很快
    your sentence:
    English:

c. 小白的 **tóng** 學…**bèn**…學得很慢
    your sentence:
    English:

d. 美 **lì**…明天有 **kǎoshì**…今天晚上在圖書館 **fù** 習功課
    your sentence:
    English:

e. 小 **Yè**…對 **shù** 學有 **xìngqu**…**xuǎn** 了兩門 **shù** 學課。
    your sentence:
    English:

5.　Indirect questions and reported questions (Use and Structure note 17.9)

Zhang Dawei asked Xie Guoqiang a lot of questions on the way to the bookstore. Afterward, Xie Guoqiang told his friend Chen Ming what Zhang Dawei had asked. Here are the English versions of the questions. Rewrite them in Mandarin, as in the example.

Example:

He asked me if the bookstore was open.　　　　　→　張大為問我書店
開不開門。

a. He asked me what time the movie begins.　　　→

b. He asked me if the math teacher was strict.　　→

c. He asked me whether that Chinese book is useful.　　→

d. He asked me if that Japanese class was hard.　　→

e. He asked me how many courses I am taking this semester.　　→

6.　Asking indirect questions (Use and Structure note 17.9)

Rewrite the question part of each dialogue exchange as a sentence with an indirect question, as in the example.

Example:

小謝：你這個學期上中文課嗎？　　　→　小謝問小張這個學期上不上中文課。
小張：上。

a. 小 **Lǐ**：你會開車嗎？　　　　→
　　小王：不會。

b. 謝太太：你們吃過 **jiǎo** 子嗎？　　→
　　小高：吃過。我很喜歡。

c. 小馬：你昨天看的那個電影有 **yìsi** 嗎？　→
　　小錢：非常有 **yìsi**。

d. 王老師：你覺得中國文 **huà** 課難不難？　→
　　小張：不太難，只是 **kǎoshì** 很多。

7.　What did they say?

Rewrite the reply in each of the dialogue exchanges in Exercise 6 as a sentence, stating what the person said, as in the example. Use the word supplied in parentheses in your sentence.

Example:

小謝：你這個學期上中文課嗎？　→　（跟）小張跟小謝說他這個學期上中文課。
小張：上。

a. (**gàosu**)：

b. (說)：

c. (**gàosu**)：

d. (說)：

8.　一點 or 有一點 (Use and Structure note 17.13)

Complete each sentence in Mandarin to match the English translation, using 一點 or 有一點 as appropriate.

a. 這本書太 **guì** 了。　*Can it be a little bit cheaper?*

b. *I've heard that this class is a little hard.* 老師也很 **yán**。

c. *It's already a little late.* 我 **yīnggāi** 回 **sùshè** 了。

d. 明天是星期天。　*You can wake up a little later.*

e. 這個 **jiǎo** 子很好吃。　*You should eat a little more.*

f. *My home is a little far from the subway station.* 我到車站去 **jiē** 你吧。

g. 你說話說得快。　*Please speak a little slower.*

9.　Reporting rumors, gossip, hearsay: I've heard that . . .

Here are some rumors. Tell Ye Youwen what you heard, as in the example.

Example:
You heard: 張大為 went back home the day before yesterday.
You say: 聽說張大為前天回家了。

a. Students are only allowed to take four courses.

b. The Chinese Culture teacher is a little strict.

c. Tomorrow night's movie is very interesting.

d. Xie Guoqiang likes Li Jiazhen.

e. The food in the student cafeteria isn't very tasty.

f. Xiao Ma has a new boyfriend.

10.   Interested or not interested? (Use and Structure note 17.14)

Here is a list of things that Gao Meili is interested in and a list of things that she is not interested in. Ask her if she is interested in each of these things, and write her response to each of your questions.

Gao Meili is interested in:	Gao Meili is not interested in:
a. French culture	b. travel
c. Japanese cinema	d. dancing
e. math	f. German literature （文學）
g. cooking Chinese food	h. singing karaoke
i. listening to music	j. watching television

a. Q:
   A:

b. Q:
   A:

c. Q:
   A:

d. Q:
   A:

e. Q:
   A:

f. Q:
   A:

g. Q:
   A:

h. Q:
   A:

i. Q:
   A:

j. Q:
   A:

11. Translation challenge I

Translate these passages into English.

a. 媽媽：**Shù** 學很有用。這個學期你 **yīnggāi xuǎn** 一門 **shù** 學課。

   Hái 子：好。我對 **shù** 學很有 **xìngqu**，不過我聽說我們學校的 **shù** 學 **lǎoshī** 都 **bǐjiào yán**。

b. 小王：我前天給你打電話你不在。你忙 **zhe** 做甚麼呢？

   小馬：**Xīn** 學期快要開 **shǐ** 了。我忙 **zhe** 買課本呢。

c. 老師：你 **zìjǐ** 的功課得 **zìjǐ** 做。不要請 **bié** 的學生 **bāng** 你做。

12. Translation challenge II

Translate these sentences into Mandarin. Use characters wherever we have learned them.

a. This semester I'm taking five courses: one music course, one American Culture course, two Japanese language courses, and one Japanese Culture course. I have three classes every day.

b. Xiao Xie: Do you have Chinese homework every day?

   Xiao Zhang: Yes. This Chinese teacher is very strict. We have homework every day. However, we only have two exams each semester.

c. Xiao Xie asked me if Xiao Mei has a boyfriend. I told him that I'm not interested in other people's lives.

Focus on communication

1. Dialogue comprehension

Study the Lesson 17 Narrative and Dialogue. Then, read the following statements and indicate whether they are true (T) or false (F).

a. (   ) 學校已經開學了。

b. (   ) 這幾天很多學生得買課本。

c. (   ) 大為剛回中國，中文說得很好。

d. (   ) 現在學校的書店開門。

e. (　) 中國文 **huà** 課的老師很有意思。

f. (　) 大為早就對中國文 **huà** 課有 **xìngqu** 了。

g. (　) 星期五大為 **bǐjiào** 忙，**yīn** 為他有很多課。

2.　What do you say?

What do you say in each of the following situations? Type your answers, using characters where we have learned them, and email them to your Chinese teacher.

a. You want to find out if the coffee shop is still open right now.

b. You want to express your long-term interest in Chinese music.

c. You want to tell your roommate that you heard that this Chinese teacher is rather strict.

d. You want to find out how many courses your roommate is taking this semester.

e. You want to explain why your Chinese is a bit rusty. (The reason is that you haven't spoken Chinese for two months.)

3.　Complete the mini-dialogues

Use the structure in parentheses to complete each mini-dialogue.

a. A: 這個 **gōngzuò** 錢不多，你為甚麼喜歡？

　　B: ＿＿＿＿＿＿＿＿＿＿＿＿＿＿＿＿＿＿＿＿＿。(**yīn** 為)

b. A: 你覺得你的學校怎麼樣？

　　B: ＿＿＿＿＿＿＿＿＿＿＿＿＿＿＿＿＿＿＿＿＿。(只是)

c. A: **Zāogāo**, 我 **wàng** 了做功課，老師一 **dìng** 會不高 **xìng**。

　　B: ＿＿＿＿＿＿＿＿＿＿＿＿＿＿＿＿＿＿＿＿＿。(沒關係)

d. A: 聽說李老師很 **yán**，是不是？你上過他的課，你覺得呢？

　　B: ＿＿＿＿＿＿＿＿＿＿＿＿＿＿＿＿＿＿＿＿＿。(不過)

4.　Multiple choice questions

Select the best expression to complete each sentence, and then translate your sentences into English.

a. 我喜歡吃家常 **cài**，＿＿＿＿＿ 我做得不好。
　　1) **suǒ** 以
　　2) **yīn** 為
　　3) 可是

　　English:

b. ＿＿＿＿星期五早上我有課，＿＿＿＿我不 **néng xuǎn** 這門課。
  1) **Yīn** 為…**suǒ** 以
  2) **Suī** 然…可是
  3) **Yīn** 為…不過

  English:

c. 書店現在沒開門，**suǒ** 以 ＿＿＿＿。
  1) 今天是星期天
  2) 一會兒就開了
  3) 我不 **néng** 去買課本

  English:

d. **Suī** 然我已經學了三年的中文了，可是＿＿＿＿。
  1) 我一直對中文很有 **xìngqu**
  2) 我還沒去過中國
  3) 我每天都有中文課

  English:

e. **Yīn** 為快 **kǎoshì** 了，＿＿＿＿。
  1) 很多人在圖書館學習
  2) 我下個星期有三個 **kǎoshì**
  3) 聽說老師 **bǐjiào yán**

  English:

5.   A conversation between Xiao Zhang and Xiao Wang

Part I.   Fill in the blanks with the correct word, choosing from those given below.

只是	**zìjǐ**	一 **dìng**	門	剛
在	沒關係	**zhe**	有	早就

小王：小張，我 ＿＿＿＿ 幾個星期沒有看見你了。你 ＿＿＿＿ 忙甚麼？

小張：我忙 ＿＿＿＿ 學習呢。這個學期我 **xuǎn** 了幾 ＿＿＿＿ **bǐjiào** 難的課。每天都有很多功課。我常常沒有時 **jiān** 想 **bié** 的事。**Zāogāo**！我 **wàng** 了買中文課本。學校書店的書都太 **guì**，我真不想 ＿＿＿＿ 那兒買。

小王：我聽說學友書店的書都很 **piányi**，＿＿＿＿ 有一點 **yuǎn**。你 ＿＿＿＿ **xìngqu** 嗎？我 ＿＿＿＿ 想去看看了，不過我不想 ＿＿＿＿ 一個人去。

小張：真的嗎？有點 **yuǎn** ＿＿＿＿，我 ＿＿＿＿ 買車，我們可以開我的新車去。

Part II.   Read the dialogue above. Then, answer the questions about it in Mandarin.

a. 小張忙 **zhe** 作甚麼？

b. 小張 **wàng** 了作甚麼？

c. 學友書店怎麼樣？

d. 小張想去那個書店嗎？他打 **suan** 怎麼去？

6.   Sequence of events

Based on the illustrations given, write out the sequence of events. Use 先…再…最後…in each paragraph.

a.

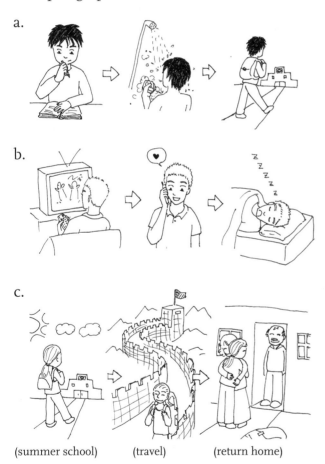

b.

c.

(summer school)   (travel)   (return home)

7. Writing I

Write a short paragraph about the classes you are taking this semester. Below is a list of expressions that you can use in your paragraph. Include at least <u>four</u> of them. Your paragraph should be at least 80 characters in length.

yīn 為…**suǒ** 以	有（一）點	只是	一 **dìng**	對…有 **xìngqu**
忙 **zhe**	不過	**bǐjiào**	有用	**xuǎn**

_____

_____

_____

_____

_____

_____

_____

_____

8. Writing II

Write a short paragraph about the classes you decided <u>not</u> to take this semester and explain your decisions. Include in your paragraph at least <u>four</u> of the expressions listed in Exercise 7. Your paragraph should be at least 80 characters in length.

_____

_____

_____

_____

_____

_____

_____

Lesson 18 Workbook

 Listening and speaking

Structure drills

1. There is a strong relationship between them (Use and Structure note 18.1)

You will hear two phrases. Say that there is a strong relationship between them, as in the example.

Example:

You will hear: 選 **zhuānyè**，**ài** 好

You will say: 選 **zhuānyè** 跟 **ài** 好有很大的關係。

Click "R" to hear the correct response: 選 **zhuānyè** 跟 **ài** 好有很大的關係。

(a)　　(b)　　(c)　　(d)　　(e)　　(f)　　(g)　　(h)

2. There is no connection (Use and Structure note 18.1)

You will hear a question asking if two things are related. Answer each question in a complete sentence saying that they are not related, as in the example.

Example:

You will hear: 這 **jiàn shì** 跟我有關係嗎？

You will say: 這 **jiàn shì** 跟你沒關係。

Click "R" to hear the correct response: 這 **jiàn shì** 跟你沒關係。

(a)　　(b)　　(c)　　(d)　　(e)　　(f)　　(g)　　(h)

3. **Rú** 果…就 *if… (then)* (Use and Structure note 18.2)

You will hear two sentences. Restate the sentences using **rú** 果 and 就 to say *if the first one happens, the second one happens*, as in the example.

> **Example:**
> *You will hear:* 你學中文。我也學中文。
> *You will say:* **Rú** 果你學中文，我就學中文。
> *Click "R" to hear the correct response:* **Rú** 果你學中文，我就學中文。

(a)   (b)   (c)   (d)   (e)   (f)   (g)

4. Describing nouns with actions or states, Part I (Use and Structure note 18.3)

You will hear a simple sentence. Restate it as a noun phrase in which the action verb describes the noun, as in the example. English translations are provided for the example.

> **Example:**
> *You will hear:* 我吃飯。 *I eat food (rice).*
> *You will say:* 我吃的飯 *the food (rice) that I eat*
> *Click "R" to hear the correct response:* 我吃的飯

(a)   (b)   (c)   (d)   (e)   (f)   (g)   (h)

5. Describing nouns with actions or states, Part II (Use and Structure note 18.3)

You will hear a simple sentence stating a completed action. Restate it as a noun phrase in which the action verb describes the noun, as in the example. English translations are provided for the example. Remember: do not include completed action 了 in your noun description.

> **Example:**
> *You will hear:* 我昨天買車了。 *I bought a car yesterday.*
> *You will say:* 我昨天買的車 *the car that I bought yesterday*
> *Click "R" to hear the correct response:* 我昨天買的車

(a)   (b)   (c)   (d)   (e)   (f)   (g)   (h)

6.   After doing an action (Use and Structure note 18.7)

You will hear a statement stating two actions that happen in sequence. Restate the information using the structure 在...以後, as in the example.

Example:
You will hear: 你先 **fù** 習功課，再 **cānjiā** 考試。
You will say: 你在 **fù** 習功課以後，再 **cānjiā** 考試。
Click "R" to hear the correct response: 你在 **fù** 習功課以後，再 **cānjiā** 考試。

(a)   (b)   (c)   (d)

7.   Before doing an action (Use and Structure note 18.7)

You will hear a statement stating two actions that happen in sequence. Restate the information using the structure 在...以前, as in the example.

Example:
You will hear: 你先 **fù** 習功課，再 **cānjiā** 考試。
You will say: 你在 **cānjiā** 考試以前，**fù** 習功課。
Click "R" to hear the correct response: 你在 **cānjiā** 考試以前，**fù** 習功課。

(a)   (b)   (c)   (d)   (e)

8.   While doing an action (Use and Structure note 18.7)

You will hear two actions that happen at the same time. Restate the information using the structure 在...時候, as in the example.

Example:
You will hear: 做功課，聽 **yīnyuè**
You will say: 我喜歡在做功課的時候聽 **yīnyuè**。
Click "R" to hear the correct response: 我喜歡在做功課的時候聽 **yīnyuè**。

(a)   (b)   (c)   (d)   (e)   (f)   (g)   (h)

9.   The most (Use and Structure note 18.8)

You will hear a question about the quality of a person, place, or action. Say that it is "the most" in terms of that quality, as in the example.

Example:
You will hear: 那個老師 **yán** 嗎？
You will say: 那個老師最 **yán**。
Click "R" to hear the correct response: 那個老師最 **yán**。

(a)   (b)   (c)   (d)   (e)   (f)   (g)   (h)   (i)   (j)

Listening for information

1.   Zhang Wen's siblings

(CD1: 13) You will hear seven questions about the siblings in Zhang Wen's family. Based on the information, answer the questions in Pinyin.

Zhang Wen	Zhang Ping	Zhang Fen	Zhang Ming	Zhang Peng
11th grade	1st year in college	3rd year in college	last semester in college	graduated last year
interested in Math	major undecided	majors in Computer Science and Music	majors in Economics	teaches in a high school

a.

b.

c.

d.

e.

f.

g.

2.   Cai Ting's roommates

(CD1: 14) Cai Ting is describing her roommates. Listen to her description and use it to complete the information in the table.

name	year in college	major
Cai Ting		
Huang An		
Zhang Xin		
Li Qiang		

3.   If…, what should you do?

You will hear five different situations. Choose the best solution for each situation.   **(CD1: 15)**

A. take it to the store to be repaired

B. just go to enjoy the others singing

C. find out about study abroad programs

D. call your teacher to explain why

E. ask him to speak slower

F. study harder

a. ( )   b. ( )   c. ( )   d. ( )   e. ( )   f. ( )

4.   Huang Licheng's birthday party

Huang Licheng has invited some friends to his twenty-first birthday party. Listen to the **(CD1: 16)** short narrative that describes the people at the party and write each person's name after the appropriate letter on the answer sheet.

A. _____   B. _____   C. _____   D. _____

E. _____   F. _____   G. _____

5. Grades

(CD1: 17) The 12th grade in Jianguo High School is a small class of seven students. Here is their grade report for Math and English. Students are indicated by number instead of name. You will hear five statements. Indicate whether each statement is true (T) or false (F) based on the information in the grade report.

student number	1/female	2/male	3/male	4/female	5/male	6/female	7/male
Math grade	88	92	88	96	80	75	93
English grade	90	85	82	90	93	77	84

a. ( )   b. ( )   c. ( )   d. ( )   e. ( )

6. Interviewing YOU

(CD1: 18) You are having a conversation with your classmate Tan Lun, who is an exchange student from Nanjing, China. He is asking you about your college life. Answer each question in Mandarin, based on your real-life situation, using characters where we have learned them.

a.

b.

c.

d.

e.

f.

g.

7. My summer job

(CD1: 19) Listen to the narrative about Ye Chen's summer job and answer the following five questions in English.

a.

b.

c.

d.

e.

8.   Dialogue I

Lin Bin, an exchange student from Sichuan, is chatting with Mark about the college (CD1: 20) application process in China and the United States. Answer the following questions based on the information in the conversation.

Note: 高考 is the name of the Chinese college entrance examination.

a. Which statement about the college entrance examination in China is correct?
   1) The entrance examination takes place before summer.
   2) The examination lasts two days.
   3) One can take the examination three times a year.

b. How did Lin Bin do on the exam?
   1) She did well in English, but not in other subjects.
   2) She entered the college that she wanted to attend.
   3) She could study the subject that she planned to major in.

c. How are high school grades considered for college application in China?
   1) Your grades may determine which colleges you can enter.
   2) Grades do not affect one's college application.
   3) Your grades determine which subject you can major in.

9.   Dialogue II

Mark is telling Lin Bin about his experience applying for college admission in the United (CD1: 21) States. Answer the following questions based on the information in the conversation.

a. Which statement about Mark is correct?
   1) He took the SAT twice, but he didn't get a good grade either time.
   2) He was tired when taking the SAT the first time.
   3) He took the SAT many times and used his best score to apply to colleges.

b. Why did Mark decide to go to this university?
   1) It is not far away from his family.
   2) He wants to major in Computer Science.
   3) He likes the weather in the east.

c. According to Mark, what are some other advantages of attending this university?
   1) It is not expensive living on campus.
   2) It is a small but diverse school.
   3) It is easier to find a job after graduation.

Reading and writing

1.   Number of strokes

Indicate the number of strokes used in writing each of the following characters.

a. 數 ＿＿＿   f. 趣 ＿＿＿

b. 興 ＿＿＿   g. 試 ＿＿＿

c. 作 ＿＿＿   h. 所 ＿＿＿

d. 最 ＿＿＿   i. 因 ＿＿＿

e. 考 ＿＿＿   j. 級 ＿＿＿

2.   Which character?

Circle the character in each line that corresponds to the meaning on the left.

a. **guǒ** (**rúguǒ** *if*)   呆   果

b. **xuǎn** *select*   選   纂

c. **jí** *level in school*   級   及

d. **qù** (**xìngqu** *interest*)   越   趣

e. **xìng** (**xìngqu** *interest*)   興   應

f. **suǒ** (**suǒyǐ** *therefore, so*) 戶   所

g. **háng** (**yínháng** *bank*)   行   街

h. **zuò** *do*   作   昨

i. **shì** (**kǎoshì** *test*)   式   試

j. **zuì** *most*   取   最

k. **shù** (**shùxué** *math*)   數   樓

l. **dìng** (**yīdìng** *certainly*) 定   走

3.   First strokes

Write the first two strokes of each of the following characters.

a. 強 ＿＿＿   f. 工 ＿＿＿

b. 定 ＿＿＿   g. 數 ＿＿＿

c. 所 ＿＿＿   h. 選 ＿＿＿

d. 因 ＿＿＿   i. 考 ＿＿＿

e. 最 ＿＿＿   j. 行 ＿＿＿

4.   Missing strokes

Complete each character by writing in the missing strokes.

a.   日   **guǒ (rúguǒ** *if*)

b.   走   **qù (xìngqu** *interest*)

c.   日   **zuì** *most*

d.   言   **shì (kǎoshì** *test*)

e.   冂   **yīn (yīnwèi** *because*)

f.   糹   **jí** (*level in school*)

g.   弓   **qiáng** *strong*

h.   巴   **xuǎn** *select*

i.   彳   **háng (yínháng** *bank*), **xíng** *okay*

j.   門   **xìng (xìngqu** *interest*)

5.   Total strokes

Rewrite this list of characters, arranging the characters in terms of their total number of strokes. Begin your list with the character with the fewest strokes.

強	試	因	趣	工	作	所	行	興	果	最	選	定	考	數	級

6.   Radicals

Here are characters that we have learned in this and previous lessons. Rewrite each character in the row next to its radical.

因　候　定　經　最　課　作　家　工　園　強
趣　試　張　差　國　選　起　級　住　道　時

宀	
辶	
口	
日	
亻	
走	
言	
工	
糸	
弓	

7.   Character sleuth

Group the following characters in terms of a part that they share in common. The shared part need not be the radical in each character. Add at least four shared parts to the list, and then write the characters that share the part afterward, as in the example. You can use a character more than once.

考　期　數　在　作　最　定　坐
趣　老　難　想　果　朋　行　昨
漢　本　做　往　起　前　怎　樣

shared part	characters
人	人，大，太，天，舍
土	
堇	
月	

8. Skimming for information

Read the following paragraph and provide the requested information. You have not learned all of the characters in the paragraph, but you have learned enough characters and grammatical structures to enable you to identify the main point.

a. Circle the characters that you have not learned.

你對哪門課有興趣，不一定要選那個專業。選專業跟很多方面有關係。第一，那個專業難不難。如果很難，你一定學不好。第二，那個專業有用沒有。沒有用的東西為甚麼要學呢？最後，那個專業容易不容易找工作。學了一個專業，可是沒有工作有甚麼用呢？這就是為甚麼專業跟興趣有關係，可是關係不大。

b. In one sentence in English, state the general topic of this passage. That is, what is this paragraph about?

9. Dictionary skills

Following the instructions in Lesson 17 of the Textbook, look up these characters in a Chinese dictionary and provide the requested information:

a. 累
   pronunciation:
   meaning:
   one two-character word or phrase in which it occurs:

b. 業
pronunciation:
meaning:
one two-character word or phrase in which it occurs:

c. 壞
pronunciation:
meaning:
one two-character word or phrase in which it occurs:

10.   Find the incorrect characters

Xiao Zhang has written this email to his older brother, but he has written eleven characters incorrectly. Read the passage aloud, circle the mistakes, and correct them on the answer sheet below.

> 因為我一真對書學很有興去，所以這個學七我先了兩們數學可。可是 **dì** 一個考是以後，我的考是分數不太好。下可以後我去找老師。老師跟我話，**dì** 一個考試的分數好不好沒有關西。**Rú** 果你一直很用功，一定 **néng** 字好，一定 **néng** 考好。

a. ____   b. ____   c. ____   d. ____   e. ____   f. ____

g. ____   h. ____   i. ____   j. ____   k. ____

11.   Scrambled sentences

Rewrite these phrases as sentences, putting the words in the correct order to match the English translations.

a. 選 / **bǐjiào** / 我 / 我 / 每個 / 強 / 都 / 數學課 / 所以 / 因為 / 數學 / 學期 / 一門
Since I am relatively strong in math, I take a math class every semester.

b. 興趣 / 你 / 甚麼 / 有 / 最 / 對
What are you most interested in?

c. 學生 / 忙 / 一年級 / 每天 / 大學 / 非常 / 都 / 的
First-year college students are extremely busy every day.

d. 以前 / 行 / 功課 / 行 / **fù** 習 / 我們 / 圖書館 / 不 / 考試 / 去
Let's go to the library to review the course work before the test, okay?

e. 工作 / 沒 / 那樣 / 有 / 的 / 興趣 / 對 / 我
I am not interested in that kind of job.

12.   Pinyin to characters to English

Rewrite the following sentences in Chinese characters and translate them into English.

a. **Guóqiáng shì xuéxiào yīniánjí de xuésheng**。

English:

b. **Tā měitiān yào qù shàng kè, yě yào qù gōngzuò, suǒyǐ tā hěn máng, yǒu de kǎoshì fēnshù yě bù hǎo**。

English:

c. **Tā yě xiǎng zhǐ shàng kè, bù gōngzuò**。

English:

d. **Zhèyàng tā de kǎoshì fēnshù huì hǎo yīdiǎn**。

English:

e. **Kěshì tā yīdìng děi qù gōngzuò**。

English:

f. **Qù gōngzuò, yǒu le qián, tā cái kěyǐ shàng xué**。

English:

Focus on structure

1.   There is a connection between these things (Use and Structure note 18.1)

Write a sentence for each of the following pairs of situations, saying that there is a relationship between them, as in the example.

Example:

A   B

選 **zhuānyè**   你的 **ài** 好   →   選 **zhuānyè** 跟你的 **ài** 好有關係。

A   B

a. 睡 **jiào** 睡得好   考試分數   →

b. 學生用功不用功   **chéngjì** 好 **huài**   →

c. 經 **jì**   數學   →

d. 老師 **yán** 不 **yán**   學生用功不用功   →

e. 你的 **ài** 好   你的興趣   →

2.   Is there a connection? (Use and Structure note 18.1)

Rewrite the sentences you wrote in Exercise 1 as questions, and translate your questions into English.

a.

   English:

b.

   English:

c.

   English:

d.

   English:

e.

   English:

3.   There isn't any connection (Use and Structure note 18.1)

Answer "no" to each of the questions that you wrote in Exercise 2 in complete Mandarin sentences.

a.

b.

c.

d.

e.

4.   What if? (Use and Structure note 18.2)

Answer each of the following questions truthfully in complete Mandarin sentences using **rú** 果 in each of your sentences.

a. **Rú** 果你選的課太難，怎麼 **bàn**？

b. **Rú** 果你在看電 **yǐng** 的時候覺得那個電 **yǐng** 沒有意思，你會做甚麼？

c. **Rú** 果你的朋友請你去機 **cháng jiē** 他可是你明天有一個考試，你會做甚麼？

d. **Rú** 果學校的書店沒有你要買的課本，怎麼 **bàn**？

e. **Rú** 果你請幾個朋友吃飯可是他們今天都太忙，你怎麼 **bàn**？

5.   Describing nouns, Part I (Use and Structure note 18.3)

Using the pattern <u>description</u> 的 (main) N, translate each of the following noun phrases into Mandarin. The main noun is underlined in each phrase.

Example:
the <u>classes</u> that I selected: 我選的<u>課</u>

a. the <u>cell phone</u> that I bought yesterday   →

b. the <u>Chinese restaurant</u> that we went to   →

c. the <u>movie</u> that I watched   →

d. the <u>students</u> who select a major in economics   →

e. the <u>car</u> that she drives   →

6.   Describing nouns, Part II (Use and Structure note 18.3)

Translate the following noun phrases into English

a. 我買的書   →

b. 我昨天看的那本書   →

c. **jiāo** 我中文的老師   →

d. 他昨天 **hē** 的 **jiǔ**   →

e. 我昨天看的電 **yǐng**   →

f. 他上個星期買的中文書   →

g. 我的 **tóngwū** 昨天買的書   →

h. 媽媽給我做的飯   →

i. **cānjiā quán** 國考試的高中生   →

7.   Describing nouns, Part III (Use and Structure note 18.3)

The noun phrases that you translated in Exercise 6 above occur as the subject or object of the verb in the following sentences. Translate these sentences into English, referring to your translations in Exercise 6.

a. 我買的書都 **bǐjiào guì**。   →

b. 我昨天看的那本書很好。   →

c. 他是 **jiāo** 我中文的老師。   →

d. 他昨天 **hē** 的 **jiǔ** 是法國 **jiǔ**。   →

e. 我昨天看的電 **yǐng** 沒有意思。　　　　　　→

f. 他上個星期買的中文書非常 **piányi**。　　　　→

g. 我的 **tóngwū** 昨天買的書是一年級的中文書。　→

h. 我最喜歡媽媽給我做的飯。　　　　　　　　　→

i. **Cānjiā quán** 國考試的高中生都很 **jǐn** 張。　　→

8. Describing nouns, Part IV (Use and Structure note 18.3)

These sentences each contain a noun phrase with a verb description. Translate them into Chinese. The noun phrase and description are underlined.

a. The student who does best on the test does not have to come to class tomorrow.

b. There are a lot of students who plan to apply to college. (Translate it this way: *The students who plan to apply to college are numerous.*)

c. The fruit that you gave me (as a present) is extremely delicious.

d. Students who graduate from college can find somewhat better jobs.

e. The student who returned to her home country this summer is coming back tomorrow.

9. Describing nouns, Part V (Use and Structure note 18.3)

Put square brackets around the description clauses in each of the following sentences, circle the main verb, and then translate the sentences into English.

a. **Cānjiā** 考試的學生不一定都 **shēn** 請大學。

b. 你 **rènshi** 的高中生 **hē** 不 **hē píjiǔ**？

c. **Bāng** 他學習的那個人已經在中國住了一年了。

d. 你 **néng** 不 **néng** 給我 **jièshào** 昨天晚上跟你吃飯的那個人？

10. Describing nouns, Part VI (Use and Structure notes 18.3, 18.11)

The following noun phrases each contain a noun that is described by more than one description. Underline each description phrase, and then translate these noun phrases into English.

a. 我昨天買的很 **guì** 的手機 →

b. 我昨天晚上看的很有意思的日本電 **yǐng** →

c. 這個學期選中文的美國學生 →

d. 那兩個 **shēn** 請去中國學習的大學生 →

e. 我覺得最有意思的那些課 →

f. 我們剛 **rènshi** 的學文學的那個人 →

11. Asking for reasons and giving explanations, Part I (Use and Structure note 18.6)

Translate the following conversations into Mandarin.

a. Lili: Why do you go to sleep so late every night?

Meili: Because I have so much homework in my economics class (*Because my economics class homework is so much.*)

b. Xiao Wang: Why are you so nervous?

Xiao Zhang: Because I'm taking a national college admissions test tomorrow.

Xiao Wang: What happens if you do poorly on the test?

Xiao Zhang: If I do poorly on the test, in the future, I won't be able to attend college.

c. Chen Ming: Why are grades so important?

Teacher: Because your high school grades are related to whether or not you get into college.

12. Asking for reasons and giving explanations, Part II
(Use and Structure note 18.6)

Translate the following conversations into English.

a. 大為：你昨天為甚麼沒去看電 yǐng？
友文：我去了，可是去晚了。因為昨天的公 **gòng qì** 車非常慢，所以我到的時候電 **yǐng** 已經開 **shǐ** 了。

b. 大為：你的 **zhuānyè** 是經 **jì**，這個學期為甚麼選了一門 **yīnyuè** 課？
國強：我選了兩門經 **jì** 課。因為經 **jì** 課的功課和考試都很多，我聽說 **yīnyuè** 課容易，所以選了一門 **yīnyuè** 課。

c. 美 **lì**：不知道為甚麼我最 **jìn** 覺得很 **lèi**。
友文：我想因為快考試了，你 **bǐjiào jǐn** 張。人 **jǐn** 張的時候就容易 **lèi**。

d. **Mài Kè**：這麼容易的考試我為甚麼考得不好呢？我太 **bèn** 了。
王明：你不 **bèn**。因為你對這門課沒有興趣，學的時候不用功，所以考得不好。

13. From this perspective (Use and Structure note 18.9)

Translate these sentences into English.

a. 我的 **tóngwū** 在學習 **fāngmiàn** 很 **cōng** 明，可是在生 **huó fāngmiàn** 很 **bèn**。我在 **sùshè** 要 **bāng** 他做很多 **shìqing**。

b. 在選 **zhuānyè** 這 **fāngmiàn**，你最好問問你的爸爸媽媽和 **bié** 的 **tóng** 學，不要 **zìjǐ jué** 定。

c. 在中文和中國文 **huà** 這些 **fāngmiàn** 國強 **bāng** 大為，在 **Yīng** 文和 **yīnyuè fāngmiàn** 國強常常請大為 **bāng** 他。

d. **Suī** 然國強常常 **bāng** 大為學中文，可是在中文 **yǔ** 法 **fāngmiàn** 國強也不 **dǒng**。他只知道怎麼說。

14. Translation challenge I

Translate these sentences into English. Begin by identifying the structures used in the sentence, including noun descriptions. The first sentence is outlined for you.

a. 美國的高中生在 **bìyè** 以前，**cānjiā** 不 **cānjiā quán** 國的考試？(___ 以前，___ 的考試)

b. 很多美國的大學生覺得 **hē jiǔ** 跟學習 **chéngjì** 沒有關係。最 **zhòng** 要的是 **hē jiǔ** 以後不要開車，學習的時候要用功。

c. 我的 **ài** 好和興趣是 **yīnyuè** 和 **chàng gē**，可是選 **yīnyuè zhuānyè jiāng** 來不容易找工作。我 **yīnggāi** 怎麼 **bàn** 呢？

d. 上大學為甚麼要選 **zhuānyè** 呢？很多大學生 **bìyè** 以後的工作跟他的 **zhuānyè** 沒有一點關係。

e. **Zhuānyè** 沒有好 **huài**，可是有的容易，有的難。為甚麼有很多學生要選很難的 **zhuānyè** 呢？

f. 我快要 **bìyè** 了，開 **shǐ shēn** 請工作。因為現在美國的經 **jì** 很不好，所以大學 **bìyè** 生很難找到 **zìjǐ** 喜歡的工作。我很 **jǐn** 張。我常常想 **rú** 果我可以一直上學就好了。

g. 我昨天在圖書館 **rènshi** 的那個中國學生跟我說 **rú** 果我在學習中文 **fāngmiàn** 有問 **tí** 可以給他打電話問他。

15. Translation challenge II

Translate these sentences into Mandarin, using the phrase or structure provided.

a. I think this matter is none of your business. (關係)

b. She is the best teacher in our school. (最)

c. If you work very hard (in your studies), in the future, you may become the number one person in your major. Every field produces a leading expert. (Use **rú** 果, also use the Chinese proverb introduced in this lesson.)

d. Before you select your major you should think about your interests. (以前)

e. The strongest students do not necessarily make the most money. (不一定)

f. If you are feeling tired you should go back and go to sleep. (**rú** 果)

g. I've heard that you are interested in Chinese economics. Do you think that in the future you will study in China? (興趣)

h. Yes. I plan to go to China to study before I graduate from college. After I graduate I will go back again and look for work. (以前, 以後)

Focus on communication

1.   Dialogue comprehension

Study the Lesson 18 Narrative and Dialogue. Then, read the following statements and indicate whether they are true (T) or false (F).

a. (   ) 選 **zhuānyè** 很 **zhòng** 要，對 **zhuānyè** 沒有興趣，就學不好。

b. (   ) 你的 **jiāng** 來跟你的 **zhuānyè** 有很大的關係。

c. (   ) **Rú** 果學習的時候你很容易 **jǐn** 張，**chéngjì** 也不好，你的 **zhuānyè** 一定選得不好。

d. (   ) 有的 **zhuānyè** 好，有的 **zhuānyè** 很 **zāogāo**。

e. (   ) 美國學生上大學以前先 **jué** 定 **zhuānyè**。

f. (   ) 大為和國強的 **zhuānyè** 都是經 **jì**。

g. (   ) **Rú** 果你經 **jì fāngmiàn** 最強，你就選經 **jì fāngmiàn** 的 **zhuānyè**。

h. (   ) 中國的高中生 **rú** 果不 **cānjiā quán** 國的考試，就不能上大學。

i. (   ) 在中國，你先 **shēn** 請大學和 **zhuānyè** 再考試。

2.   What do you say?

What do you say in each of the following situations? Type your answers, using characters where we have learned them, and email them to your Chinese teacher.

a. You want to tell your friend who just did really badly on a test that grades are not the most important thing.

b. You wonder what you should do because economics is not a major that you are interested in.

c. You want your friend to know that you had nothing to do with the situation (matter) that he mentioned.

d. You want to explain to your parents that math is not your strongest subject so you will not pick math as your major.

e. As a father, assure your son that if he begins to earn money right now, he can definitely afford his favorite car in the future.

f. You want to find out why your friend from China already knows her major before she enters college.

g. You express the unlikelihood that you will dive into the job market right after graduation because you first plan to travel in China for three months.

h. You want to encourage your younger brother that if he studies diligently from now on, he can definitely apply to a good college.

i. Tell your roommate that all of the restaurants she picks are great.

j. You were wondering if you could switch to a different teacher if you don't like the one you chose.

3. Complete the mini-dialogues

Use the structure in parentheses to complete each mini-dialogue. You can respond in any way that makes sense and uses the targeted structure.

a. A: 這個 **jiǎo** 子真好吃！

B: _____ 當然好吃！(description 的 N)

b. A: 你甚麼時候可以 **sòng** 我回家？

B: _____。(以後)

c. A: 你不 **cōng** 明，當然沒有女朋友！

B: _____。(A 跟 B 沒有關係)

d. A: 中文、日文和法文哪個難？

B: _____。(最)

e. A: **Rú** 果書店不賣我要的課本，怎麼 **bàn**？

B: **Bié jǐn** 張，_____。(不會)

4. Why and how?

Fill in the blanks with 為甚麼, 這麼, 怎麼, or 怎麼 **bàn** to complete each question. (Use 怎麼 only once.) Then answer each question truthfully.

a. 從學校到你家 _____ 走最快？

Answer: _____

b. 上 **cì** 的中文考試你 _____ 考得不好？

Answer: _____

c. **Rú** 果你很 **lèi**，沒有時 **jiān** 做飯，_____？

Answer: _____

d. 你 _____ 對中文有興趣？

Answer: _____

e. 你想去法國 **lǚyóu**，可是你沒有錢，_____？

Answer: _____

f. 上個學期你的 **chéngjì** 為甚麼 _____ **zāogāo**（or _____ 好）？

Answer: _____

5.   Multiple choice questions

Select the expression that best completes each sentence and then translate the sentence into English.

a. 中國的高中學生先 **cānjiā quán** 國的考試，_____ **shēn** 請大學和 **zhuānyè**。
   1) 再
   2) 所以
   3) 因為

English:

b. _____ 星期五早上我沒有 **shì**，我 _____ 跟你去那個新的書店。
   1) 因為…所以
   2) **Suī** 然…可是
   3) **Rú** 果…就

English:

c. 我對數學沒有興趣，所以 _____。
   1) 我的 **zhuānyè** 是數學
   2) 數學 **fāngmiàn** 的課我都不選
   3) 我不 **néng bìyè**

English:

d. **Suī** 然有的 **zhuānyè jiāng** 來可以 **zhèng bǐjiào** 多的錢，可是 _____。
   1) 我一直對經 **jì** 很有興趣
   2) **zhuānyè** 和你的 **jiāng** 來有很大的關係
   3) 選一個你最喜歡的 **zhuānyè bǐjiào zhòng** 要

English:

e. **Rú** 果 _____，就吃一點水果吧。
   1) 你已經吃過飯了
   2) 喝了一點水
   3) 你在吃飯

English:

6. 小王的 **chéngjì**

Below is Xiao Wang's report card from last semester. He tends to do well in the subjects that he has the most interest in and vice versa. Translate and answer the questions in Mandarin.

Chinese	Chinese Culture	Economics	Mathematics	Chinese Music
A+	A	B+	C–	A–

a. How many courses did Xiao Wang choose last semester?

    Q: _____

    A: _____

b. In which subject did Xiao Wang get the highest grade?

    Q: _____

    A: _____

c. What area was Xiao Wang strongest in?

    Q: _____

    A: _____

d. What factor influences his grades?

    Q: _____

    A: _____

e. What course was Xiao Wang least interested in?

    Q: _____

    A: _____

f. In the future, what area can Xiao Wang look for a job in?

    Q: _____

    A: _____

7.   This is my friend who...

You are showing photos of your college friends to your parents. Follow the example sentence and use <u>description</u> 的 N to complete each sentence.

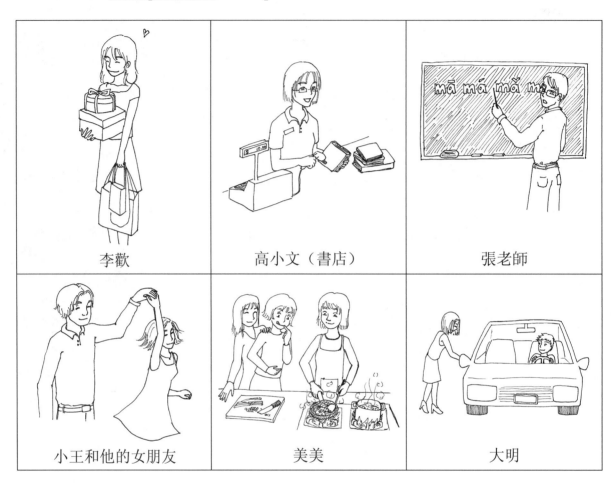

| 李歡 | 高小文（書店） | 張老師 |
| 小王和他的女朋友 | 美美 | 大明 |

Example:
常常做飯給我們吃的是美美。

a. _____是張老師。

b. _____是大明。

c. _____是小王和他的女朋友。

d. _____是李歡。

e. _____是高小文。

8.   Do you agree? Why or why not?

Read each statement and write a simple response stating why you agree or do not agree with it. Start your sentence with 我也覺得 / 我不覺得 + statement, 因為....

a. 選 **zhuānyè** 是大學生最 **zhòng** 要的 **shìqing**。

b. 選 **zhuānyè** 跟 **jiāng** 來的工作有很大的關係。

c. **Rú** 果大家都選這個 **zhuānyè**，這個 **zhuānyè** 一定是最好的。

d. 大學一年級和二年級選的課，可以 **bāng** 你 **jué** 定你的 **zhuānyè**。

e. **Rú** 果選 **bǐjiào** 容易的 **zhuānyè**，大學的生 **huó** 會 **bǐjiào** 快 **lè**。

f. **Rú** 果還沒有 **jìn** 大學就選 **zhuānyè**，你不一定會喜歡那個 **zhuānyè**。

9.   Writing

Write a paragraph about how you decided on your major and why you chose it. You can use some of the answers you have used in the previous exercise. If you haven't decided on your major, explain what you are interested in and what major you might choose. Below is a list of words/expressions that you can use in your paragraph. Include at least <u>five</u> of them. Your paragraph should be at least 100 characters in length.

因為...所以	A 跟 B 有關係	只是	**jué** 定	對...有興趣
選	**rú** 果...就	**bǐjiào**	有用	不過

_____

_____

_____

_____

_____

_____

Lesson 19 Workbook

Listening and speaking

1. I've done it already (Use and Structure note 19.2)

You will hear a suggestion that you finish doing some action. Reply that you have already finished, as in the example.

Example:
You will hear: 你要看 **wán** 這本書。
You will say: 這本書我已經看 **wán** 了。
Click "R" to hear the correct response: 這本書我已經看 **wán** 了。

(a)   (b)   (c)   (d)   (e)   (f)   (g)   (h)   (i)   (j)

2. I did it, but I wasn't successful (Use and Structure note 19.2)

You will hear a question asking if you have successfully completed some task. You will say that you did the action, but that you did not successfully complete the task, as in the example.

Example:
You will hear: 那本書你找到了嗎？
You will say: 那本書，我找了，可是沒找到。
Click "R" to hear the correct response: 那本書，我找了，可是沒找到。

(a)   (b)   (c)   (d)   (e)   (f)   (g)   (h)

3. Extremely! (Use and Structure note 19.3)

You will hear a question asking about the characteristic of some person or thing. Say that the person or thing is *extremely* so, as in the example.

Example:
You will hear: 今天的 **kǎoshì** 難嗎？
You will say: 今天的 **kǎoshì** 難 **jí** 了。
Click "R" to hear the correct response: 今天的 **kǎoshì** 難 **jí** 了。

(a)   (b)   (c)   (d)   (e)   (f)   (g)   (h)   (i)   (j)

4. Both…and (Use and Structure note 19.6)

You will hear two qualities followed by a noun. Say that the noun has *both* the first quality *and* the second quality, as in the example.

Example:
You will hear: **piányi**、好吃、中國飯
You will say: 中國飯 **yòu piányi yòu** 好吃。
Click "R" to hear the correct response: 中國飯 **yòu piányi yòu** 好吃。

(a)   (b)   (c)   (d)   (e)   (f)   (g)   (h)

5. Bǎ with resultative verbs (Use and Structure note 19.7)

You will hear a sentence saying that you should complete some task. Restate the sentence with **bǎ**, as in the example.

Example:
You will hear: 你要看 **wán** 這本書。
You will say: 我 **bǎ** 這本書看 **wán** 了。
Click "R" to hear the correct response: 我 **bǎ** 這本書看 **wán** 了。

(a)   (b)   (c)   (d)   (e)   (f)   (g)   (h)   (i)   (j)

6. Put the object in a location (Use and Structure note 19.7)

You will hear a sentence stating the location of some object. Restate the sentence with **bǎ**, saying that you have put the object in the location.

Example:
You will hear: 書放在書 **jià** 上了。
You will say: 我 **bǎ** 書放在書 **jià** 上了。
Click "R" to hear the correct response: 我 **bǎ** 書放在書 **jià** 上了。

(a)   (b)   (c)   (d)   (e)   (f)   (g)   (h)   (i)   (j)

7. Negation of bǎ sentences (Use and Structure notes 19.7, 19.11)

You will hear a sentence with **bǎ** saying that someone has done some action. Negate the sentence, saying that the person has not done the action, as in the example.

Example:
You will hear: 小謝 **bǎ** 那本書看 **wán** 了。
You will say: 小謝沒 **bǎ** 那本書看 **wán**。
Click "R" to hear the correct response: 小謝沒 **bǎ** 那本書看 **wán**。

(a)   (b)   (c)   (d)   (e)   (f)   (g)   (h)

8. Don't do it! (Use and Structure note 19.7)

You will hear a sentence saying that I have put an object in some location. Reply by telling me politely not to put the object in that location, as in the example.

Example:
You will hear: 我 **bǎ** 書放在地上了。
You will say: 請你不要 **bǎ** 書放在地上。
Click "R" to hear the correct response: 請你不要 **bǎ** 書放在地上。

(a)   (b)   (c)   (d)   (e)   (f)   (g)   (h)   (i)   (j)

9. You have to do it (Use and Structure note 19.8)

You will hear a question asking whether it is necessary to do something. Reply that you have to do it, as in the example.

Example:
You will hear: 那本書你一定要看嗎？
You will say: 對，那本書我非看不可。
Click "R" to hear the correct response: 對，那本書我非看不可。

(a)   (b)   (c)   (d)   (e)   (f)   (g)

10. As soon as I do this, I do that (Use and Structure note 19.10)

You will hear a statement saying that after you do one action, you do another action. Restate the sentence with 一…就 to say that *as soon as* you do the first action, you do the second one *right afterward,* as in the example.

Example:
You will hear: 我下了課就去圖書館。
You will say: 我一下課，就去圖書館。
Click "R" to hear the correct response: 我一下課，就去圖書館。

(a)   (b)   (c)   (d)   (e)   (f)   (g)   (h)   (i)   (j)

11.   Whenever (Use and Structure note 19.10)

You will hear a statement saying that when you do one action, you do another action. Restate the sentence with 一…就 to say that *whenever* you do the first action, you do the second one, as in the example.

Example:
You will hear: 我開車的時候聽 **yīnyuè**。
You will say: 我一開車就聽 **yīnyuè**。
Click "R" to hear the correct response: 我一開車就聽 **yīnyuè**。

(a)   (b)   (c)   (d)   (e)   (f)   (g)   (h)

Listening for information

1.   Moving things around the room

(CD1: 24)

Gaofeng and his roommate are sitting in their dorm room. Gaofeng is telling his roommate to move things to different places in the room. Listen to each of Gaofeng's instructions and draw an arrow from the place where each item is to the place where Gaofeng tells his roommate to put it.

Gaofeng

2.   What are they doing?

(CD1: 25) This is the room where Xiao An, Pai Hai, Wen Shan, and Wang Tong live. Their friends Cheng Li, Lao Dong, and Xiao Wang are visiting them. Look at the picture to find out what each person is doing and then answer the questions in the recording in English.

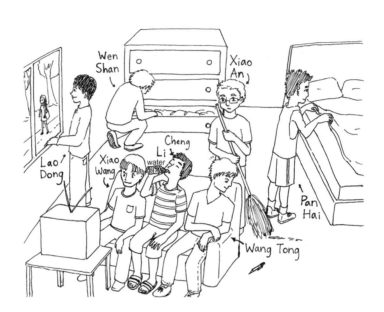

a.

b.

c.

d.

e.

f.

g.

3. Aiping's room

You will hear six statements that describe Aiping's room. Listen to the statements and (CD1: 26) indicate whether they are true (T) or false (F) based on the drawing.

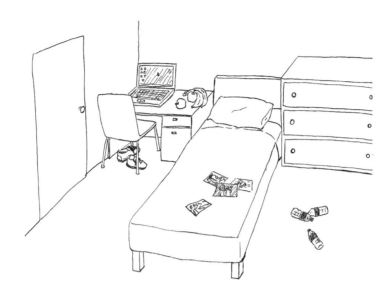

a. ( )   b. ( )   c. ( )   d. ( )   e. ( )   f. ( )

4. Our afternoon

Listen to Xianmin's narration about his afternoon with his girlfriend Xinxin, and write the (CD1: 27) events in English in chronological order as Xianmin describes them.

a. _____ → b. _____ → c. _____ →

d. _____ → e. _____

5. My girlfriend is visiting

Shucheng is telling his roommate what they need to do before his girlfriend arrives. Listen (CD1: 28) to his instructions and write the tasks in English in the order in which they are mentioned.

a.

b.

c.

d.

e.

6. Conversation

(CD1: 29) A classmate is asking you about your living situation. Write the answers in complete sentences in Mandarin, based on your situation, writing characters wherever we have learned them. If you live at home, describe your home situation.

a.

b.

c.

d.

e.

f.

7. Listen and reply

(CD1: 30) Xiao Fang has a new roommate. Listen to her description of her new roommate to her mom and answer the questions that follow in English, based on the description.

a.

b.

c.

d.

e.

8. Dialogue I

(CD1: 31) You will hear a dialogue between two classmates who are taking the same course. Answer the questions based on the dialogue.

a. What is the homework?
   1) complete the Lesson 2 workbook
   2) preview the Lesson 3 text
   3) complete the Lesson 3 workbook
   4) preview the Lesson 2 text

b. What is the woman's plan?
   1) She will talk to the teacher.
   2) She will withdraw from the course.
   3) She will do her laundry.
   4) She will get help from the man.

c. Which statement about the woman's clothes is accurate?
   1) She cannot find the clothes that she wants.
   2) She does not have time to wash her clothes now.
   3) All of her clothes are dirty.
   4) She needs to buy some new clothes.

9.   Dialogue II

You will hear a dialogue between a brother and sister. Answer the questions based on the **(CD1: 32)** dialogue.

a. Where did the brother last see his cell phone?
   1) at school
   2) in the room
   3) in the restaurant
   4) in the office

b. What did the sister do?
   1) She cleaned his room.
   2) She helped him to remember something.
   3) She scolded him for losing the phone.
   4) She told him where to find the phone.

c. Where is the cell phone?
   1) next to the desk
   2) under a pile of papers
   3) in the office
   4) under the chair

Reading and writing

Focus on Chinese characters

1.   Number of strokes

Indicate the number of strokes used in writing each of the following characters.

a. 始 ____   f. 屋 ____

b. 能 ____   g. 間 ____

c. 同 ____   h. 房 ____

d. 洗 ____   i. 舍 ____

e. 雖 ____   j. 床 ____

2.   Which character?

Circle the character in each line that corresponds to the meaning on the left.

a. **jiān** (**fángjiān** *room*)   間   問

b. **fāng** (**fángjiān** *room*)   房   放

c. **lǐ** (**lǐbian** *inside*)   裏   裹

d. **sù** (**sùshè** *dormitory*)   伯   宿

e. **biān** (**lǐbian** *inside*)   邊   這

f. **shǐ** (**kāishǐ** *begin*)   始   如

g. **wài** (**wàibian** *outside*)   外   仆

h. **chuáng** *bed*   床   庄

i. **shè** (**sùshè** *dormitory*)   含   舍

j. **wū** (**tóngwū** *roommate*)   屋   房

k. **tóng** (**tóngwū** *roommate*)   筒   同

l. **suī** (**suīrán** *although*)   難   雖

3.   First strokes

Write the first two strokes of each of the following characters.

a. 雖 ____   f. 屋 ____

b. 放 ____   g. 所 ____

c. 裏 ____   h. 房 ____

d. 床 ____   i. 能 ____

e. 邊 ____   j. 宿 ____

4.   Missing strokes

Complete each character by writing in the missing strokes.

a.   自   **biān** (**lǐbian** *inside*)

b.   阝   **jiān** (**fángjiān** *room*)

c.   个   **shè** (**sùshè** *dormitory*)

d.   宀   **sù** (**sùshè** *dormitory*)

e.   夕   **wài** (**wàibian** *outside*)

f.   方   **fàng** *put*

g.   白   **néng** *able to, can*

h.   女   **shǐ** (**kāishǐ** *begin*)

i.   冂   **tóng** (**tóngwū** *roommate*)

j.   呂   **suī** (**suīrán** *although*)

5.   Total strokes

Rewrite this list of characters, arranging the characters in terms of their total number of strokes. Begin your list with the character with the fewest strokes.

舍	雖	屋	同	床	間	放	房	能	始	宿	外	洗	邊	裏

6. Radicals

Here are characters that we have learned through this lesson. Rewrite each character in the row next to its radical.

邊　定　能　選　外　房　間
始　屋　放　所　床　洗　同

戶	
宀	
辶	
口	
月	
夕	
門	
女	
尸	
攵	
广	
氵	

7. Character sleuth

Group the following characters in terms of a part that they share in common. The shared part need not be the radical in each character.

外　放　洗　多　問　們　能　容　期　選　房
前　媽　用　先　始　館　朋　宿　好　家　間

shared part	characters
人	人，大，太，天，舍
夕	
門	
月	
方	
先	
女	
宀	

8. Find the words and phrases

You won't be able to completely understand the following passage, but it contains many characters that we have learned.

a. Circle at least fifteen <u>words</u> that we have learned that are <u>composed of two or more characters each</u> and write them on the answer sheet below.

"今年" is an example of a word that is composed of two or more characters.

"我也" is composed of two characters in a row that we have learned, but it is <u>not</u> a word.

> 晚上吃晚飯的時候我的手機沒有了。我想下午下課以後我去圖書館了。在圖書館一做完作業我就來吃飯了。我一定在圖書館學習的時候把手機放在桌子上了。我回圖書館去找我的手機。找了半天，可是沒找到。我不可以沒有手機。明天下了課，我非得去買手機不可。我很不高興地回宿舍了。一打開宿舍的門，我就看見我的手機在宿舍的桌子上。我不用買新的了。我高興極了。

Words in this paragraph composed of two or more characters:

1. _____   2. _____   3. _____   4. _____   5. _____

6. _____   7. _____   8. _____   9. _____   10. _____

11. _____   12. _____   13. _____   14. _____   15. _____

b. In one sentence in English, state the general topic of this passage.

9. Dictionary skills

Following the instructions in Lesson 17 of the Textbook, look up these characters in a Chinese dictionary and provide the requested information.

a. 把
pronunciation:
meaning:
one two-character word or phrase in which it occurs:

b. 完
pronunciation:
meaning:
one two-character word or phrase in which it occurs:

c. 衣
pronunciation:
meaning:
one two-character word or phrase in which it occurs:

10. Find the incorrect characters

Xiao Zhang has written this email to his parents but he has written ten characters incorrectly. Read the passage aloud, circle the mistakes, and correct them on the answer sheet below.

> 我這級天非常忙，沒友時問去買可本。今天非去不可了，**yīn** 為明天九要開始上課了。
> 一吃 **wán** 早飯，我就到書點去了。**Bié** 的書都賣到了，就是中問課的書賣 **wán** 了，
> **yīn** 為巽中文課的學生恨多。

a. ____   b. ____   c. ____   d. ____   e. ____

f. ____   g. ____   h. ____   i. ____   j. ____

11. Scrambled sentences

Rewrite these phrases as sentences, putting the words in the correct order to match the English translations.

a. 課本 / 同屋 / 我的 / 的 / 都 / 在 / 他床 / 下邊 / 的

My roommate's textbooks are all under his bed.

b. 在 / 可是 / **zhōumò** / 她 / 宿舍 / 她 / 洗 **yīfu** / 雖然 / 住 / 每個 / 回家

Although she lives in a dorm, she goes home every weekend to do laundry (wash clothes).

c. 非常 / 學 / 的時候 / 我 / 開始 / 開車 / 開車 / 慢 / 剛 / 開得/

When I just started to learn how to drive a car I drove extremely slowly.

d. 能 / 我 / 你 / 不 / **bāng** / 課 / 能 / 選

Can you help me select courses?

e. 的 / 在 / 他 / 都 / 床上 / 東西 / 放

All of his things are on the bed.

12. Translation

Read the following passage and translate it into English.

小 **Yè** 沒有同屋，她一個人住。她的宿舍不大，**dàn** 是很 **gānjìng**。房間裏的東西不多，
一個床、一個 **guì** 子、一個書 **jià**、一張 **zhuō** 子和兩 **bǎ yǐ** 子。**Zhuō** 子上有書、**bǐ**、**liàn**
習本，還有一個電 **nǎo**。

13. Pinyin to characters

Rewrite the following sentences in Chinese characters.

a. Jīntiān suīrán shì xīngqīliù, bù yòng qù shàng kè, kěshì Dàmíng qǐ chuáng qǐ de hěn zǎo。

b. Tā yào gēn tā èr niánjí de jǐ ge péngyou yīqǐ qù tā Zhōngguó tóngwū de jiā。

c. Dào Zhōngguó rén de jiā qù kànkan, qù chī fàn, tāmen dōu hěn gāoxīng。

Focus on structure

1.   She's been doing it a long time (Use and Structure note 19.1)

Here is a list of the things that Meili has done and the amount of time she has spent on each activity. Write a sentence in Mandarin for each activity, describing how long she has done it.

activity	duration
a. washed clothes	more than a half hour
b. watched television	more than three hours
c. studied Chinese	more than one year
d. slept	more than eight hours

a.

b.

c.

d.

2.   Bird watching (Use and Structure note 19.2)

Xie Guoqiang has a new hobby: bird watching. He is keeping a list of birds that can be seen in and around Beijing, and he checks off birds as he sees them. Write a sentence for each bird, saying whether he has seen it or not. The resultative verb that you will use in each sentence is 看到.

bird	sighted
a. golden oriole (**jīn yīng**)	
b. egret (**bái lù**)	✓
c. woodpecker (**zhuó mù niǎo**)	
d. spotted turtle dove (**bān jiū**)	✓

a.

b.

c.

d.

3.   Have you completed the task? (Use and Structure note 19.2)

Here are tasks that Guoqiang has been engaged in. Ask him in complete Mandarin sentences if he has reached the indicated conclusion or result, as in the example.

Example:
看書, finished reading   →   你看 **wán** 書了嗎？ or 你看 **wán** 書了沒有？

a. 找他的 **shǒujī**, found it   →

b. 買電 **yǐng piào**, bought it   →

c. **shōushi** 房間, finished (and it is now presentable for his guests)   →

d. 寫功課, finished   →

e. 選課, finished   →

4. Done! (Use and Structure note 19.2)

Guoqiang has completed all of the tasks. Answer *yes* to each of the five questions in Exercise 3 using a complete sentence in Mandarin.

a.

b.

c.

d.

e.

5. When did Guoqiang complete the tasks?

Guoqiang finished some of these tasks a while ago, and some of them just a moment ago. For a few of the tasks, he's almost done. Take your answers in Exercise 4 and rewrite them, adding in the time adverb in the appropriate location. Then translate each of your responses into English.

a. 剛　　→
   English:

b. 早就　　→
   English:

c. 現在　　→
   English:

d. 剛　　→
   English:

e. 早就　　→
   English:

6. Not yet done! (Use and Stucture notes 19.2, 19.4, 19.7)

Here are activities that Youwen has been doing, followed by the result or conclusion that she wants to reach. Write a sentence for each of these activities saying that she has been doing it for a long time but she's still not done.

a. **shōushi** 房間...**shōushi gānjìng**

b. 做功課...做 **wán**

c. 找她的 **shǒujī**...找到

d. 看書...看 **wán**

7. All except for this (Use and Structure note 19.5, 19.7)

Xiao Chen is getting his dorm ready for a party. For every part of the preparation, he has only one more thing to do. Here is his list of tasks and remaining activities. Complete each sentence in Mandarin and then translate the entire sentence into English. Use the expression 就是 *only, it is only* in each of your Mandarin sentences.

a. 功課都做好了。 *I just haven't finished reviewing the Chinese characters.*
   Mandarin:
   English: _____. *I just haven't finished reviewing the Chinese characters.*

b. 我 **bǎ** 房間 **shōushi** 好了。 *I just haven't put the clothes in the dresser.*
   Mandarin:
   English: _____. *I just haven't put the clothes in the dresser.*

c. 吃的，**hē** 的都買好了。 *I just haven't bought the beer.*
   Mandarin:
   English: _____. *I just haven't bought the beer.*

d. 同學都已經 **gàosu** 了。 *I just haven't invited my teachers.*
   Mandarin:
   English: _____. *I just haven't invited my teachers.*

e. **Bié** 的都好了。 *We just haven't selected the music.*
   Mandarin:
   English: _____. *We just haven't selected the music.*

8. What they do in the time before the party
(Use and Structure notes 19.2, 19.7)

Xiao Chen and his friends are all going to be busy in the time before the party. Here is what they are doing. Translate their activities into English.

a. 在小 **Chén** 的同學來以前，他得先 **bǎ** 漢字 **fù** 習 **wán**。

b. 在小高去小 **Chén** 家以前，她先給媽媽爸爸打電話。

c. 在大為去晚會以前，他得先 **jiē** 小 **Yè** 和小高。

d. 在小王去小 **Chén** 那兒以前，他先 **bāng** 小 **Chén** 買幾 **píng** 可 **lè**。

9. Both...and (Use and Structure note 19.6)

Here are comments and observations that Xiao Chen's guests make during the party. Write them in complete Mandarin sentences, using **yòu** AdjV₁ **yòu** AdjV₂.

a. 宿舍（**piàoliang**，**gānjìng**） →

b. **cài**（多，好吃） →

c. 地 **tiě**（**piányi**，快） →

d. 水果（好看，好吃） →

e. 那個日本飯館（**yuǎn**，**guì**） →

10. Have to do it? No need to do it? (Use and Structure notes 19.8, 19.9)

Here is a list of activities. Meili has put a * next to all of the activities she absolutely has to do, and she has put a ☺ next to all of the activities she need not do. Write a Mandarin sentence for each activity saying that she has to do it (非…不可) or need not do it (不用). If the verb phrase consists of a verb + object, state the object before 非…不可.

a. review Chinese * →

b. go to the library ☺ →

c. finish reading the economics textbook * →

d. clean up the room ☺ →

e. watch that new Chinese movie * →

f. go downtown to buy a subway map ☺ →

11. When will you do it? As soon as... (Use and Structure note 19.10)

Xiao Xie's mother is asking him when he is going to do a number of things. He says he will do them as soon as he finishes another activity. Here is a list of her questions and the activity that he needs to finish first before he does the task that she mentions. Use this information to write Xiao Xie's responses, using 一 VP₁ 就 VP₂ in each response, as in the example.

Example:
你甚麼時候 **shuì** 覺？（看 **wán** 這本書） → 我一看 **wán** 這本書就 **shuì** 覺。

a. 你甚麼時候去上課？（吃 **wán** 早飯） →

b. 你甚麼時候做功課？（找到我的課本） →

c. 你甚麼時候找工作？（這個學期 **wán** 了） →

d. 你甚麼時候選 **zhuānyè**？（對課有興趣） →

e. 你甚麼時候請你的同屋來家吃飯？（放 **jià**） →

12.   Complete the sentences

Fill in the blanks with one of the following words or phrases to complete each sentence.

就是	半天	非	一定	不用	在

a. 上課的時候不可以 **hē kāfēi**。你得 _____ 上課以前 **hē wán**。

b. 這個店的 **yīfu** 不多，我選了 _____ 也沒選到一 **jiàn** 我想買的。

c. 明天 _____ 上課，所以今天晚上可以晚一點 **shuì**。

d. **Rú** 果昨天考試容易一點，我 _____ 會考得 **bǐjiào** 好。

e. 我會說中文、日文、法文、**Dé** 文，_____ 不會說 **Yīng** 文。

f. 功課明天就得給老師，所以今天晚上我 _____ 寫 **wán** 不可。

Focus on communication

1.   Dialogue comprehension

Study the Lesson 19 Narrative and Dialogue. Then, read the following statements and indicate whether they are true (T) or false (F).

a. (   ) 小張和小謝這幾天忙 **zhe** 選課還有買課本。

b. (   ) 小張和小謝今天晚上請同學來開晚會，所以他們在 **shōushi** 宿舍。

c. (   ) 他們現在都在房間裏。

d. (   ) 小張找書找了十二個鐘頭了。

e. (   ) 他們的房間 **luànjí** 了。這兒、那兒都是書。

f. (   ) 他們 **jué** 定先 **shōushi** 房間，不找課本了。

g. (   ) **Zhuō** 子上和地上的書 **yīnggāi** 放在書 **jià** 上，**yīfu yīnggāi** 放在 **guì** 子裏。

h. (   ) 房間 **shōushi** 好以後，小張 **sǎo** 地，小謝 **shōushi xié** 子。

2.   What do you say?

What do you say in each of the following situations? Type your answers, using characters where we have learned them, and email them to your Chinese teacher.

a. You are mad that your younger brother messes up your room. Ask him to straighten it up before you come back tonight.

b. Your hands are full with grocery bags. Ask someone nicely if he can open the door for you.

c. You want to know if your classmate finished selecting his classes.

d. Your friend offers you beer at a party. You decline because you feel sleepy as soon as you drink beer.

e. You wonder if your friend has seen the shoes you purchased yesterday. You've been looking for them for a long time.

f. You tell your friend that he's going to regret it if he does not try this restaurant. (In other words, he must try it!)

g. It's been two weeks since school began. Your teacher wonders why you haven't bought the textbooks yet. What does the teacher say?

h. You are checking out a potential apartment for rent. You don't like it because it's small and expensive.

i. You ask if your roommate can sweep the floor clean because you are busy putting books back on the shelf.

j. You explain to your friend that you've been to France and Germany but you haven't been to China.

k. You brought home from school a bag of dirty clothes. Ask your mom if she can wash them for you.

3.   Complete the mini-dialogues

Use the structure in parentheses to complete each mini-dialogue.

a. A: 你不是去買 **xié** 嗎？怎麼沒買到？

   B: 那些 **xié** _____，我都不喜歡。（**yòu…yòu**）

b. A: 你打 **suan** 甚麼時候開始寫功課？

   B: 我 _____。（一…就）

c. A: 你看見我的日文課本了嗎？我已經找了半天了。

   B: 沒看見。我 _____ 就來 **bāng** 你找。（**bǎ**）

d. A: 你看，這是我昨天買的 **yīfu**，你覺得怎麼樣？

   B: _____！多少錢？我也想買一 **jiàn**！（**jí** 了）

e. A: _____？（不用）

   B: 你怎麼 **wàng** 了？今天是 Veterans Day，放一天 **jià**。

4. Before and after

Below are two pictures of Xie Weizhong's room, before and after he cleaned it up.

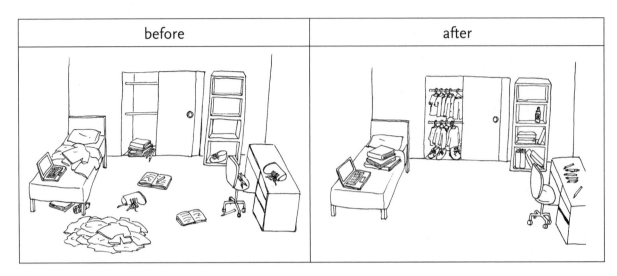

before	after

Part I. Look at the BEFORE picture. Translate each of the following questions into Mandarin and then answer them in Mandarin.

a. What is in the closet?

   Q:

   A:

b. Where is Xie Weizhong's computer?

   Q:

   A:

c. Where are all the books?

   Q:

   A:

d. What's on the floor?

   Q:

   A:

e. How many pencils are there in Xie Weizhong's room? Where are they?

   Q:

   A:

Part II.   Look at the BEFORE picture and decide whether the following statements are true or false. If a statement is false, please correct it.

Example:
Guì 子裏有很多 **xié**.   →   *False:* **Guì** 子裏<u>沒有</u>xié.

a. 謝為中的電 **nǎo** 在床下邊。   →

b. 床上有 **xié**，**yīfu** 還有電 **nǎo**。   →

c. 謝為中的 **bǐ** 都在 **yǐ** 子上。   →

d. 謝為中的床上有 **xié**，地上有 **xié**，**zhuō** 子上也有 **xié**。   →

e. 謝為中的 **guì** 子裏沒有 **yīfu**。   →

f. 謝為中的書 **jià** 上有一 **píng** 水。   →

Part III.   Look at the AFTER picture. Write <u>four</u> sentences to describe how Xie Weizhong has cleaned up his room. You need to use the **bǎ**-structure.

Example:
謝為中 **bǎ** 水放在書 **jià** 上。

a.

b.

c.

d.

Part IV.   Look at the AFTER picture and write a few sentences to answer this question:
請問，你覺得謝為中 **bǎ** 房間 **shōushi** 好了嗎？為甚麼？

_____

_____

_____

5. A conversation between Xiao Ye's mother and Xiao Ye

Part I. Fill in the blanks.   Select a word from the following list to complete each sentence.

只是	**wán**	不用	多	沒
yīn 為	就是	的	**yòu**	開

Yè太太： 友文，昨天晚上我給你打電話你怎麼不在？

小Yè：　　媽，昨天小張和小謝在他們的宿舍 ＿＿ 晚會，我們都去了。

Yè太太： 晚會有意思嗎？

小Yè：　　有意思，＿＿，他們的宿舍太小，去的人太多，沒有 **yǐ** 子坐。

Yè太太： 你們吃甚麼？

小Yè：　　小謝做了很多吃的，很多東西都 ＿＿ 吃 **wán**。

Yè太太： 友文，開學已經一個 ＿＿ 星期了，忙不忙？

小Yè：　　還好。我的課選好了，課本也買好了，＿＿ 宿舍還沒有 **shōushi** 好。

Yè太太： 沒關係，慢慢 **shōushi**。這個 **zhōumò** 回家吃飯吧！我打 **suan** 做你 **zuì** 喜歡 ＿＿ **hóngshāo ròu**。

小Yè：　　這個 **zhōumò** 不行，＿＿ 我下個星期有考試。下個 **zhōumò** 吧！我一考 ＿＿ 試就回家。

Yè太太： 要不要爸爸去學校 **jiē** 你？

小Yè：　　＿＿，坐地 **tiě** ＿＿ 快 **yòu piányi**。

Yè太太： 那也好。那下個星期六見。

小Yè：　　媽，再見。

Part II. Q&A.   Read the dialogue above. Then, answer the questions in Mandarin.

a. 昨天晚上小 **Yè** 為甚麼不在宿舍裏？

b. 小 **Yè** 覺得小張和小謝的宿舍怎麼樣？

c. 他們開學多 **jiǔ** 了？

d. 開學到現在，小 **Yè** 甚麼 **shì** 還沒有做 **wán**？

e. 這個 **zhōumò** 小 **Yè** 會回家嗎？為甚麼？

f. 小 **Yè** 怎麼回家？

6. Writing

Look at this picture and imagine what this mother is saying to her son right now. Use the following structures/words in your paragraph:

luàn	非…不可	yòu…yòu	shōushi	bǎ

_____

_____

_____

_____

_____

_____

_____

_____

Lesson 20 Workbook

 Listening and speaking

(audio online)

Structure drills

1. The whole time (Use and Structure note 20.1)

You will hear a statement followed by a word referring to time. Restate the sentence, saying that the action was true for that whole period of time, as in the example.

> **Example:**
> *You will hear:* 我同屋沒睡覺，**yè**
> *You will say:* 我同屋一 **yè** 沒睡覺。
> *Click "R" to hear the correct response:* 我同屋一 **yè** 沒睡覺。

(a)   (b)   (c)   (d)   (e)   (f)   (g)   (h)   (i)   (j)

2. Are you able to do it? (Use and Structure note 20.6)

You will hear a statement about some action that has reached a result or conclusion. Ask your roommate if she can do this action to the result or conclusion, as in the example.

> **Example:**
> *You will hear:* 看 **dǒng** 中文書
> *You will say:* 中文書你看得 **dǒng** 看不 **dǒng**？
> *Click "R" to hear the correct response:* 中文書你看得 **dǒng** 看不 **dǒng**？

(a)   (b)   (c)   (d)   (e)   (f)   (g)   (h)

3. Focusing on a detail of a past event with 是…的
   (Use and Structure note 20.9)

You will hear a sentence about some action. Restate the sentence with 是…的 to focus on some detail of the action, as in the example.

Example:
You will hear: 我昨天去了。
You will say: 我是昨天去的。
Click "R" to hear the correct response: 我是昨天去的。

(a)   (b)   (c)   (d)   (e)   (f)   (g)   (h)   (i)   (j)

4. Asking about a detail of a past event with 是…的
   (Use and Structure note 20.9)

You will hear a statement with 是…的 that focuses on some detail of a past event, followed by a question word or phrase. Use that word or phrase to ask the corresponding question with 是…的, as in the example.

Example:
You will hear: 我是在圖書館 **rènshi** 他的。（在哪兒？）
You will say: 你是在哪兒 **rènshi** 他的？
Click "R" to hear the correct response: 你是在哪兒 **rènshi** 他的？

(a)   (b)   (c)   (d)   (e)   (f)   (g)   (h)   (i)   (j)

5. When did it begin? 從 + time + 開始

You will hear an action followed by a time phrase. Say that the action started at that time, as in the example.

Example:
You will hear: **lā dù** 子，昨天晚上
You will say: 我從昨天晚上開始 **lā dù** 子。
Click "R" to hear the correct response: 我從昨天晚上開始 **lā dù** 子。

(a)   (b)   (c)   (d)   (e)   (f)   (g)   (h)   (i)   (j)

6. Focusing on when something began: 是從 + time + 開始的
(Use and Structure note 20.9)

You will hear an action followed by a time expression. Say that the action began at that time, using 是...的 to focus on the starting time, as in the example.

Example:

You will hear: **lā dù** 子，昨天晚上
You will say: 我是從昨天晚上開始 **lā dù** 子的。
Click "R" to hear the correct response: 我是從昨天晚上開始 **lā dù** 子的。

(a)   (b)   (c)   (d)   (e)   (f)   (g)   (h)   (i)   (j)

7. Saying *besides X* with **chú** 了 X 以外，也 VP (Use and Structure note 20.10)

You will hear a statement followed by a statement with additional information on the same topic. Rephrase the information with **chú** 了 X 以外, as in the example.

Example:

You will hear: 你學中文，我們也學中文。
You will say: **chú** 了你以外，我們也學中文。
Click "R" to hear the correct response: **chú** 了你以外，我們也學中文。

(a)   (b)   (c)   (d)   (e)   (f)   (g)   (h)   (i)   (j)

Listening for information

(CD1: 36)

1. Are you sick?

You will hear seven questions asking about the people in the drawings. Answer the questions in English.

Ke Feng	Mr. Zhang	Ding Ding	Mrs. Huang	Xiao Zheng

a.

b.

c.

d.

e.

f.

g.

2. We all got sick

(CD1: 37)

Xiao Ping and her three roommates all got sick. Listen to Xiao Ping's narration about everyone's illness. Fill in the missing information in the form, based on the information that she presents.

who	symptoms	action/current status
Yaxin		
		getting better
	headache	
Lingling		

3. Lunch time

(CD1: 38)

Li Tairan is talking about her weekend. Answer the questions that follow, based on the information she provides.

a.

b.

c.

d.

e.

4. Giving explanations

(CD1: 39) You will hear descriptions of five people. Each description will be followed by a question. Answer each question in English based on the information in the description.

a.

b.

c.

d.

e.

5. Questions about getting sick

(CD1: 40) Answer the questions you hear in complete sentences in Mandarin, using characters where we have learned them.

a.

b.

c.

d.

e.

f.

6. Listen and reply

(CD1: 41) Peng Tongda did not feel well, so he went to see a doctor. You will hear what the doctor said to him. Answer the questions in English based on the doctor's diagnosis and instructions.

a.

b.

c.

d.

e.

7. Dialogue I

You will hear a dialogue between a teacher and a student in class. Answer the questions **(CD1: 42)** based on the dialogue.

a. What symptoms does the student have?
   1) a stomach ache
   2) a sore throat
   3) a fever
   4) a headache

b. What did the teacher suggest the student do first?
   1) take the test
   2) go back to the dorm
   3) see a doctor
   4) take some medicine

c. What will the student do?
   1) drink more water
   2) prepare for the test
   3) go with a classmate to see a doctor
   4) call the teacher when feeling better

8. Dialogue II

You will hear a dialogue between two classmates in the dorm. Answer the questions based **(CD1: 43)** on the dialogue.

a. What is the main reason why the male student called the female student?
   1) to complain that he cannot fall asleep
   2) to find out if his friend was sleeping
   3) to ask her out
   4) to ask questions about the homework

b. What will they do after the phone call?
   1) go to the library together
   2) do the homework
   3) go to sleep
   4) have some coffee

c. What did the male student do right before he made the phone call?
   1) drank some coffee
   2) tried to go to sleep
   3) called other friends
   4) completed the Chinese homework

Reading and writing

1. Number of strokes

Indicate the number of strokes used in writing each of the following characters.

a. 慣 _____   f. 別 _____

b. 酒 _____   g. 睡 _____

c. 院 _____   h. 菜 _____

d. 服 _____   i. 喝 _____

e. 次 _____   j. 淨 _____

2. Which character?

Circle the character in each line that corresponds to the meaning on the left.

a. **jìng (gānjìng** *clean*)   淨   靜

b. **huài** *bad*   還   壞

c. **bié** *don't*   別   另

d. **bǎ** *take*   把   吧

e. **tóu** *head*   題   頭

f. **hóng** *red*   江   紅

g. **shāo** *simmer* (**fā shāo** *have a fever*)   燒   澆

h. **jiǔ** *alcohol, wine*   酒   西

i. **fú (shūfu** *comfortable*)   股   服

j. **yuàn (diànyǐngyuàn** *movie theater*)   院   完

k. **gān (gānjìng** *clean*)   乾   幹

l. **guàn (xíguàn** *accustomed to*)   慣   慣

3. First strokes

Write the first two strokes of each of the following characters.

a. 菜 ___ f. 紅 ___

b. 慣 ___ g. 壞 ___

c. 睡 ___ h. 喝 ___

d. 次 ___ i. 乾 ___

e. 把 ___ j. 燒 ___

4. Missing strokes

Complete each character by writing in the missing strokes.

a. 月〡 **fú** (**shūfu** *comfortable*)

b. 忄田 **guàn** (**xíguàn** *accustomed to*)

c. 冫 **cì** *time*

d. 氵 **jìng** (**gānjìng** *clean*)

e. 目 **shuì** (**shuì jiào** *sleep*)

f. 阝 **yuàn** (**yīyuàn** *hospital*)

g. 口日 **hē** *drink*

h. 火土 **shāo** (**fā shāo** *have a fever*)

i. 豆 **tóu** *head*

j. 口 **bié** *don't*

5. Total strokes

Rewrite this list of characters, arranging the characters in terms of their total number of strokes. Begin your list with the character with the fewest strokes.

服	乾	把	院	頭	酒	慣	次	菜	燒	紅	睡	淨	喝	別	壞

6. Radicals

Here is a list of characters that we have learned through this lesson. Rewrite each character in the row next to its radical.

慣　剛　壞　別　酒　把　洗　忙
漢　坐　到　快　找　地　慢　打

氵	
扌	
刂	
忄	
土	

7. Character sleuth

Group the following characters in terms of a part that they share in common, as in the example. The shared part need not be the radical in each character. You can use a character more than once.

經　用　些　看　睡　哪　學　宿　服　明　給
容　開　院　都　那　紅　字　園　定　能　朋

shared part	characters
人	人，大，太，天
糸	
阝	
二	
月	
宀	
元	
目	

8. Find the words and phrases

You won't be able to completely understand the following passage, but it contains many characters that we have learned, including at least fifteen words composed of two or more characters.

a. Circle the <u>words</u> we have learned that are <u>composed of two or more characters each</u> and write them on the answer sheet below.

"今年" is an example of a word that is composed of two or more characters.

"我也" is composed of two characters in a row that we have learned, but it is <u>not</u> a word.

我的朋友老李非常喜歡學校旁邊的中國飯館。他每次去都吃他最喜歡的紅燒肉。
昨天他又跟朋友一起去了那家中國飯館。他的朋友說你已經吃了好幾次紅燒肉了。
今天別吃了。吃別的菜吧。他沒有吃紅燒肉，吃了炒白菜，還喝了一點酒。吃完飯
他的肚子就不舒服，晚上睡不著。他想這可能是因為沒有吃紅燒肉。下次還得吃紅
燒肉。

Words in this paragraph composed of two or more characters:

1. ＿＿＿＿   2. ＿＿＿＿   3. ＿＿＿＿   4. ＿＿＿＿   5. ＿＿＿＿

6. ＿＿＿＿   7. ＿＿＿＿   8. ＿＿＿＿   9. ＿＿＿＿   10. ＿＿＿＿

11. ＿＿＿＿   12. ＿＿＿＿   13. ＿＿＿＿   14. ＿＿＿＿   15. ＿＿＿＿

b. In one sentence in English, state the general topic of this passage.

9.   Dictionary skills

Following the instructions in Lesson 17 of the Textbook, look up these characters in a Chinese dictionary and provide the requested information.

a. 發
   pronunciation:
   meaning:
   one two-character word or phrase in which it occurs:

b. 病
   pronunciation:
   meaning:
   one two-character word or phrase in which it occurs:

c. 包
   pronunciation:
   meaning:
   one two-character word or phrase in which it occurs:

10.   Find the incorrect characters

Xiao Zhang has written this email to a friend back home, but he has written twelve different characters incorrectly (some more than once). Read the passage aloud, circle the mistakes, and correct them on the answer sheet below. If the same mistake occurs twice, count it as a single mistake.

> 這個星斯學小的店 **yǐng** 院有"家"這個店 **yǐng**。我沒看過，不只到這個電 **yǐng** 好壞。我文我的同屋看過每有。他說他看過，他很習歡，已紅看了好九次了。他還話他可一跟我在看一次。

a. ____   b. ____   c. ____   d. ____   e. ____   f. ____

g. ____   h. ____   i. ____   j. ____   k. ____   l. ____

11.   Scrambled sentences

Rewrite these phrases as sentences, putting the words in the correct order to match the English translations.

a. 東西 / 床 / 在 / 別 / 把 / 的 / 放 / 我的 / 上 / 你

Don't put your things on my bed.

b. 飯館 / 吧 / 去 / 那 / 吃/ 我們 / 下次 / 家 / 飯

Let's eat in that restaurant next time.

c. 酒 / 喜歡 / 為甚麼 / 喝 / 中國人 / 紅

Why do Chinese people like to drink red wine?

d. 把 / 的 / 乾淨 / 你 / 你 / **yī** 服 / 洗 / 得

You should wash your clothes (clean).

e. 做 / 好 / 媽媽 / 非常 / 你 / 吃 / 菜 / 的

The food that your mother cooks is extremely delicious.

12.   Translate into English

Read the following passage and translate it into English.

小王的女朋友是他在一個一年級的學生晚會上 **rènshi** 的。她是去年從 **Yīng** 國來的。她也是來中國學中文的。她來中國以前在 **Yīng** 國的時候就開始學中文了。她說中文說得非常好。在那個晚會上他們一起 **chàng gē**、**tiào wǔ**、說了很多話、也吃了很多東西。晚上很晚才回宿舍。

13.   Translate into Mandarin

Rewrite the following sentences in Chinese characters.

a. I am not used to using chopsticks (筷子) to eat Chinese food.

b. How come your dorm is so clean?

c. You have a fever. Don't go to class today. (Write **fā** in pinyin.)

d. Don't drink alcohol before going to sleep.

e. My roommate has already been sleeping for ten hours.

Focus on structure

1.   How many times? (Use and Structure note 20.2)

Here is a list of activities that Ye Youwen has done this week and the number of times she has done each one. Rewrite this information in complete Mandarin sentences, using characters where we have learned them.

a. ate Sichuan food (twice)   →

b. cleaned her room (once)   →

c. washed clothes (three times)   →

d. listened to music (many times)   →

e. drank beer (once)   →

f. took the subway (five times)   →

2. 還是 and **huòzhě** (Use and Structure note 20.5)

Translate these sentences into Mandarin, using 還是 or **huòzhě** in each sentence, as appropriate.

a. Would you like to drink coffee or tea?

b. Tonight we can watch television or listen to music.

c. You can see a doctor tonight or tomorrow morning.

d. Do you prefer to bathe at night or in the morning?

e. Are you going to major in Chinese or Japanese?

3. Resultative verbs in the potential form
  (Use and Structure notes 19.2, 20.6)

Translate each of the following sentences into English.

a. 我打不開這個門。

b. 今天晚上的功課太多了。我做不 **wán**。

c. 這 **jiàn yī** 服太 **zāng**。我洗不乾淨。

d. 老師說話說得那麼快，你聽得 **dǒng** 嗎？

e. **Hànbǎobāo** (hamburgers) 在中國吃得到嗎？

f. 明天是我的生日。今天晚上一定睡不 **zháo**。

g. 這個字寫得太小。我看不見是哪個字。

h. 我找不到那個電 **yǐng** 院。請 **gàosu** 我怎麼走。

4.   Resultative verbs and the potential form (Use and Structure notes 19.2, 20.6)

Complete the following sentences by filling in each blank with one of the following, <u>or leave it empty</u>, to match its English translation:

了	沒	不	得

a. 你這 **jiàn** 衣服 ＿＿ 洗 ＿＿ 乾淨 ＿＿，你看，這裏還有一點兒 **zāng**。
This shirt was not washed clean. Look, there's still a dirty spot here.

b. 我想你大 **gài** 是 ＿＿ 吃 ＿＿ 壞 ＿＿ **dù** 子 ＿＿，所以一直上 **cè** 所。
I think you probably have stomach flu. That's why you keep going to the bathroom.

c. 這麼多 **jiǎo** 子，你 ＿＿ 吃 ＿＿ 完 ＿＿ 嗎? ＿＿ 吃 ＿＿ 完 ＿＿ 沒關係，明天再吃。
So many dumplings! Can you finish them all? It's okay if you can't. We can eat them tomorrow.

d. 我已經找了好幾個月的工作，還是 ＿＿ 找 ＿＿ 到 ＿＿ 一個喜歡的 ＿＿。
I have been looking for a job for months but still can't find one that I like.

e. 小張可能是太 **lèi** 了，剛做完功課就在床上 ＿＿ 睡 ＿＿ **zháo** ＿＿。
Xiao Zhang is probably too tired. He fell asleep on his bed right after he finished the homework.

f. 小謝這幾天 **yè** 裏常 **késou**、有好幾天 ＿＿ 睡 ＿＿ 好 ＿＿。
Xiao Xie has been coughing the past few nights. He hasn't slept well for days.

g. 這門課太難了，我上課的時候常常 ＿＿ 聽 ＿＿ **dǒng** ＿＿，下課得問同學。
This class is too difficult. A lot of times I couldn't understand in class and had to ask my classmates after class.

h. 王老師，您寫的字太小了，我 ＿＿ 看 ＿＿ 見 ＿＿。可以寫大一點嗎?
Teacher Wang, the characters you wrote are too small, I can't see them. Could you write them a little bigger?

i. 不行，不行，我已經 ＿＿ 吃 ＿＿ **bǎo** ＿＿ 了 ＿＿，不能再吃了。
No way, I'm already full. I can't eat any more.

5.   Details of a past event (Use and Structure note 20.9)

Xiao Xie's father is quizzing him about his activities last weekend. Express each question in Mandarin, using 是…的 in each question.

a. What day did you eat in a restaurant?

b. Who did you have dinner with?

c. Where did you eat?

d. What time did you return to the dorm?

e. What time did you go to sleep?

6.   Your personal information (Use and Structure note 20.9)

Answer questions a.–d. in Mandarin, using 是…的 in each sentence.

a. Where were you born?

b. What month and date were you born?

c. What year were you born?

d. When did you begin to study Chinese?

Translate e.–f. into Mandarin.

e. When did you graduate from high school?

f. When did you select your major?

7.   **Chú** 了 X 以外 (Use and Structure note 20.10)

Rewrite each sentence using the structure **chú** 了 X 以外, as in the example, and translate your new sentences into English.

Example:

我喜歡吃中國菜，也喜歡吃美國菜   →   **Chú** 了中國菜以外，我也喜歡吃美國菜。

English: Besides Chinese food, I also like to eat American food.

a. 我媽媽很會做 **chǎo bái** 菜，還有 **hóng** 燒 **dòufu**   →

English:

b. 我 **fā** 燒，頭也很 **téng**   →

English:

c. **Zhuō** 子上有書，地上也有書   →

English:

d. 我選了幾門 **zhuānyè** 課和一門 **yīnyuè** 課   →

English:

e. 他每天都忙 **zhe** 工作和學習   →

English:

f. 你得多喝水，也 **yīnggāi** 去看 **yī** 生，**shēntǐ** 才會好   →

English:

8.   Complete the sentences

Fill in the blanks with words from the following list to complete each sentence. Then, translate each sentence into English.

次	一	**huòzhě**	馬上	大 **gài**	還是	不	沒	因為

a. 菜 _____ 就來了，請您再 **děng** 一下。

English:

b. 他這麼不用功，還常常不去上課，**chéngji** _____ 很 **zāogāo**。

English:

c. 小張 _____ **bìng** 了，所以今天沒有來上課。

English:

d. 你習慣早上 **xǐ zǎo** _____ 晚上 **xǐ zǎo**？

English:

e. 我不能喝 **kāfēi**，一喝就睡 _____ **zháo**。前天我喝了一小 **bēi kāfēi** 以後，_____

yè _____ 睡。

English:

f. **Bìyè** 以後，我想去中國 _____ 去 **Táiwān** 找工作。
English:

g. 我說了好幾 _____，洗好的 **yī** 服得放在 **guì** 子裏，你怎麼都不聽？
English:

9.   Translation challenge I

Translate these sentences into English.

a. 我今天一天忙 **zhe fù** 習功課，因為明天我有三個考試。

b. **Chú** 了我以外，小 **Yè** 也沒 **cānjiā** 今天早上的考試。我們都起晚了。

c. **Chú** 了 **dù** 子不 **shū** 服以外，我不 **fā** 燒，也不頭 **téng**。可能是昨天晚上吃得太多了。

d. 今天的中文功課太多了，吃晚飯以前做不 **wán**。

e. 因為我對中國很有興趣，所以下個學期我要選一門中國文 **huà huòzhě** 中國經 **jì** 的課。

f. 我 **dài** 他到學校的 **yī** 院看 **bìng**。**Yī** 生說他不習慣吃 **là** 的，所以 **dù** 子 **téng**，很快就會好，還給了他一些 **yào**。

g. 這個電 **yǐng** 我很喜歡，已經看了三次了。

h. 美 **lì** 學漢字學得很快，也學得很好。她每天把 **xīn** 學的漢字每個字寫三次。

10.   Translation challenge II

Translate these sentences into Mandarin.

a. I was sick all day yesterday and didn't finish my homework.

b. You ate too much. Next time don't eat so much.

c. This is my first time eating spicy food.

d. Q: When you traveled in China could you understand the people?

 A: Except for Sichuan people, I understood everything.

e. I finished reading that book but I didn't understand it.

f. Where did the two of you meet?

g. I'm not interested in music. Whenever I listen to music I fall asleep.

Focus on communication

1. Dialogue comprehension

Study the Lesson 20 Narrative and Dialogue. Then, read the following statements and indicate whether they are true (T) or false (F).

a. (　) 小張昨天晚上到朋友家去吃飯了。

b. (　) 小張昨天晚上沒有睡覺，因為朋友請他吃飯、喝酒。

c. (　) 小謝覺得小張大 **gài** 吃壞 **dù** 子了。

d. (　) 小張吃了晚飯以後開始 **dù** 子 **téng**。

e. (　) 今天是小謝 **dài** 小張去看 **bìng** 的。

f. (　) 小張不 **fā** 燒也不 **késou**，就是 **dù** 子有點 **téng**。

g. (　) **Yī** 生覺得小張昨天晚上吃的東西，可能不太乾淨，**huòzhě** 四 **chuān** 菜太 **là** 了。

h. (　) **Yī** 生問了小張以後，給了他一些 **yào**。

2. What do you say?

What do you say in each of the following situations? Type your answers, using characters where we have learned them, and email them to your Chinese teacher.

a. Your roommate looks pale to you. You want to know what's going on.

b. You complain about your sleep problem: you wake up several times in the middle of night.

c. You wonder when your friend started driving because he doesn't seem to be a very experienced driver.

d. You complain about a severe headache and an upset stomach.

e. You need to explain your symptoms to the doctor: you have a fever and have been coughing since last week.

f. You want to let your friend know that you might arrive late, either 3 p.m. or 3:30 p.m.

g. You are telling the hostess that you're too full to eat when she insists that you get a second helping of food.

3.   大家都 **bìng** 了

It's the flu season and everyone in Xiao Zhang's class is sick. Use the information in the pictures to complete each sentence below. Then translate the sentences into English.

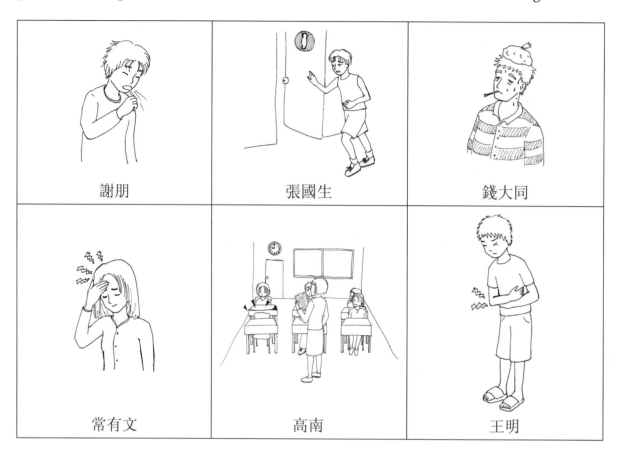

a. _____ **fā** 燒了，**shēntǐ** 很不 **shū** 服。

   English:

b. _____ **bìng** 了好幾天了，都沒有來上課。

   English:

c. _____ 可能是吃壞 **dù** 子了。昨天一天 **lā** 了好幾次 **dù** 子。

   English:

d. _____ 這幾天一起床就一直 **késou**。

   English:

e. _____ 頭很 **téng**，吃了 **yào** 也沒有用。

   English:

f. _____ 的 **dù** 子 **téngjí** 了，已經三天不能吃東西了。她打 **suan** 今天去看 **bìng**。

   English:

4.   Complete the mini-dialogues

Use the structure in parentheses to complete each mini-dialogue.

a. A: 你說你選了中文課，還有呢？

   B: _____。（**chú** 了...以外）

b. A: 你 **zhōumò** 做甚麼？

   B: 我常常 _____。（**huòzhě**）

c. A: 今天回家請寫 **dì** 五課、**dì** 六課的功課，明天給我。

   B: 老師，功課太多了，我 _____！（ActV 得/不 + RVE）

d. A: 吃中國飯你怎麼不用 **kuài** 子？

   B: _____。（不習慣）

e. A: 明天是你生日，我們去那家日本飯館吃飯吧。

   B: **Huàn** 一家好不好？那家飯館我 _____。（好幾次）

5.   Meet your new teammates

You will be participating in a three-week volunteer program in China this winter break. Today is the orientation and you are meeting the other team members for the first time.

Part I.   Write down the questions that you can ask your teammates. Use 是...的 in your questions for c.–f.

Example:

   Where are you from?   →   你是從哪兒來的?

a. What is your name?   →

b. Why do you want to go to China?   →

c. Who did you come with?   →

d. When did you begin to study Chinese? →

e. How did you hear about this job?   →

f. How did you get here today?   →

g. Write at least one more question: →

Part II.   Below is information about four other volunteers. Translate the questions into Mandarin and then answer them in Mandarin.

	country	year they began studying Chinese	where they learned Chinese	who they came here with
Zhēnní	France	2006	Paris (**Bālí**)	alone
Tāngmǔ	USA	last September	college	one classmate
Jiékè	Britain	this summer	Beijing	two friends
Mòlì	Japan	last month	Tokyo	her older sister

a. Who came here with her older sister?

Q:

A:

b. Where is **Tāngmǔ** from? (use 是…的)

Q:

A:

c. Did **Jiékè** study Chinese in Tokyo?

Q:

A:

d. How long has **Zhēnní** been learning Chinese?

Q:

A:

Part III.   It's your turn to introduce yourself. Write at least four sentences about yourself.

6. Writing

Xiao Wang is not feeling well.

Part I.　This is a story about Xiao Wang. Rearrange the sentences in the right order to form a cohesive paragraph.

a. 雖然沒有 **lā dù** 子，可是，頭一直很 **téng**，**dù** 子也不太 **shū** 服。

b. 從飯館回來以後我有點兒不 **shū** 服，就去睡覺了。

c. 早上我的同屋說我大 **gài** 喝太多酒了。

d. **Yè** 裏睡不 **zháo**，起來好幾次。

e. 我下 **wǔ** 三點才吃 **wǔ** 飯，所以晚飯吃得不多。

f. 我吃了 **yào** 就覺得好一點了。

g. 昨天晚上小張請我們幾個人去一家 **xīn** 開的飯館吃飯，因為他找到工作了。

h. 他給了我一 **piàn** 頭 **téng yào**，還叫我多喝一點 **chá**。

i. 不過因為太高興，喝了好幾 **píng pí** 酒。

Part II.　Below is a dialogue between Xiao Wang and his roommate. Fill in the roommate's part, based on the paragraph in Part I.

Roommate:　你 _____？
Xiao Wang:　我昨天晚上沒睡好，頭 **téngjí** 了。

Roommate:　**Chú** 了 _____？
Xiao Wang:　我 **dù** 子也不太 **shū** 服。

Roommate:　_____？
Xiao Wang:　昨天吃了晚飯以後就開始不 **shū** 服。

Roommate:　_____？
Xiao Wang:　我是在一家 **xīn** 開的飯館吃的晚飯。

Roommate:　_____？
Xiao Wang:　我吃得不多，就喝了三 **píng pí** 酒。

Roommate:　三 **píng**？我想，你 _____。
Xiao Wang:　喝太多了？那怎麼 **bàn** 呢？

Roommate:　_____。
Xiao Wang:　謝謝。我現在就吃。

Part III.   Xiao Wang is feeling sick this morning so he missed his class today. Help him write an email message to his Chinese teacher apologizing for not being at class today. He needs to explain why he missed the class. The email message should be at least 100 characters in length.

李老師，您好：

我是您二年級中文課的學生。對不起，＿＿＿＿＿＿＿＿＿＿＿＿＿＿＿＿＿＿

＿＿＿＿＿＿＿＿＿＿＿＿＿＿＿＿＿＿＿＿＿＿＿＿＿＿＿＿＿＿＿＿＿＿＿＿＿

＿＿＿＿＿＿＿＿＿＿＿＿＿＿＿＿＿＿＿＿＿＿＿＿＿＿＿＿＿＿＿＿＿＿＿＿＿

＿＿＿＿＿＿＿＿＿＿＿＿＿＿＿＿＿＿＿＿＿＿＿＿＿＿＿＿＿＿＿＿＿＿＿＿＿

＿＿＿＿＿＿＿＿＿＿＿＿＿＿＿＿＿＿＿＿＿＿＿＿＿＿＿＿＿＿＿＿＿＿＿＿＿

＿＿＿＿＿＿＿＿＿＿＿＿＿＿＿＿＿＿＿＿＿＿＿＿＿＿＿＿＿＿＿＿＿＿＿＿＿

＿＿＿＿＿＿＿＿＿＿＿＿＿＿＿＿＿＿＿＿＿＿＿＿＿＿＿＿＿＿＿＿＿＿＿＿＿

明天 **rú** 果您有時間，我可以去找您問幾個問 **tí** 嗎？謝謝！

王明明

Lesson 21 Workbook

 Listening and speaking

(audio online)

Structure drills

1. More and more (Use and Structure note 21.1)

You will hear a sentence stating the quality of some subject. You will say that the subject has more and more of that quality, as in the example.

Example:
You will hear: 天 **qì lěng** 了。
You will say: 天 **qì yuè** 來 **yuè lěng** 了。
Click "R" to hear the correct response: 天 **qì yuè** 來 **yuè lěng** 了。

(a)   (b)   (c)   (d)   (e)   (f)   (g)   (h)   (i)   (j)

2. Saying that two things are alike (Use and Structure note 21.4)

You will hear two phrases describing different things. Say that they are alike, as in the example.

Example:
You will hear: 我的中文書，你的中文書
You will say: 我的中文書跟你的中文書一樣。
Click "R" to hear the correct response: 我的中文書跟你的中文書一樣。

(a)   (b)   (c)   (d)   (e)   (f)   (g)   (h)   (i)   (j)

3. Saying that two things are not alike (Use and Structure note 21.4)

You will hear two phrases describing different things. Say that they are not alike, as in the example.

Example:

You will hear: 我的中文書，你的中文書

You will say: 我的中文書跟你的中文書不一樣。

Click "R" to hear the correct response: 我的中文書跟你的中文書不一樣。

(a)   (b)   (c)   (d)   (e)   (f)   (g)   (h)   (i)   (j)

4. Asking whether two things are alike (Use and Structure note 21.4)

You will hear two phrases describing different things. Ask whether they are alike or not, as in the example.

Example:

You will hear: 你的中文書，我的中文書

You will say: 你的中文書跟我的中文書一樣不一樣？

Click "R" to hear the correct response: 你的中文書跟我的中文書一樣不一樣？

(a)   (b)   (c)   (d)   (e)   (f)   (g)   (h)   (i)   (j)

5. Saying that two things are alike in some way (Use and Structure note 21.4)

You will hear a sentence describing the quality of two things. Restate the sentence, saying that these two things have the same quality, as in the example.

Example:

You will hear: 今天很 **lěng**，昨天也很 **lěng**。

You will say: 今天跟昨天一樣 **lěng**。

Click "R" to hear the correct response: 今天跟昨天一樣 **lěng**。

(a)   (b)   (c)   (d)   (e)   (f)   (g)   (h)   (i)   (j)

6. Comparisons with **bǐ** (Use and Structure note 21.7)

You will hear a sentence describing two noun phrases. Restate the sentence with **bǐ**, as in the example, saying that one has more of some quality than the other.

Example:

You will hear: 我的書三十塊錢，他的書三十五塊錢。

You will say: 他的書 **bǐ** 我的 **guì**。

Click "R" to hear the correct response: 他的書 **bǐ** 我的 **guì**。

(a)   (b)   (c)   (d)   (e)   (f)   (g)   (h)   (i)   (j)

7. Saying *a lot more* (Use and Structure note 21.7)

You will hear a sentence describing two noun phrases. Restate the sentence with **bǐ**, as in the example, saying that one noun phrase has a lot more of some quality than the other.

Example:
You will hear: 中文課有五個考試，文化課只有一個考試。
You will say: 中文課的考試 **bǐ** 文化課的多得多。
Click "R" to hear the correct response: 中文課的考試 **bǐ** 文化課的多得多。

(a)   (b)   (c)   (d)   (e)   (f)   (g)   (h)

Listening for information

1. World weather report

The following chart displays the temperatures on January 21 in seven cities around the world. **(CD1: 47)** You will hear seven statements comparing the weather in the cities. Based on the chart, indicate whether each statement is true (T) or false (F).

January 21	
city	temperature
Beijing	28°F/12°F
Shanghai	42°F/33°F
Taipei	62°F/55°F
Paris	48°F/38°F
London	50°F/41°F
New York	43°F/32°F
Houston	74°F/69°F

a. ( )   b. ( )   c. ( )   d. ( )   e. ( )   f. ( )   g. ( )

2. Today's weather

(CD1: 48) You will hear a short weather forecast for four major US cities: Seattle, Boston, Miami, and Chicago. Complete the following table based on the report, adding in the name of each city and the temperature under the picture that illustrates the weather.

city				
temperature				

3. Buenos Aires

(CD1: 49) You will hear a short description from a travel agency about the climate of Buenos Aires. Write the answers to the questions in Mandarin, based on the description.

a. **Bùyínuòsī** 最 **lěng** 的天 **qì** 在哪一個月？

b. **Bùyínuòsī** 的 **chūn** 天從哪一個月開始？

c. **Bùyínuòsī** 的 **qiū** 天是哪幾個月？

d. **Bùyínuòsī** 的 **dōng** 天有幾個月？

e. **Bùyínuòsī**，二月的天 **qì** 怎麼樣？

4.   Two rooms

The room on the left is Xiao Pan's dorm room. The room on the right belongs to Qi Sheng. You will hear six statements comparing their rooms. Based on the pictures indicate whether each statement is true (T) or false (F).

(CD1: 50)

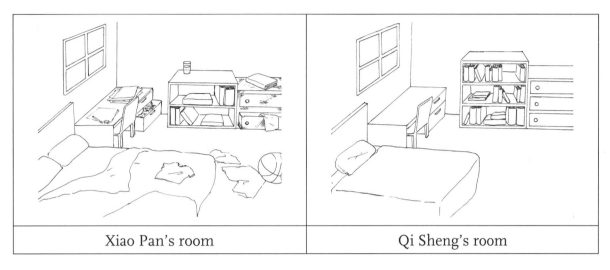

| Xiao Pan's room | Qi Sheng's room |

a. (   )   b. (   )   c. (   )   d. (   )   e. (   )   f. (   )

5.   Your hometown

The recording asks you six questions about your hometown. Write down your answers in Mandarin, using characters where we have learned them.

(CD1: 51)

a.

b.

c.

d.

e.

f.

6.   Telephone message

Your friend Sun Ping left a phone message for you regarding a trip. Listen to the message and write a reply to him in Mandarin.

(CD1: 52)

Your reply:

7.   Interview

(CD1: 53–54) Zhou Yu and Lanlan are being interviewed by a school newspaper reporter. Listen to their replies and do the following:

a. In English, state the topic of the interview: _____

b. In Mandarin, write a short paragraph comparing the replies of the two students on this topic.

8.   Dialogue

(CD1: 55) Two students at a university in the south are talking about the weather. Listen to their conversation and answer the questions based on the dialogue.

a. What is their plan?
　　1) to go to the park in the rain
　　2) to stay in the dorm
　　3) to wait until the rain stops
　　4) to eat something first

b. What season is it?
　　1) spring
　　2) summer
　　3) fall
　　4) winter

c. How is the weather during the winter in the south?
　　1) It only snows a little bit.
　　2) It is the longest season.
　　3) It is not very cold.
　　4) It seldom rains.

d. How is the weather in the north where the male student comes from?
　　1) It rains in the spring.
　　2) It is hot in the summer.
　　3) The winter season is about three months long.
　　4) It gets cold in the fall.

e. What is the average temperature in July in the south?

1) 90–100°
2) 80–90°
3) 70–80°
4) 60–70°

Reading and writing

Focus on Chinese characters

1.   Number of strokes

Indicate the number of strokes used in writing each of the following characters.

a. 亮 _____   f. 化 _____

b. 近 _____   g. 出 _____

c. 衣 _____   h. 夏 _____

d. 概 _____   i. 髒 _____

e. 離 _____   j. 應 _____

2.   Which character?

Circle the character in each line that corresponds to the meaning on the left.

a. **gāi (yīnggāi** *should*)   刻   該

b. **jìn** *close*   近   進

c. **piào (piàoliang** *pretty, beautiful*)   漂   票

d. **chū** *exit, produce*   山   出

e. **gài (dàgài** *probably*)   槩   概

f. **rú (rúguǒ** *if*)   如   姑

g. **zāng** *dirty*   髒   體

h. **shū (shūfu** *comfortable*)   舒   舍

i. **yīng (yīnggāi** *should*)   憔   應

j. **suì** *years of age*   歲   戚

k. **xià (xiàtiān** *summer*)   夏   頁

l. **huà (wénhuà** *culture*)   比   化

3. First strokes

Write the first two strokes of each of the following characters.

a. 概 _____   f. 應 _____

b. 如 _____   g. 該 _____

c. 歲 _____   h. 近 _____

d. 出 _____   i. 夏 _____

e. 衣 _____   j. 髒 _____

4. Missing strokes

Complete each character by writing in the missing strokes.

a.   言   **gāi** (**yīnggāi** *should*)

b.   鹵   **lí** *separated from*

c.   斤   **jìn** *close*

d.   骨   **zāng** *dirty*

e.   百   **xià** (**xiàtiān** *summer*)

f.   𠂉   **shū** (**shūfu** *comfortable*)

g.   广   **yīng** (**yīnggāi** *should*)

h.   亠   **liàng** (**piàoliang** *pretty, beautiful*)

i.   丿   **huà** (**wénhuà** *culture*)

j.   氵   **piào** (**piàoliang** *pretty, beautiful*)

5. Total strokes

Rewrite this list of characters, arranging the characters in terms of their total number of strokes. Begin your list with the character with the fewest strokes.

離	近	舒	概	漂	出	髒	衣	化	應	如	亮	夏	歲	該

6. Radicals

Here is a list of characters that we have learned through this lesson. Rewrite each character in the row next to its radical.

酒　朋　洗　概　法　近　服　能

如　髒　應　始　床　校　漂　選

氵	
木	
女	
广	
辶	
月	

7. Character sleuth: Look for the phonetic

Group the characters below in terms of their rhyme. Write the characters that rhyme with each other in the column on the right. Write the shared part of each character in the column on the left. For all of these characters, the shared part is the "phonetic," the part of the character that suggests the pronunciation of the character. The first line is completed for you

問，園，跟，吧，放，見，紅，鐘，馬，很，間，現，

塊，工，媽，中，們，院，把，嗎，房，快，門

'rime'	characters that rhyme and share a common part
女	如

8.   Getting the gist of a paragraph

You won't be able to completely understand the following passage, but you know enough characters and words to be able to identify the topic of the paragraph and some of the supporting details. Read the paragraph for the main ideas and answer the questions that follow in English. Do not look up any characters we have not learned.

有的人常常把下雪想得很漂亮，房子上是雪、路上也是雪。我想這些人大概沒有看見過下雪。第一，下雪的時候常常很冷。天氣太冷讓人覺得很不舒服。第二，下雪以後出去、進來、走路、開車都很不方便。第三，下雪以後，很快路上就很髒，鞋、衣服、汽車都很容易髒。下雪的時候可能很漂亮，但是漂亮的時間不長。我真的不喜歡下雪。

This paragraph is about 雪. It is the <u>topic</u> of this paragraph. We have not yet presented the meaning of this character in this book. If you don't recognize it, don't look it up or ask anyone for its meaning.

a. How does the author's opinion about this topic compare with that of other people?

b. How many arguments does the author give to support his opinion?

c. Where in the paragraph does the author directly state his opinion?

d. What do you think 雪 means? What evidence do you have for this meaning?

9.   Dictionary skills

Following the instructions in Lesson 17 of the Textbook, look up these characters in a Chinese dictionary and provide the requested information.

a. 雪
  pronunciation:
  meaning:
  one two-character word or phrase in which it occurs:

b. 長
  pronunciation:
  meaning:
  one two-character word or phrase in which it occurs:

c. 短
  pronunciation:
  meaning:
  one two-character word or phrase in which it occurs:

10.   Find the incorrect characters

Xiao Zhang continues his email correspondence with his classmates back in the USA. He hasn't yet proofread this message, but when he does, he will find that thirteen characters are incorrect. Read the passage aloud, circle the mistakes, and correct them on the answer sheet below.

> 作天晚上下 **xuě** 了。下了一 **yè**。今天早上我一起床就住 **chuānghu** 外邊看。我覺的很票亮。路上沒友很多車，可是人非常都。他們都 **chuān** 了很多一服。有的人 **sǎo xuě**，有的人 **wán xuě**。我很我的同屋也到外邊去 **wán xuě**。**Wán** 了差不多一個中頭。**Wán** 得很高興，可是國了一回兒我覺得非常 **lěng**。回宿舍我們喝了很多 **rè chá**、吃了一點東酒以後，才覺得書服了。

a. ____   b. ____   c. ____   d. ____   e. ____   f. ____   g. ____

h. ____   i. ____   j. ____   k. ____   l. ____   m. ____

11.   Scrambled sentences

Rewrite these phrases as sentences, putting the words in the correct order to match the English translations.

a. 我 / 我 / 家 / 很近 / 離 / 很早 / 來得 / 學校 / 所以 / 都 / 每天

My home is close to school, so I arrive very early every day.

b. 去 / 夏天 / 中國 / 學習 / 今年 / 要 / 我 / 到 / 中文

I want to go to China this summer to study Chinese.

c. 對 / 真 / 我 / 為甚麼 / 知道 / 大學生 / 這麼 / 有興趣 / 不 / 很多 / 喝酒

I really don't know why many college students are so interested in drinking.

12.   Pinyin to characters

Rewrite the following sentences in Chinese characters.

a. **Tā de yīfu dōu hěn piàoliang, wǒ xiǎng yīdìng yě dōu hěn guì**。

b. **Zhège xuéqī nǐ yīnggāi xuǎn Zhōngguó wénhuà kè**。

c. **Wǒ de sùshè hěn shūfu yě hěn piàoliang, zhǐ shì yǒu yīdiǎn zāng**。

Focus on structure

1.   State the opposite

Fill in the blanks with the opposite of each word.

Example:

大 ↔ 小。

a. 好 ↔ _____   b. 乾淨 ↔ _____   c. **bèn** ↔ _____

d. **rè** ↔ _____   e. 多 ↔ _____   f. **duǎn** ↔ _____

g. **guì** ↔ _____   h. 近 ↔ _____   i. 容易 ↔ _____

2.   Getting more and more… (Use and Structure note 21.1)

Describe each situation in a complete sentence that includes **yuè** 來 **yuè**, as in the example.

Example:

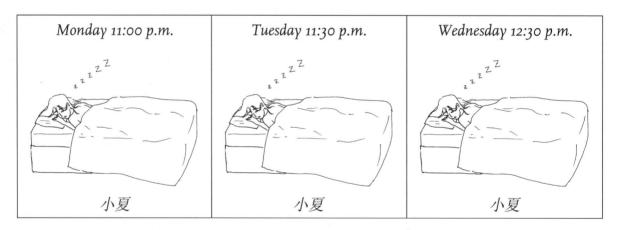

| Monday 11:00 p.m. | Tuesday 11:30 p.m. | Wednesday 12:30 p.m. |

小夏睡覺的時間 **yuè** 來 **yuè** 晚。

a. Median house price in California:

November 2007	November 2008	November 2009
$500,000	$450,000	$300,000

b. 天 **qì yùbào**：

今天：70°F	明天：73°F	後天：75°F

---

c. 北京的 **dōng** 天：

January 2007: −5°C	January 2008: −6°C	January 2009: −7°C

---

d. 在 **Jiāzhōu** 開車：

REGULAR 1.85
PLUS 1.93
SUPREME 2.01
2003

REGULAR 2.03
PLUS 2.45
SUPREME 2.98
2007

REGULAR 2.82
PLUS 3.05
SUPREME 3.27
2009

---

e. 張小弟：

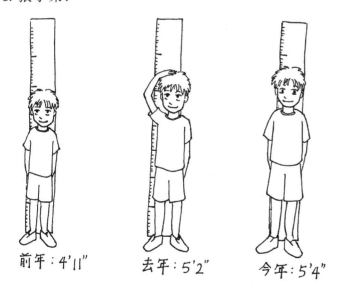

前年：4'11"　　去年：5'2"　　今年：5'4"

---

3.   More and more (Use and Structure note 21.1)

Answer each question in a complete sentence that includes the phrase **yuè** 來 **yuè**.

a. 你覺得中文考試怎麼樣?

b. 如果你吃壞了 **dù** 子，可是你沒有吃 **yào**，你的 **dù** 子可能會怎麼樣?

c. 如果你沒有時間 **shōushi** 房間，你的房間可能會怎麼樣?

4.   真 **zāogāo** (Use and Structure note 21.3)

Complete each sentence using V + 不了, based on the information in the illustration and the English translation.

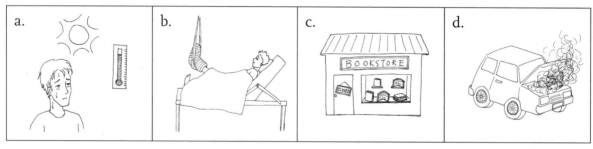

a. 今年的夏天真 _____ ，我快 _____了。
   It's so hot this summer. I almost can't stand it.

b. 小王 _____ **qiú** 也 _____ 學校了。
   Xiao Wang can't play ball and he can't go to school either.

c. 書店已經 _____ 了。我們 _____ 書了。
   The bookstore is not open. We can't buy the books.

d. 小謝的車 _____ ，現在他 _____ 家了。
   Xiao Xie's car broke down (it is 'bad'). Now he can't go home.

5.   It can't happen (Use and Structure note 21.3)

Fill in the blank with the appropriate V + 不了 expression, choosing from those given below, to complete each sentence to match the English translation.

> | 去不了 | 走不了 | 上不了 | 晚不了 | 來不了 |

a. 我現在還有一點 **shì**，_____ 。你們別 **děng** 我了，先走吧。
   I have something to do now and cannot leave. Don't wait for me. Go on ahead.

b. 對不起，這個星期天我得回家。我 _____ 你家了。
   Sorry, I have to go home this Sunday. I can't go to your home.

c. 國強給我打電話說他今天晚上得去工作，_____ 了。
   Guoqiang phoned me and said that he has to go to work tonight and he cannot come (here).

d. 電 **yǐng** 八點開始。現在才六點半。我們 _____ 。
   The movie starts at 8 o'clock. It's only 6:30 right now. We won't be late.

e. 我有點不舒服。請你 **gàosu** 老師今天的課我 _____ 了。
   I'm not feeling well. Please tell the teacher I won't be able to attend today's class.

6.   Saying that two things are the same (Use and Structure note 21.4)

Answer the following questions in complete Mandarin sentences, based on the information given.

month	Jan	Feb	Mar	Apr	May	Jun	Jul	Aug	Sep	Oct	Nov	Dec
temperature (Celsius)	−4.6	−2.7	4.5	13.1	19.8	24.4	25.8	24.4	19.4	12.4	4.1	−2.7

a. Which two months are equally cold?

b. Which two months of the year are equally hot?

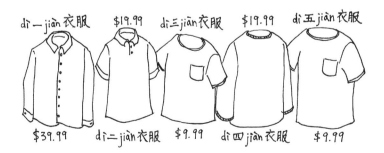

c. Which two shirts are equally expensive?

d. Which two shirts are the same?

7.   Making comparisons (Use and Structure note 21.7)

Answer each of the following questions in a complete sentence, based on the illustration. Use **bǐ** in each of your answers.

a. 誰的 **guì** 子 **luàn**？

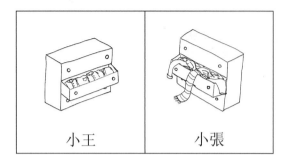

| 小王 | 小張 |

b. 誰的房間乾淨？

| 關小東 | 王小真 |

c. 誰的家近？

8.   More comparisons (Use and Structure notes 21.4 and 21.7)

Here are some facts about Gao Meili and her roommate Ye Youwen. Answer the questions that follow in complete Mandarin sentences, based on this information.

Gao Meili	Ye Youwen
age: 21 height: 5'4" courses this semester: 4 tests next week: 2 very smart	age: 20 height: 5'5" courses this semester: 5 tests next week: 1 very smart

a. Are Gao Meili and Ye Youwen the same age? (Hint: equally big)

b. Are Gao Meili and Ye Youwen the same height?

c. Who has more classes this semester? (Hint: Whose courses are more numerous?)

d. Who has more tests next week?

e. Who is smarter, Gao Meili or Ye Youwen?

9.   Asking about comparisons (Use and Structure notes 21.4 and 21.7)

Translate the questions in Exercise 8 into Mandarin.

a.

b.

c.

d.

e.

10.   Rhetorical questions (Use and Structure note 21.5)

Ask the following rhetorical questions in Mandarin.

a. Isn't it the case that Gao Meili and Ye Youwen are the same age (equally big)?

b. Isn't it the case that Gao Meili and Ye Youwen are the same height (equally tall)?

c. Isn't it the case that Gao Meili is smarter than Ye Youwen?

11.   Who made you do it? (Use and Structure note 21.8)

Xiao Zhang is explaining to his parents that different people have made him do certain things. Express each situation in Mandarin, as in the example:

Example:

老師, *put on some more clothes*   →   老師 **ràng** 我多 **chuān** 一點衣服。

a. 我的同屋, put my clothes in the dresser

b. 老師, do homework every day

c. 我的同屋, go to the hospital to see a doctor

d. **Yī** 生, take medicine every day this week (How do you say "take" medicine in Mandarin? Review Lesson 20.)

12.   That's the difference between A and B (Use and Structure note 21.9)

Sum up each of these sentences by saying "that's the difference between A and B," as in the example.

Example:

Chūn 天常常 **guā fēng**，**qiū** 天不 **guā fēng**。   →   這就是 **chūn** 天和 **qiū** 天的不同。

a. 美國人喜歡早上洗 **zǎo**。中國人喜歡晚上洗 **zǎo**。 →

b. 北京一年四 **jì**，南 **Jiāzhōu** 一年一 **jì**。   →

c. 美 **lì** 很用功，她的妹妹太喜歡 **wán**。   →

Focus on communication

1.   Dialogue comprehension

Study the Lesson 21 Narrative and Dialogue. Then, read the following statements and indicate whether they are true (T) or false (F).

a. (   ) 大為是一年多以前來北京的。

b. (   ) 北京 **dōng** 天不下 **xuě**，夏天不下 **yǔ**。

c. (   ) 最近幾年北京天 **qì rè** 的時間 **yuè** 來 **yuè** 長也 **yuè** 來 **yuè** 早。

d. (   ) 北京一年四 **jì** 最 **duǎn** 的是 **qiū** 天。

e. (   ) 大為最喜歡北京的 **chūn** 天。

f.　(　) 今天的最高 **wēndù** 只有三、四 **dù**。

g.　(　) 明天很 **lěng**，還會下 **yǔ**。

h.　(　) 後天大概不會下 **yǔ**。

i.　(　) 國強喜歡下 **xuě**，因為下雪的時候可以出去 **wán**。

j.　(　) 下 **xuě** 以後，大為大概不想出去，因為太 **lěng** 了。

k.　(　) 大為是從南 **Jiāzhōu** 來的。

l.　(　) 在 **Jiāzhōu** 的時候，大為如果想去 **hǎi** 邊，應該很 **fāngbiàn**。

m.　(　) 大為 **bǐjiào** 喜歡他家 **xiāng** 的天 **qì**。

n.　(　) 小王覺得他的中文老師 **guǎn** 得太多了。

o.　(　) 國強覺得，中文老師只是關 **xīn** 小王。

2.　What do you say?

What do you say in each of the following situations? Type your answers, using characters where we have learned them, and email them to your Chinese teacher.

a. Complain about how you can't stand today's high temperature anymore.

b. Advise your little brother to wear more clothes because it's cold outside.

c. Tell your mother that you're already twenty-one, so of course you know how to clean up your room.

d. Remind your roommate that the doctor wanted him to (told him to) finish taking the cold medicine.

e. You wonder why your Chinese teacher cared about what time you go to bed.

f. You brought your friend who just had her wisdom tooth removed some soup. Explain that you made the chicken soup (**jī tāng**) because you were afraid that she'd be unable to eat other food.

g. Comment on the weather in your area these past few days.

h. Explain why you like (or dislike) rain.

i. Compare the winter in your hometown with Beijing's, based on what you have read in this lesson.

j. Complain about the weather these days. The highest temperature has been only 2–3 degrees below zero.

3. Complete the mini-dialogues

Use the structure in parentheses to complete each mini-dialogue.

a. 小夏：　你們都坐我的車回家吧。小王，我先 **sòng** 你還是先 **sòng** 小張？

　　小王：　先 **sòng** 我。我家 ＿＿＿＿＿＿＿＿＿＿＿＿＿＿＿＿＿＿＿＿。（A **bǐ** B…）

b. 小高：　我有一年多沒看見你！你 ＿＿＿＿＿＿＿＿＿＿＿＿ 了！（**yuè** 來 **yuè** AdjV）

　　小 **Lín**：哪裏，哪裏。你也是。

c. 小張：　這個學期你怎麼不上中文課了？

　　小馬：　**Yǔ** 法 **yuè** 來 **yuè** 難，我 ＿＿＿＿＿＿＿＿＿＿！所以不上了。（V＋不了）

d. 小謝：　你覺得我應該買哪一 **jiàn** 衣服？

　　小夏：　都可以。＿＿＿＿＿＿＿＿＿＿＿＿＿＿＿＿＿＿。（A 跟 B一樣…）

e. 小高：　你要不要跟我們出去？我們要去買東西。

　　小 **Lín**：我不能去。我媽媽 ＿＿＿＿＿＿＿＿＿＿＿＿＿＿＿＿。（**ràng**…）

4. Making connections

Complete the sentences with the clauses given below. For the first part of the sentence, make your choice from the column on the left. For the second part of the sentence, make your choice from the column on the right. Then, translate the sentences into English.

A. 我最喜歡 **qiū** 天   F. 沒有時間做功課

B. 這門課很有用，也很有意思   G. 去圖書館做功課

C. **Zhōumò** 我常常在宿舍睡覺   H. 天 **qì** 不 **lěng** 也不 **rè**，非常舒服

D. 昨天我跟小王一起做功課、看電 **shì**   I. 功課 **tè** 別多

E. 我一天都忙 **zhe shōushi** 房間   J. 還一起吃晚飯

a. ＿＿＿＿＿＿＿＿＿＿＿＿＿＿＿，因為 ＿＿＿＿＿＿＿＿＿＿＿＿＿＿＿＿＿。

b. ＿＿＿＿＿＿＿＿＿＿＿＿＿＿＿，**érqiě** ＿＿＿＿＿＿＿＿＿＿＿＿＿＿＿＿。

c. ＿＿＿＿＿＿＿＿＿＿＿＿＿＿＿，**huòzhě** ＿＿＿＿＿＿＿＿＿＿＿＿＿＿＿。

d. ＿＿＿＿＿＿＿＿＿＿＿＿＿＿＿，所以 ＿＿＿＿＿＿＿＿＿＿＿＿＿＿＿＿＿。

e. ＿＿＿＿＿＿＿＿＿＿＿＿＿＿＿，只是 ＿＿＿＿＿＿＿＿＿＿＿＿＿＿＿＿＿。

5.   天 **qì yùbào**

Part I.   Six weathermen are presenting weather forecasts for their cities. Identify each weatherman on the basis of their forecast and write their name in the blank space in their forecast. Then translate each forecast into English.

王子強   謝易南   舒國定

常歡   夏如如   張明非

a. 大家好，我是 _____。明天的天 **qì** 還是跟這幾天一樣，非常舒服。雖然有一點兒 **fēng**，可是不大，是出去 **wán** 的好天 **qì**。
English:

b. 大家好，我是 _____。大家可能覺得，今年的 **dōng** 天怎麼這麼 **cháng**。明天 **tè** 別 **lěng**，最高 **wēndù** 只有 **líng** 下四、五 **dù**。最 **zāogāo** 的是，很可能會下大 **xuě**，如果沒有 **shì**，就在家裏別出去，在路上開車的時候，最好開慢一點。
English:

c. 大家好，我是 _____。最近這幾天又 **mēn** 又 **rè**，我想很多人都快 **shòu** 不了了。明天還是很 **rè**，不過下 **wǔ** 會下一點兒 **yǔ**。應該會 **ràng** 大家高興一點。
English:

d. 大家好，我是 _____。下 **yǔ** 下了一天了，大家今天一定覺得很不 **fāngbiàn**。明天 **chú** 了下 **yǔ** 以外，還會 **guā** 大 **fēng**。這樣的天 **qì** 要到 **zhōumò** 才會有一點不同。
English:

e. 大家好，我是 _____。明天會 **bǐ** 今天 **lěng** 得多，**érqiě** 可能會下 **xuě**，出去的時候，別 **wàng** 了多 **chuān** 一點衣服。
English:

f. 大家好，我是 _____。不知道你是不是跟我一樣，也覺得 **chūn** 天快到了。最近 **bái** 天 (*daytime*) **yuè** 來 **yuè cháng**。明天也是一個好天 **qì**，不 **lěng** 不 **rè**，舒服 **jí** 了。
English:

Part II. It's your turn to be the weatherman! Check the weather forecast online or on TV, and write about tomorrow's weather in Mandarin. Your weather forecast should be at least 100 characters in length.

_____

_____

_____

_____

_____

6. 一年四 **jì** 我最（不）喜歡…

Part I. Students in Xiao Zhang's class each talked about the season they like or dislike the most. Complete each sentence based on the illustrations.

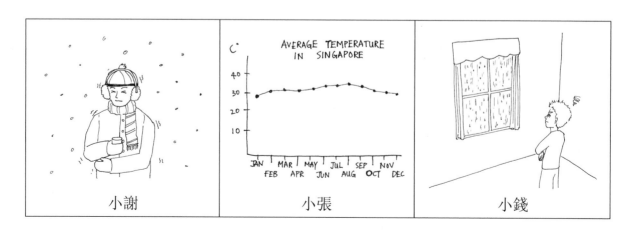

| 小謝 | 小張 | 小錢 |

| 小常 | 小高 | 小王 |

a. 小謝最不喜歡 **dōng** 天，因為 **dōng** 天 _____

_____。

b. 小張家 **xiāng** 的天 **qì**，一年四 **jì** 都 _____

_____。

c. 小錢不喜歡 **qiū** 天，因為 **qiū** 天 _____

_____。

d. 小常最不喜歡夏天，因為夏天 _____

_____。

e. 小高最喜歡夏天，因為夏天 _____

_____。

f. 小王最喜歡 **dōng** 天，因為 **dōng** 天 _____

_____。

Part II. It's your turn. Tell us your (least) favorite season in your hometown and explain why. Your paragraph should be at least 120 characters in length.

_____

_____

_____

_____

_____

7.   你家 **xiāng** 的天 **qì** 怎麼樣？

Interview a friend and find out the year-round weather in his/her hometown. Write down the questions you can ask.

Questions about his/her hometown:

a. _____

b. _____

Questions about each season: length, temperature, what s/he likes and dislikes about it:

a. _____

b. _____

c. _____

d. _____

8.   Writing

After your Exercise 7 interview, write a short passage about the weather in your friend's hometown. Your passage should be at least 100 characters in length.

_____

_____

_____

_____

_____

_____

_____

_____

9. Form a cohesive paragraph

Rewrite these sentences, putting them in the correct order to form a <u>persuasive paragraph</u> about studying Chinese.

a. **dì** 二，中國和美國是兩個很不一樣的國家，在學習中文的時候你可知道一些中國文化。

b. **dì** 一，現在中國的經 **jì yuè** 來 **yuè** 好，中國和美國的關係也很好。很多工作都要會說中文的人。

c. 多學一些不同的文化很有意思。

d. 選不選中文 **zhuānyè** 沒有關係，但是你在上大學的時候最好學一些中文。為甚麼呢？

e. 這樣，你會 **bǐjiào** 有興趣，可以學得很快、當然也就可以學得很好。

f. 你會說中文，**bìyè** 以後就容易找工作。

g. 人少的時候，老師和學生的關係，同學和同學的關係都 **bǐjiào** 好。

h. **dì** 三，中文課和數學課、經 **jì** 課很不一樣，中文課，每個課的學生 **bǐjiào** 少。

Lesson 22 Workbook

 Listening and speaking

(audio online)

Structure drills

1. Even the object (Use and Structure note 22.7)

Example:

You will hear: 我沒有手 **jī**。
You will say: 我 **lián** 手 **jī** 都沒有。
Click "R" to hear the correct response: 我 **lián** 手 **jī** 都沒有。

(a)　(b)　(c)　(d)　(e)　(f)　(g)

2. Even the subject (Use and Structure note 22.7)

Example:

You will hear: 我媽媽喜歡 **chàng kǎlā OK**。
You will say: **lián** 我媽媽都喜歡 **chàng kǎlā OK**。
Click "R" to hear the correct response: **lián** 我媽媽都喜歡 **chàng kǎlā OK**。

(a)　(b)　(c)　(d)　(e)　(f)　(g)　(h)

3. Even the time (Use and Structure note 22.7)

Example:

You will hear: 他星期天去上課。
You will say: 他 **lián** 星期天都去上課。
Click "R" to hear the correct response: 他 **lián** 星期天都去上課。

(a)　(b)　(c)　(d)　(e)　(f)　(g)　(h)

4. My roommate did the opposite (Use and Structure notes 22.5, 22.6)

Example:
You will hear: 我走進來。
You will say: 我走進來的時候，我的同屋走出去了。
Click "R" to hear the correct response: 我走進來的時候，我的同屋走出去了。

(a)   (b)   (c)   (d)   (e)   (f)

5. Add the object (Use and Structure note 22.6)

Example:
You will hear: 他 **shēn** 出來，手
You will say: 他 **shēn** 出手來。
Click "R" to hear the correct response: 他 **shēn** 出手來。

(a)   (b)   (c)   (d)   (e)   (f)   (g)   (h)   (i)   (j)

6. Not as much as (Use and Structure note 22.9)

Example:
You will hear: 昨天比今天冷。
You will say: 今天沒有昨天冷。
Click "R" to hear the correct response: 今天沒有昨天冷。

(a)   (b)   (c)   (d)   (e)   (f)   (g)   (h)   (i)   (j)

7. It has that quality all right, but... (Use and Structure note 22.8)

Example:
You will hear: 昨天比今天冷。
You will say: 今天冷是冷，可是沒有昨天那麼冷。
Click "R" to hear the correct response: 今天冷是冷，可是沒有昨天那麼冷。

(a)   (b)   (c)   (d)   (e)   (f)   (g)   (h)   (i)   (j)

Listening for information

1. 生 **mìng** 在 **yú yùndòng**

(CD1: 58)   You will hear six statements, each of which describes a person's sport preference. Listen to the statements and match each statement with the appropriate person. The statements include one word that we have not presented in the textbook, but you should be able to figure out its meaning as you do this exercise.

person	sport
Mèng Píng	American football
Yè Àiyún	baseball
Qín Fēng	rowing
Lín Yīchén	volleyball
Lǐ Shìchéng	skiing
Sòng Zhèng	soccer

2.   Exercise schedule

(CD1: 59)   You will hear five statements, each of which describes a person's exercise schedule and sports participation. Listen to the statements and fill in the correct information for each person. The statements include one word that has not been introduced in the textbook, but you should be able to work around it.

name	what kind of sport or exercise they do	how often they practice	when the competitions are
Huáng Dézhèng			
Língling			
Hú Zǔwén			
Luó Yǔ			
Jì Wénfāng			

3. Where are they going?

You will hear five directional phrases, each describing the action in one of the drawings. **(CD1: 60)** Circle the correct directional arrow in each drawing, based on the information that you hear.

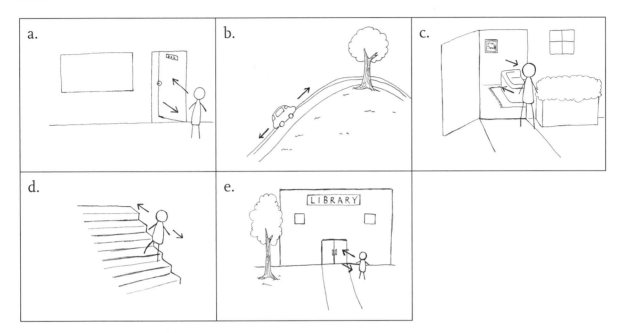

a.

b.

c.

d.

e.

4. Who goes where?

You will hear five statements, each describing the situation in one of the following pictures. **(CD1: 61)** Based on the information in the recordings, provide the names of the people involved in each situation, and draw an arrow indicating the direction of movement for the person who changes location.

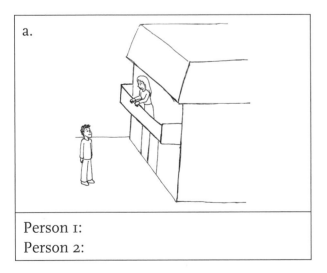

a.

Person 1:
Person 2:

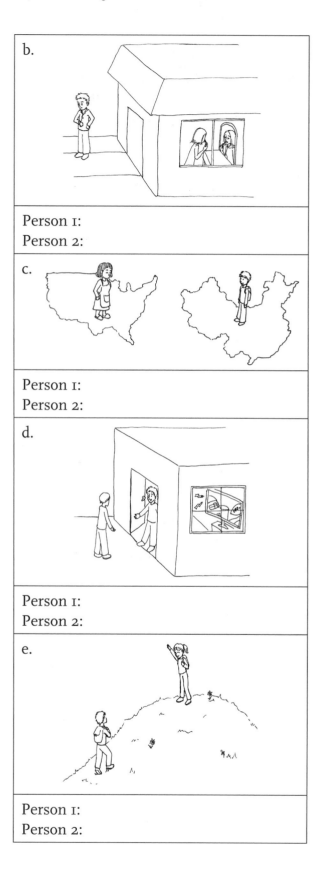

b.

Person 1:

Person 2:

c.

Person 1:

Person 2:

d.

Person 1:

Person 2:

e.

Person 1:

Person 2:

5. Colder or warmer?

You will hear five statements, each describing today's weather in one of five cities in China. (CD1: 62) Based on this information, write the names of the cities over the temperatures listed below. The five cities are: Hángzhōu, Chéngdū, Lìjiāng, Tiānjīn, and Wǔhàn.

city					
temperature	65°F	60°F	54°F	48°F	32°F

6. Even…

You will hear five statements using the sentence pattern **lián**…也/都. In the right-hand (CD1: 63) column of the table below, there are five inferences. In the statement column, write in the number of the statement that leads to each inference.

statement	inference
	→ 他不怕冷。
	→ 她下個星期有三個考試。
	→ 他很會打 **qiú**。
	→ 她沒有時間去看電 **yǐng**。
	→ 他一定很會做飯。

7. What about you?

Your friend is asking you about sports and exercise. Answer each question truthfully in a (CD1: 64) complete sentence in Mandarin, using Chinese characters where we have learned them.

a.

b.

c.

d.

e.

f.

8.   Interview

(CD1: 65) You will hear an interview between a campus newspaper reporter and Zheng Ming, who just returned to Shanghai after studying English for a year in Los Angeles. Summarize Zheng Ming's responses in English on the following three topics:

Summary

1. taking courses

2. campus life

3. studying

9.   Dialogue

(CD1: 66) You will hear a conversation between Pan Li and Luo De, who have just met in a building on campus. The conversation contains a word we have not introduced, but you should be able to follow the conversation even if you do not know what this word means.

a. How do you get to the gym?
   1) You take the elevator.
   2) You just turn left.
   3) You enter the gate.
   4) You go up to the third floor.

b. Where can you play ping-pong?
   1) You go into the room on the right.
   2) You go down to the first floor.
   3) You leave this building and go someplace else.
   4) You go up one floor.

c. What did Luo De tell Pan Li?
   1) He does not play tennis well, but he likes it.
   2) He plays tennis four times a week.
   3) He has a hard time finding a tennis court here.
   4) He has not played tennis for years.

d. What do Pan Li and Luo De plan to do?
   1) They will watch a game on Saturday.
   2) They will meet on Saturday to play ping-pong.
   3) They will go to the gym together.
   4) They will take a look at the ping-pong room.

Reading and writing

Focus on Chinese characters

1.   Number of strokes

Indicate the number of strokes used in writing each of the following characters.

a. 或 ____   f. 怕 ____

b. 教 ____   g. 進 ____

c. 冷 ____   h. 自 ____

d. 玩 ____   i. 週 ____

e. 比 ____   j. 而 ____

2.   Which character?

Circle the character in each line that corresponds to the meaning on the left.

a. **huò** (**huòzhě** *or, perhaps*)   或   國

b. **jìn** *enter*   近   進

c. **wán** *play*   完   玩

d. **jiā** *add* (**cānjiā** *participate*)   加   咖

e. **fāng** (**dìfang** *place*)   房   方

f. **shǒu** *hand*   手   毛

g. **zì** (**zìjǐ** *self*)   白   自

h. **ràng** *make, let, tell*   讓   攘

i. **pà** *fear, afraid*   怕   伯

j. **mò** (**zhōumò** *weekend*)   末   木

k. **bǐ** *compared to*   北   比

l. **ér** *and*   而   兩

3. First strokes

Write the first two strokes of each of the following characters.

a. 而 ____   f. 且 ____

b. 教 ____   g. 手 ____

c. 者 ____   h. 末 ____

d. 冷 ____   i. 方 ____

e. 或 ____   j. 讓 ____

4. Missing strokes

Complete each character by writing in the missing strokes.

a.   亻   **pà** *fear, afraid*

b.   干   **wán** *play*

c.   𠃊   **bǐ** *compared to*

d.   コ   **jiā** *add* (**cānjiā** *participate*)

e.   豆   **huò** (**huòzhě**) *or, perhaps*

f.   彳   **zì** (**zìxíngchē** *bicycle*)

g.   土   **jiào** *teach*

h.   几   **zhōu** (**zhōumò** *weekend*)

i.   冫   **lěng** *cold*

j.   亻   **jìn** *enter*

5.   Total strokes

Rewrite this list of characters, arranging the characters in terms of their total number of strokes. Begin your list with the character with the fewest strokes.

週	進	教	或	者	冷	自	手	怕	末	加	比	讓	方	玩	而	且

6.   Radicals

Here is a list of characters that we have learned through this lesson. Rewrite each character in the row next to its radical.

進　　冷　　怕　　讓　　玩　　放　　選　　慣
教　　房　　課　　數　　試　　近　　淨　　現

冫	
亻	
言	
戶	
辶	
攵	
王	

7.   Character sleuth: Look for the phonetic

Group the characters below in terms of their rhymes or near-rhymes. Write the characters that rhyme with each other in the column on the right. Write the shared part of each character in the column on the left. For all of these characters, the shared part is the "phonetic," the part of the character that provides a clue to its pronunciation. The first set of rhymes is completed for you. There are thirteen additional sets of characters that rhyme or partially rhyme and share a phonetic component among these characters.

買　　房　　跟　　哪　　賣　　完　　媽　　作
女　　紅　　爸　　門　　放　　工　　現　　吧
把　　功　　很　　間　　們　　方　　問　　國
嗎　　玩　　或　　那　　見　　如　　昨　　馬

phonetic	characters that rhyme or almost rhyme and share a phonetic component
女	如，女

8. Getting the gist of a paragraph

You won't be able to completely understand the following passage, but you know enough characters and words to be able to identify the topic of the paragraph and some of the supporting details. Read the paragraph for the main ideas and answer the questions that follow in English. Do not look up any characters we have not learned.

> 學習中文和學習數學有相同的地方，也有不同的地方。相同的是要去上課、看書、做功課。不同的是第一，學數學，懂了就可以了，你就可以做數學題了。學中文就很不一樣。你可能懂了，但是你還是不會說。所以學中文的時候你要多聽錄音、多練習說。第二，學數學的時候，你可以不用每天都去上課。週末多用一些時間自己看看書，也可以懂。但是學中文每天都要去上課。一天不去上課你就不知道別的同學在說甚麼了。

a. What is the general purpose of this paragraph?

b. What are the main expressions used in the paragraph that identify its purpose?

c. The author presents two facts to support one side of the argument. Which side of the argument do these facts support?

9.　Dictionary skills

Following the instructions in Lesson 17 of the Textbook, look up these characters in a Chinese dictionary and provide the requested information.

a. 相

pronunciation:

meaning:

one two-character word or phrase in which it occurs:

b. 己

pronunciation:

meaning:

one two-character word or phrase in which it occurs:

c. 第

pronunciation:

meaning:

one two-character word or phrase in which it occurs:

10.　Find the incorrect characters

Xiao Zhang has written this email to his parents back in the USA, telling them about his recent basketball game with Xiao Wang and Guoqiang. He hasn't yet proofread this message, but when he does, he will find that eleven different characters are incorrect, several more than once. Read the passage aloud, circle the mistakes, and correct them on the answer sheet below.

巴巴媽媽你們好，

這個週未小王讓我和國強跟他一起去大 **lánqiú**。雖然是 **dōng** 天，可是我們還再外邊打。開始國強不想去，可是我們非讓他去不課。那天 **tè** 別冷。他話 **lián** 手都 **shēn** 不出來，怎麼能打 **qiú** 呢？可是我 **gàosu** 他一開是打 **qiú**，一開是 **pǎo bù**，他就不覺的冷了。我們打了一回兒，不 **dàn** 不覺得冷，而且覺得很 **rè**，很舒服。我想下個週末我們還會一走去打 **qiú**。

你們最進怎麼樣？

---

a. ＿＿＿　　b. ＿＿＿　　c. ＿＿＿　　d. ＿＿＿　　e. ＿＿＿　　f. ＿＿＿

g. ＿＿＿　　h. ＿＿＿　　i. ＿＿＿　　j. ＿＿＿　　k. ＿＿＿

11. Scrambled sentences

Rewrite these phrases as sentences, putting the words in the correct order to match the English translations.

a. 得 / 我 / 高 / 王 / 老師 / 多 / 比

I'm a lot taller than Professor Wang.

b. 去 / 我們 / 個 / 吧 / 週末 / 玩 / 下 / 公園

Let's go to the park and have some fun next weekend.

c. 外邊 / 很 / 有 / 宿舍 / 自行車 / 的 / 多

There are a lot of bicycles outside of the dorm.

12. Comprehension

Read the following paragraph and indicate whether the statements below are true (T) or false (F), based on the information in the passage.

中文的 "自行車" 是 "自 jǐ 走的車" 的意思。"行" 就是 "走"。我剛來美國的時候，看見可以過馬路的地方都有 "Xing" 這個字。我想可能是現在在美國學中文的人很多，但是因為漢字很難寫，所以他們不寫漢字。或者是因為 "Xing" 很不容易說，所以寫在馬路上，讓他們每天都看。

a. (　) The narrator has just arrived in the USA.

b. (　) The narrator thinks that few Americans study Chinese.

c. (　) The narrator thinks that perhaps the character 行 is hard for Americans to write.

d. (　) There is an overlap in meaning between the word 行 in Chinese and the use of "Xing" in English.

e. (　) The narrator thinks that "Xing" means *bicycles* in English.

Focus on structure

1.   Similarities and differences (Use and Structure notes 22.1, 22.2)

Write a sentence for each of the following lines, stating that A and B have similarities and differences when it comes to C, as in the example, and translate your sentence into English.

Example:
A: 美國的大學生   B: 中國的大學生   C: **duànliàn shēntǐ**

美國的大學生跟中國的大學生在 **duànliàn shēntǐ** 上有 **xiāng** 同的地方，也有不同的地方。

When it comes to exercising, American students and Chinese students have similarities and differences.

a. A: 北京   B: **Tái** 北   C: 天 **qi**

Your sentence: _____

English: _____

b. A: 美國   B: 中國   C: 文化

Your sentence: _____

English: _____

c. A: 美國大學生   B: 中國大學生   C: 學習

Your sentence: _____

English: _____

d. A: 日本人   B: 中國人   C: 吃飯

Your sentence: _____

English: _____

e. A: **Yīng** 文   B: 中文   C: **yǔ** 法

Your sentence: _____

English: _____

2.   Stating similarities (Use and Structure note 22.2)

Continuing the comparisons you introduced in Exercise 1, write a Mandarin sentence stating that *the similarity is that*:

a. the summer is very hot

b. American students and Chinese students are hardworking

c. before students graduate they have to select a major

d. both use chopsticks to eat

e. the subject (**zhǔyǔ**) is before the verb (**dòngcí**), and the object (**bīnyǔ**) is after the verb

3. Stating differences and linking information with 而 (Use and Structure notes 22.2, 22.4)

Continuing the comparisons you introduced in Exercise 1, write a Mandarin sentence for each pair that you are comparing, stating that *the differences are....* Link the differences with 而.

a. Beijing has four seasons and Taipei doesn't have winter.

b. American people use given names to call (叫) their friends and Chinese people use family name + given name (**xìngmíng**) to call their friends.

c. American students select their major when they are in their third year, and Chinese students select their major before they begin to attend college. (Use 才 and 就 in this sentence.)

d. Chinese people like to eat hot and spicy food and Japanese people do not.

e. English has "the" and "a" and Chinese does not.

4. Directional complements (Use and Structure notes 22.5 and 22.6)

Write a sentence using a verb of motion with a directional complement describing the motion in each of the following pictures from Xiao Wang's perspective. Do not include the phrases "toward Xiao Wang" or "away from Xiao Wang" in your sentences.

| a. | ride down, toward Xiao Wang |

b.		ride up, away from Xiao Wang
c.		jump down, toward Xiao Wang (**tiào** *jump*)
d.		drive up, away from Xiao Wang
e.		ride across, toward Xiao Wang
f.		run in, toward Xiao Wang
g.		ride out, away from Xiao Wang

h.		run out, toward Xiao Wang
i.		walk in, away from Xiao Wang
j.		walk up, toward Xiao Wang

5.   They can't do it (Use and Structure note 22.6)

Rewrite each of your sentences in Exercise 4 from Xiao Wang's perspective, saying that the subject is unable to do the action.

a.

b.

c.

d.

e.

f.

g.

h.

i.

j.

6. Walk out of the park

Rewrite each of your sentences in Exercise 4 from Xiao Wang's perspective, adding in the location that serves as the reference point of the action. As an example, (a) has been completed for you.

a. 他 **qí** 下山來。

b.

c.

d.

e.

f.

g.

h.

i.

j.

7. Even they can do these activities (Use and Structure note 22.7)

Translate a.–d. into English, and translate e.–h. into Mandarin, using characters where we have learned them. Complete i.–k. with the phrases provided in parentheses.

a. 自行車容易 **qí**。**Lián** 我 **mèimei** 都能 **qí**。

b. 我 **dìdi** 很喜歡打 **qiú**。**Lián páiqiú** 也喜歡（打）。

c. 他不 **dǒng** 中文。**Lián** "你好" 也不 **dǒng**。

d. 我的同屋每天都去 **jiàn shēn**房 **duànliàn shēntǐ**。她 **lián** 週末都去。

e. In my hometown, it is cold in the spring. It is even very cold in April.

f. My older sister is very hardworking. She even studies on Friday night.

g. In my school, a lot of students participate in school sports teams. Even the first-year students participate.

h. Yesterday's test was too long. Even the smartest students didn't finish it.

i. 大為每天都去 **pǎo bù**，＿＿＿＿＿＿＿＿＿＿＿＿＿＿。（下 **xuě** 的時候）

j. 國強的房間 **luànjí** 了，＿＿＿＿＿＿＿＿＿＿＿＿＿＿。（坐的地方）

k. 小張昨天很不舒服。一吃東西就 **lā dù** 子，＿＿＿＿＿＿＿＿＿＿。（水）

8.   Comparisons with 沒有 (Use and Structure note 22.9)

Write a complete Mandarin sentence for each line, saying that NP₁ is *not as* AdjV as NP₂.

NP₁	NP₂	AdjV
a. American football	soccer	interesting
b. June	August	hot
c. my older sister	my older brother	hardworking
d. taking a bus	driving a car	convenient
e. my room	your room	messy
f. my hobbies	my roommate's hobbies	many

9.   It is AdjV all right, but... (Use and Structure note 22.8)

Using the information in Exercise 8, say that NP₁ has the quality of the adjectival verb, but that it doesn't have as much as NP₂, following the example below.

Example:

NP₁	NP₂	AdjV
movie tickets	*football game tickets*	*expensive*

電 **yǐng piào guì** 是 **guì**，可是沒有 **zúqiú** 比 **sài piào** 那麼 **guì**。
Movie tickets are expensive all right, but they are not as expensive as football game tickets.

a.

b.

c.

d.

e.

f.

10.   Scrambled sentences

Rewrite these phrases into sentences, putting them in the right order to match the English translations.

a. 做 / 沒有 / 開始 / 忙 **zhe** / 玩 **qiú** / 功課 / 學期 / 時間 / 學生 / 一 / 都 / 而

Once the semester begins, the students are all busy doing their course work and do not have time to play ball.

b. 喜歡 / **shēntǐ** / 喜歡 / **duànliàn** / 到 **dǐ** / 你 / 不

Do you really like to work out or not?

c. 嗎 / 了 / **pǎo** 上 / 你 / 他 / 小張 / 去 / 看得見 / 山 (2 sentences)

Xiao Zhang ran up the mountain. Can you see him?

d. 真 / 冷 / 下 **xuě** / 可是 / 冷 / 漂亮 / 北京 / 是 / 的時候 / **dōng** 天

Winter in Beijing is indeed cold, but it's really beautiful when it snows.

e. **xiāng** 同 / 在 / 和 / 習慣 / 她 / 生 **huó** / 很不 / 上 / 她 **mèimei**

When it comes to daily habits, she and her younger sister are very different.

Focus on communication

1.   Dialogue comprehension

Study the Lesson 22 Narrative and Dialogue. Then, read the following statements and indicate whether they are true (T) or false (F).

a. (   ) 美國的大學生和中國的大學生都喜歡 **duànliàn shēntǐ**，只是他們喜歡的 **yùndòng** 不太一樣。

b. (   ) **Pīngpāng qiú** 和 **páiqiú** 是美國大學生和中國大學生都喜歡的 **yùndòng**。

c. (   ) 美國大學週末常常有校 **duì** 的比 **sài**。

d. (   ) 小王跟大為要去打 **lánqiú**。

e. (   ) 國強不想去，因為他手 **téng**，**shēn** 不出來。

f. (   ) 前兩天比這幾天冷。

g. (   ) 大為覺得自 **jǐ duànliàn** 得比國強多。

h. (   ) 國強的 **yùndòng** 就是打 **qiú**、**qí** 自行車和坐電 **tī**。

i. (   ) 國強最後 **jué** 定跟他們一起去打 **qiú**。

2.   What do you say?

What do you say in each of the following situations? Type your answers, using characters where we have learned them, and email them to your Chinese teacher.

a. State at least three kinds of sports that you like.

b. Ask someone how frequently s/he works out at the gym.

c. Advise your friend that s/he should exercise more.

d. Argue that you exercise by walking to school every day and never taking the elevator.

e. Tell people not to jump (**tiào** in **tiàowǔ** *dance*) down.

f. You are competing with your sibling/roommate/friend. Brag about two things that you do much better than s/he does.

g. You are arguing with your friend about winter in your city. You agree that he has a point, but you have a different opinion about winter.

3.   Complete the mini-dialogues

Use the structure in parentheses to complete each mini-dialogue.

a. A: 王老師，中文和 **Yīng** 文最大的不同是甚麼？

   B: ＿＿＿＿＿＿＿＿＿＿＿＿＿＿＿＿＿＿＿＿＿＿＿＿。（…而…）

b. A: 你最近在忙甚麼？怎麼都沒看見你？

   B: 我每天都忙 **zhe** ＿＿＿＿＿＿＿＿＿＿＿＿＿＿＿＿。（**lián**…都…）

c. A: 你昨天說 **dù** 子 **téng**，現在呢？還 **téng** 不 **téng**？

   B: 現在好多了。＿＿＿＿＿＿＿＿＿＿＿＿＿＿＿。（沒有…那麼…）

d. A: 四 **chuān** 菜真好吃！

   B: ＿＿＿＿＿＿＿＿＿＿＿＿＿＿＿＿＿＿＿。（A 是 A, 可是…）

e. A: 我問了你那麼多次，你 ＿＿＿＿＿＿＿＿＿＿＿＿＿？（到 **dǐ**）

   B: 我怎麼會不喜歡你呢！你想太多了。

4. Multiple choice

Select the appropriate line to complete each sentence, and then translate the sentence into English.

a. 我和我 **mèimei** 很不一樣。我很喜歡走路 **duànliàn shēntǐ**，而 ＿＿＿＿＿＿＿＿＿＿。
  1) 我昨天走路走了一個 **zhōngtou**
  2) 她只喜歡坐車、坐電 **tī**
  3) 她今年是一年 **jí** 的學生

  English:

b. 小美的 **shēntǐ** 很好，她每天 **yùndòng**，**lìng** 外，＿＿＿＿＿＿＿＿＿＿。
  1) 她還 **cān** 加學校的校 **duì**
  2) 小美這個學期選了四門課
  3) 小張不喜歡 **yùndòng**

  English:

c. 加 **zhōu** 漂亮是漂亮，可是 ＿＿＿＿＿＿＿＿＿＿＿＿＿＿＿＿。
  1) 天 **qì** 真好
  2) 我比 **jiào** 喜歡 **Niǔyuě**
  3) 在加 **zhōu** 開車很方 **biàn**

  English:

d. **Yùndòng** 對 **shēntǐ** 很好，而且 ＿＿＿＿＿＿＿＿＿＿＿＿＿＿。
  1) 今天這麼冷，我就不出去 **yùndòng** 了
  2) 美國大學生跟中國大學生在 **yùndòng** 上有 **xiāng** 同的地方，也有不同的地方
  3) 我覺得 **yùndòng** 以後 **tè** 別舒服

  English:

e. 下 **xuě** 的時候，我喜歡在家睡覺或者 ＿＿＿＿＿＿＿＿＿＿＿＿＿＿。
  1) 喝一 **bēi rè chá**，看外邊的 **xuě**
  2) 路上很髒，不能出去玩兒
  3) 冷得手都 **shēn** 不出來

  English:

5.   Sports event schedule

Here is a sports schedule at a college in California. Answer the questions that follow in Mandarin, based on this schedule.

team	date	opponent
soccer	2/18	UC Irvine
basketball	2/18	UC Davis
basketball	2/19	UC Santa Barbara
sailing	2/22	UC Berkeley
volleyball	3/1	CSU Long Beach
sailing	3/2	UC Santa Cruz
cycling	3/2	UC Davis
cycling	3/4	Caltech
volleyball	3/5	UC Riverside
volleyball	3/9	UCLA

a. 這個學校有甚麼校 **duì**？

b. 小週 **tè** 別喜歡看 **zúqiú** 比 **sài**，你想他哪天一定會去看比 **sài**？

c. 二月二十二號這個學校跟哪個學校比 **sài**？比甚麼？

d. 小王 **cān** 加學校的 **lánqiú duì**，你想他哪幾天大概不能去上課？

e. **Lánqiú** 比 **sài** 早還是自行車比 **sài** 早？

f. 今天是二月二十八號，你覺得我還能買到 **páiqiú** 比 **sài** 的票嗎？為甚麼？

6.   Read and retell

Part I.   Read the paragraph and fill in the blanks with a verb + directional complement based on the English translation.

今天是小 **Yè** 的生日。小張讓小 **Yè** 下了課以後就在 **kāfēi** 館 **děng** 他。小張 _____

_____ (walked into the coffee shop) 的時候，看見小謝和小高 _____

(run out)。小 **Yè** 說，小謝和小高聽說今天是她的生日，他們要讓她高興一下。小張

讓小 **Yè** 把手 _____ (extend out)，他給小 **Yè** 買了一 **jiàn** 漂亮的衣服。小 **Yè**

非常高興。他們兩個人一起 _____ (walk out of the coffee

shop)，看見小謝的車 _____ (drive over)，小高讓他們 _____

_____ (enter in)，小謝打 **suan dài** 他們去吃晚飯。

Part II.   Read the paragraph again. Imagine what was said during those situations:

a. Xiao Xie wonders what Xiao Ye is doing in the coffee shop and Xiao Ye explains.

b. Xiao Zhang is surprised to see Xiao Xie and Xiao Gao rushing out and asks them where exactly (到 **dǐ**) they are going and why they are running so fast.

c. Xiao Zhang tells Xiao Ye that he heard it was her birthday today and he bought her a little something.

d. Xiao Ye gushes about the beautiful gift and thanks Xiao Zhang.

e. Xiao Gao suggests to Xiao Xie that they drive over to the coffee shop to take Xiao Zhang and Xiao Ye to the mountain top.

f. Xiao Gao tells Xiao Zhang and Xiao Ye to hurry and get into the car.

g. Xiao Xie tells them that he is driving them up the mountain for dinner.

7.   Talk about your favorite sports/workout

Part I.   Answer the following questions truthfully.

a. 你喜歡 **yùndòng** 嗎？你最喜歡甚麼 **yùndòng**？

b. 你是甚麼時候開始做這個 **yùndòng** 的？

c. 你為甚麼喜歡這個 **yùndòng**？

d. **Yùndòng** 以後，你覺得怎麼樣？

e. 這個 **yùndòng** 有甚麼好的地方？有沒有不方 **biàn** 的地方？是甚麼？

f. 你一個星期做幾次這個 **yùndòng**？

g. 你在哪兒做這個 **yùndòng**？

h. 下 **yǔ** 或者天 **qì** 不好的時候，如果不能 **yùndòng**，你怎麼 **duànliàn shēntǐ**？

i. **Chú** 了你最喜歡的這個 **yùndòng** 以外，你還想試試甚麼 **yùndòng**，為甚麼？

Part II.   Use your answers above to write a paragraph about your favorite sports. Your paragraph should be at least 120 characters in length.

_____

_____

_____

_____

_____

_____

_____

_____

_____

_____

8.   Writing a comparison paragraph

Part I.   Form a cohesive paragraph. Rearrange these sentences so that they become a cohesive paragraph that compares college life in the past with life nowadays.

a. 還可以跟朋友一起出去玩，很晚才回宿舍也沒有關係。

b. 不同的是，以前的大學生跟朋友在宿舍、**cāntīng**、**kāfēi** 館 **tán** 話，去圖書館找上課要用的書。

c. 雖然很多 **shì** 都得自 **jǐ** 做，**lián** 衣服都得自 **jǐ** 洗。

d. **Lìng** 外，有了電 **nǎo** 以後，選課、買書，都比以前方 **biàn**。

e. 以前的大學生跟現在的大學生在生 **huó** 上有 **xiāng** 同的地方，也有不同的地方。

f. 可是在學校住可以自 **jǐ jué** 定吃飯、睡覺的時間。

g. 而現在的大學生上 **wǎng** 跟朋友 **tán** 話、找上課要用的東西。

h. **Xiāng** 同的是年 **qīng** 人都喜歡住校的生 **huó**。

Part II.   Write your own comparison paragraph: Following the structure of the above paragraph, write a similar paragraph to compare high school life and college life from your own experience. Your paragraph should be at least 120 characters in length.

_____

_____

_____

_____

_____

_____

_____

_____

_____

_____

Lesson 23 Workbook

 Listening and speaking

Structure drills

1. Even more (Use and Structure note 23.2)

You will hear a comparison between two people, places, or things, followed by a new person, place, or thing. Say that the new item has *even more* of some quality than the first item, as in the example.

Example:
You will hear: 中文比 **Yīng** 文難。（日文）
You will say: 日文比中文 **gèng** 難。
Click "R" to hear the correct response: 日文比中文 **gèng** 難。

(a)   (b)   (c)   (d)   (e)   (f)   (g)   (h)   (i)   (j)

2. 只要 S/VP₁ 就 VP₂ *as long as*, Part I (Use and Structure note 23.4)

You will hear two statements. Rephrase them using 只要 to say that as long as the first statement is true, the second one is true.

Example:
You will hear: 你喜歡，你就可以買。
You will say: 只要你喜歡，就可以買。
Click "R" to hear the correct response: 只要你喜歡，就可以買。

(a)   (b)   (c)   (d)   (e)   (f)   (g)   (h)   (i)   (j)

3. 只要 S/VP₁ 就 VP₂ *as long as*, Part II (Use and Structure note 23.4)

Restate each sentence with 只要 S/VP₁ 就 VP₂, as in the example.

Example:

You will hear: 你去看電 **yǐng**，我也去。

You will say: 只要你去看電 **yǐng**，我就去。

Click "R" to hear the correct response: 只要你去看電 **yǐng**，我就去。

(a)   (b)   (c)   (d)   (e)   (f)   (g)   (h)   (i)   (j)

4. 一點兒都 NEG V *not even a little*, Part I (Use and Structure note 23.5)

You will hear a sentence describing the quality of some person, place, or thing. Restate the sentence to say that s/he or it has none of that quality, as in the example.

Example:

You will hear: 你不 **pàng**。

You will say: 你一點兒都不 **pàng**。

Click "R" to hear the correct response: 你一點兒都不 **pàng**。

(a)   (b)   (c)   (d)   (e)   (f)   (g)   (h)

5. 一點兒 NP 都 NEG V *not even a little* NP, Part II
(Use and Structure note 23.5)

You will hear a sentence talking about something that I have not done. Rephrase the sentence to say that I didn't even do a little of the action.

Example:

You will hear: 我沒喝酒。

You will say: 我一點兒酒都沒喝。

Click "R" to hear the correct response: 我一點兒酒都沒喝。

(a)   (b)   (c)   (d)   (e)   (f)   (g)

Listening for information

1. Listen and draw

You will hear five statements, each of which mentions an object with a certain color. Listen (CD1: 69)
to the sentences and draw each item, indicating its color, in the corresponding box.

a.	b.	c.	d.	e.

2.   Shopping spree

(CD1: 70) Xiao Ping, Jia Ting, and Lai Xinxin went shopping last weekend. Listen to what they bought and write in the information on the following form.

name	item	size	price	color
Xiao Ping				
Jia Ting				
Lai Xinxin				

3.   What is the condition?

(CD1: 71) You will hear five statements, each describing a condition that leads to some result. In the "condition" column of the following table, write down the letter of the condition that leads to each of the results in the "result" column.

condition	result
	→ **dù** 子就不 **téng** 了。
	→ 就可以買這條 **lán qún** 子。
	→ 身體一定會很好。
	→ 媽媽就讓他出去玩。
	→ 就可以選這門課。

4.   My sisters and I

(CD1: 72) Listen to the passage about me and my sisters, and write down each of our clothing sizes.

person	3rd younger sister (**xiǎo mèi**)	2nd younger sister (**èr mèi**)	1st younger sister (**dà mèi**)	me
size				

5. Not at all

You will hear five statements, each describing a different situation. In the "conclusion" column of the following table, write the letter of the statement that can be used to sum up or conclude each of the following situations.

(CD1: 73)

situation	conclusion
我兩點才吃 **wǔ** 飯。	
我昨天晚上睡了十個鍾頭。	
這個考試只要十分鐘就寫完了。	
那家新 **cāntīng** 又貴，服務又慢。	
這條 **qún** 子太 **duǎn** 了。	

6. Conversation

Answer the questions you hear truthfully, based on your personal experience and interests. (CD1: 74)

a.

b.

c.

d.

e.

f.

7. Listen and write

You will hear a phone message from Aunt Lin. Write an email to answer her questions in Mandarin, using characters where we have learned them. (CD1: 75)

Email to Aunt Lin

8. Meizhen's shopping experience

(CD1: 76) Meizhen is talking about her shopping experience. Based on her narrative, indicate whether each of the following statements is true (T) or false (F).

a. (   ) Meizhen wears a size 5.

b. (   ) The skirt is 50% off.

c. (   ) Meizhen likes the color red.

d. (   ) Meizhen bought some things, but she didn't buy a skirt.

e. (   ) Meizhen went shopping last weekend.

9. Dialogue

(CD1: 77) Zhijie is phoning Wenna to invite her to an event. Listen to their conversation and select the correct answer to each of the following questions.

a. What event will they attend tomorrow night?
   1) an evening party
   2) a dance party
   3) a singing performance
   4) a musical

b. How did the woman learn about the event?
   1) from the campus newspaper
   2) from her friend
   3) from a radio broadcast
   4) from some school posters

c. What will the woman probably wear tomorrow night?
   1) a long skirt
   2) a short skirt
   3) a pair of red pants
   4) a traditional dress

d. Why does the man want to go to the event?
   1) His friends organized the event.
   2) He was asked to buy the tickets.
   3) He is going on a date with the female speaker.
   4) His sister is singing at the event.

e. What is their plan for tomorrow?
   1) They will take the subway.
   2) They will meet at the auditorium.
   3) They will drive there.
   4) They will walk together.

Reading and writing

1.   Number of strokes

Indicate the number of strokes used in writing each of the following characters.

a. 新 _____   f. 貴 _____

b. 員 _____   g. 綠 _____

c. 特 _____   h. 連 _____

d. 鐵 _____   i. 穿 _____

e. 事 _____   j. 球 _____

2.   Which character?

Circle the character in each line that corresponds to the meaning on the left.

a. **shì** (**shìyàng** *style*)   式   試

b. **yùn** *move* (**yùndòng** *movement*)   動   運

c. **xīn** *heart*   心   新

d. **wán** *finish, end*   玩   完

e. **yòu** *also, both*   友   又

f. **lián** *even*   車   連

g. **tiě** *iron* (**dìtiě** *subway*)   錄   鐵

h. **tiáo** (*classifier for streets, skirts*)   佟   條

i. **tǐ** (**shēntǐ** *body*)   體   髒

j. **shēn** (**shēntǐ** *body*)   身   夏

k. **yuán** (**fúwùyuán** *server, clerk*)   員   貴

l. **qì** (**tiānqì** *weather*)   汽   氣

3.   First strokes

Write the first two strokes of each of the following characters.

a. 春 ____   f. 累 ____

b. 山 ____   g. 綠 ____

c. 市 ____   h. 條 ____

d. 務 ____   i. 心 ____

e. 葉 ____   j. 動 ____

4.   Missing strokes

Complete each character by writing in the missing strokes.

a.   勹   **shēn (shēntǐ** *body*)

b.   干   **shì (shìyàng** *style*)

c.   宀   **wán** *finish, end*

d.   田   **lèi** *tired*

e.   宀   **chuān** *wear, put on*

f.   王   **qiú** *ball*

g.   ﾉ丶   **guì** *expensive*

h.   ﾉ一   **qì (tiānqì** *weather*)

i.   二   **chūn** *spring*

j.   亠   **shì (shì zhōngxīn** *city center*)

5.   Total strokes

Rewrite this list of characters, arranging the characters in terms of their total number of strokes. Begin your list with the character with the fewest strokes.

動	特	葉	事	綠	穿	式	新	身	完	員	體	心	累	氣	鐵	貴	又	運	條

6. Radicals

Here is a list of characters that we have learned through this lesson. Rewrite each character in the row next to its radical.

完　員　穿　春　經　運　綠　連
進　玩　邊　定　喝　最　球　週

口	
日	
宀	
辶	
糸	
王	

7. Character sleuth: Look for the phonetic

Group the characters below in terms of their rhymes or near-rhymes. Write the characters that rhyme with each other in the column on the right. Write the shared part of each character in the column on the left. For all of these characters, the shared part is the "phonetic," the part of the character that provides a clue to its pronunciation. The first set of rhymes is completed for you. There are nine additional sets of characters that rhyme or partially rhyme and share a phonetic component among these characters.

女　如　現　玩　把　門　放　紅
房　國　工　式　或　完　近　爸
見　試　跟　院　新　方　問　很

phonetic	characters that rhyme or almost rhyme and share a phonetic component
女	如

8.   Getting the gist of a paragraph

You won't be able to completely understand the following passage, but you know enough characters and words to be able to identify the topic of the paragraph and some of the supporting details. Read the paragraph for the main ideas and answer the questions that follow in English. Do not look up any characters we have not learned.

我真的不知道為甚麼有這麼多的人喜歡打球。打球到底有甚麼意思呢？很多人在一起，跑來、跑去。不是把球踢出去，就是把球搶過來，又髒、又熱、又累。有的時候還會傷了身體，不得不去看醫生。如果真的那麼喜歡球，每個人自己買一個拿回家不是很好嗎？

---

a. What is the general topic of this paragraph?

b. What is the narrator's opinion about this topic?

c. Circle one or two sections of the passage that reveal the narrator's opinion.

9.   Dictionary skills

Following the instructions in Lesson 17 of the Textbook, look up these characters in a Chinese dictionary and provide the requested information.

a. 街
pronunciation:
meaning:
one two-character word or phrase in which it occurs:

b. 花
pronunciation:
meaning:
one two-character word or phrase in which it occurs:

c. 種
pronunciation:
meaning:
one two-character word or phrase in which it occurs:

10.   Find the incorrect characters

Xiao Zhang has written this email to his parents back in the USA, telling them about one of his classmates, but he has typed ten characters incorrectly. Read the passage aloud, circle the mistakes, and correct them on the answer sheet below.

爸爸，媽媽，你們好！

你們身體好嗎？北京的天汽 **yuè** 來 **yuè** 冷。宿舍，叫 **shì** 都很舒朋，可是去外力得多穿衣服。**Guā fēng** 的時候覺得 **gèng** 冷。我有一個同學非常怕冷。因為怕冷，所以他很少跟我們至宿舍外邊去雲動。團為很少運動，所以他也很容以累。如果有人請他出去吃反，看電 **yǐng**，買東四，他說如果坐地鐵去，他就去。如果走路去，他就不去。

a. _____   b. _____   c. _____   d. _____   e. _____

f. _____   g. _____   h. _____   i. _____   j. _____

11.   Scrambled sentences

Rewrite these phrases as sentences, putting the words in the correct order to match the English translations.

a. 以後 / 去 / 晚飯 / 男朋友 / 新 / 市中心 / 買 / 她 / 衣服 / 和 / 的 / 的 / 吃完 / 小葉

After finishing dinner, Xiao Ye and her boyfriend went downtown to buy new clothes.

b. 的 / 天氣 / 春天 / 好 / 舒服 / 好 / 沒有 / 的 / 那麼 / 夏天 / 是 / 可是

The weather in the summer is good all right, but it is not as comfortable as the spring.

c. 都 / 打球 / 週末 / 沒有 / 時間 / 我們 / 連

We don't even have time to play ball on the weekend.

12.   Comprehension

Read the following paragraph and indicate whether the statements below are true (T) or false (F), based on the information in the passage.

有的人很喜歡買東西。有用的東西也買，沒有用的也買。只要看見他喜歡的東西，他就非買不可。我就 **rènshi** 一個這樣的人。他最喜歡買不同式樣的衣服。雖然買了很多，但是沒有時間穿。以前差不多每個週末他都出去買衣服，最近不買了。因為他買了很多，所以現在他連一點錢都沒有了。他的房間雖然很大，但是連再放一 **jiàn** 衣服的地方都沒有了。他說以後有了錢，他還會買。你說這樣的人有意思嗎？

a. (   ) The narrator's friend only likes to buy one style of clothing.

b. (   ) The narrator's friend buys clothes that he doesn't wear.

c. (   ) The narrator's friend can't buy any more clothes because his house isn't big enough to store more clothes.

d. (   ) The narrator's friend only buys clothes if they are on sale.

e. (   ) The narrator thinks that buying clothes is interesting.

Focus on structure

1.   Even more (Use and Structure note 23.2)

Translate a.–c. into English and d.–f. into Mandarin.

a. 天氣 **yùbào** 說明天比今天還冷。

b. 我覺得這 **shuāng xié** 子比那 **shuāng xié** 子 **gèng** 舒服一點。

c. **Qí** 自行車比走路快。坐出 **zū** 車 **gèng** 快。

d. Japanese is hard all right, but Chinese is even harder. (Use **gèng**.)

e. The red skirt is even prettier than the blue one. (Use 還.)

f. She is even smarter than her older sister. (Use 還.)

2.   I have no alternative (Use and Structure note 23.3)

Your roommate is wondering about your choice of action. Explain to her why this is your only option.

a. 你的同屋：你今天怎麼穿這 **jiàn** 衣服？

  你說：＿＿＿＿＿＿＿＿＿＿＿＿＿＿＿＿＿＿，所以我不得不穿這 **jiàn** 衣服。

b. 你的同屋：你不是不喜歡吃中國飯嗎？為甚麼你會去那個飯館吃飯？

  你說：＿＿＿＿＿＿＿＿＿＿＿＿＿＿＿＿＿，所以我不得不去。

c. 你的同屋：週末要不要跟我一起去看 **lán** 球比 **sài**？

  你說：我不能去。＿＿＿＿＿＿＿＿＿＿＿＿＿＿＿＿＿

d. 你的同屋：天氣這麼冷你還要出去運動？

  你說：**Yī** 生說＿＿＿＿＿＿＿＿＿＿＿，所以我＿＿＿＿＿＿＿＿＿＿。

3. Giving your opinion (Use and Structure note 23.4)

Xiao Zhang is expressing his concerns to Xiao Xie. Translate each of Xiao Zhang's sentences into English, and translate Xiao Xie's responses into Mandarin, using the expression 只要…就 in each of the responses.

a. 小張：我對我的 **zhuānyè** 沒有興趣了。

Xiao Xie: Whether you are interested or not is not important. As long as your grades are good, it's okay.

b. 小張：天氣 **yùbào** 說明天會很冷。

Xiao Xie: As long as it doesn't snow, it's okay.

c. 小張：我們的房間又 **luàn** 又髒！

Xiao Xie: It doesn't matter whether it's clean or not. As long as we have a place to sleep, it's okay.

d. 小張：明天是小葉的生日。你說我應該給她買甚麼東西？

Xiao Xie: It's not important what you buy. As long as you buy her something, she will be happy.

e. 小張：我看書看得太慢了。

Xiao Xie: It doesn't matter if you read slowly. As long as you <u>understand what you are reading</u>, it's okay. *(Use a resultative verb in the potential form for the underlined expression.)*

4. Not even a little (Use and Structure note 23.5)

Answer each of the following questions in complete Mandarin sentences, using the expression 一點都 NEG VP, and then translate your answers into English.

a. 你覺得這 **jiàn** 衣服 **liú** 行嗎？
Your reply in Mandarin:
English:

b. 你覺得春天穿這 **jiàn** 衣服 **héshì** 嗎？
Your reply in Mandarin:
English:

c. 你覺得昨天的考試難不難？
Your reply in Mandarin:
English:

d. 你對美式 **zú** 球有興趣嗎？
Your reply in Mandarin:
English:

e. 你 **pīngpāng** 球打得怎麼樣？
Your reply in Mandarin:
English:

5.   Scrambled sentences

Rewrite these phrases into sentences, putting them in the right order to match the English translations.

a. 是 / **gù** 客 / 看起來 / 這個 / 年 **qīng** 人 / **shāng** 店 / 的 / 都

It looks like the customers for this store are all young people.

b. **héshì** / 不 / 很 / 可是 / 式樣 / 都 / **liú** 行 / 大小 / 一點

The size is right, but the style isn't very current.

c. 是 / 那本 / 一點 / 看完了 / 可是 / 我 / 不 / **dǒng** / 書 / 看完了 / 都

I finished that book all right, but I didn't understand it at all.

d. **jiǎn jià** / **shāng** 店 / 都 / **gù** 客 / 讓 / 春 **jié** / 多 / 點 / 東西 / 到了 / 打 **zhé** / 買

When the Chinese New Year is approaching, the stores all give discounts and reduce prices to get the customers to buy more things.

e. 一點 / 覺得 / **huángsè** 的 / 綠 **sè** / 我 / 的 / **liú** 行 / 還 / 比

I think the yellow one is a little more stylish than the green one.

Focus on communication

1.   Dialogue comprehension

Study the Lesson 23 Narrative and Dialogue. Then, read the following statements and indicate whether they are true (T) or false (F).

a. (   ) 最近去買東西特別好，因為很多 **shāng** 店都在打 **zhé**。

b. (   ) 小葉喜歡 **guàng jiē**，而小張和小高不喜歡。

c. (　) 小張覺得 **pá** 山、打球沒有 **guàng shāng** 店那麼累。

d. (　) 小葉喜歡的 **qún** 子 **yánsè** 和式樣都好，就是比 **jiào** 貴。

e. (　) 小葉覺得自己 **pàng** 了，所以不想買 **qún** 子了。

f. (　) 小高覺得自己太 **shòu** 了，小葉 **zhèng héshì**。

g. (　) 小葉特別喜歡穿 **lánsè** 的衣服。

h. (　) 小高覺得小葉穿 **lánsè** 的不好看，所以讓她試一下別的 **yánsè** 的。

i. (　) 小葉試穿的這條 **qún** 子很多人買，因為今年 **liú** 行這個式樣。

j. (　) 紅色的 **qún** 子小葉穿起來 **shòu** 一點，**gèng** 好看，所以小葉就買了。

2.　What do you say?

What do you say in each of the following situations? Type your answers, using characters where we have learned them, and email them to your Chinese teacher.

a. Talk about one language that's even more difficult than Chinese.

b. Explain that you are obliged to do something so you can't come to the party tomorrow.

c. You gained a few pounds over the holiday break. Find some excuses to explain it.

d. Request a different size item of clothing from what you are trying on.

e. Suggest your friend try a pair of shoes in a different color because the green shoes don't look good.

f. Say something nice about what your friend is wearing right now. (For example, you look good in xxx color, etc.)

3.　Complete the mini-dialogues

Use the structure in parentheses to complete each mini-dialogue.

a. A: 你今天為甚麼出來買衣服？你不是最不喜歡 **guàng jiē** 嗎？

　　B: ＿＿＿＿＿＿＿＿＿＿＿＿＿＿＿＿＿＿＿＿＿＿＿＿。（不得不）

b. A: 真 **zāogāo**，這麼多 **yánsè**，我到 **dǐ** 要選哪一個？

　　B: ＿＿＿＿＿＿＿＿＿＿＿＿＿＿＿＿＿＿＿＿。（只要...就...）

c. A: 那門課不是很難嗎？你為甚麼要選？

　　B: ＿＿＿＿＿＿＿＿＿＿＿＿＿＿＿＿＿＿＿＿。（一點兒都不）

d. A: 我穿這條紅 **qún** 子怎麼樣，還可以嗎？

   B: _____。（看起來）

e. A: 這 **shuāng xié** 你穿特別好看，你一定要買！

   B: 好看是好看，可是_____。（**gèng**）

4. Multiple-choice

Choose the correct answer based on the context, and then translate the sentence into English.

a. 這麼冷的天，我真不想出去，可是 _____，我不得不去。
   1) 天氣太冷
   2) 我不怕冷
   3) 小張的球 **duì** 少一個人

English:

b. 我覺得一門課難一點兒沒關係，只要 _____。
   1) 有用就好
   2) 有一點難
   3) 老師也很 **yán**

English:

c. 她最近忙 **zhe** 學習、考試，_____
   1) 到 **dǐ** 去不去晚會？
   2) 連吃飯的時間都沒有。
   3) 可是真的沒有時間。

English:

d. 這 **jiàn** 衣服穿在你身上真漂亮，而且 _____。
   1) 一點兒都不 **piányi**
   2) 買一 **jiàn** 吧
   3) 打完 **zhé** 以後就 **gèng piányi** 了

English:

e. 打 **zhé jiǎn jià** 的時候好是好，可是 _____。
   1) 人太多了
   2) 我可以買到很 **piányi** 的東西
   3) 你喜歡就好

English:

5. Customer or clerk?

Identify each statement as something the **gùkè** or the 服務員 would say.

a. 這條 **qún** 子太大了，有沒有小一號的？   [ ] **gùkè**   [ ] 服務員

b. 您這麼高，這條 **cháng qún** 子 **zhèng héshì**。   [ ] **gùkè**   [ ] 服務員

c. 您想買甚麼 **yánsè** 的？   [ ] **gùkè**   [ ] 服務員

d. 我不穿 **huángsè** 的，還有別的 **yánsè** 的嗎？   [ ] **gùkè**   [ ] 服務員

e. 這是今年最 **liú** 行的 **yánsè**，您試一試，一定好看。   [ ] **gùkè**   [ ] 服務員

f. 買一 **jiàn** 給女朋友吧？她一定會很高興的。   [ ] **gùkè**   [ ] 服務員

g. 這 **shuāng xié** 好看是好看，可是我已經有太多 **xié** 了。   [ ] **gùkè**   [ ] 服務員

h. 這就是我要的，謝謝！   [ ] **gùkè**   [ ] 服務員

i. 這 **shuāng xié** 打完 **zhé** 以後一點都不貴，想買要快！   [ ] **gùkè**   [ ] 服務員

6. What are your preferences?

Use the following questions as the basis for an interview with one of your classmates. Write a paragraph about her based on her answers. Your paragraph should be at least 120 characters in length.

a. 你最喜歡甚麼 **yánsè**？

b. 你常常穿甚麼 **yánsè** 的衣服？

c. 你的 **guì** 子裏沒有甚麼 **yánsè** 的衣服？

d. 紅 **sè** 讓你想到甚麼？

e. 你會買綠 **sè** 的車還是 **lánsè** 的車？為甚麼？

f. 你覺得 **lánsè** 的房間看起來舒服，還是紅 **sè** 的？

g. 你現在用的 **bǐ** 是甚麼 **yánsè** 的？

h. 你喝過綠 **chá** 嗎？你喜歡喝紅 **chá** 還是喜歡喝綠 **chá**？

_____

_____

_____

_____

_____

_____

7. Shopping experience

As a customer, explain why you are hesitant about buying a certain item (size, color, price, etc.). As a salesperson, try your best to talk your customer into making a purchase.

Example:
A mini-skirt.
Customer: 這條 **qún** 子很好看，就是太 **duǎn** 了。
Salesperson: 怎麼會太 **duǎn**？今年就 **liú** 行 **duǎn qún**，穿在你身上 **zhèng héshì**。

a. A blue shirt (size small, $59.99)

Customer: _____

_____

Salesperson: _____

_____

b. A pair of yellow shoes (size 11, $35.00)

Customer: _____

_____

Salesperson: _____

_____

c. A long red skirt (size medium, $34.99)

Customer: _____

_____

Salesperson: _____

_____

d. A refurbished iPhone 3GS (16GB, $199.00)

Customer: _____

_____

Salesperson: _____

e. A brand new IBM laptop ($1,200)

Customer: _____

_____

Salesperson: _____

_____

8.   Xiao Ye's weight loss plan

Part I.   Read the paragraph and select the expressions that best complete the story.

葉小文最近每天 ＿＿＿＿＿（①都 ②也）走路去上課，在學校也不 ＿＿＿＿＿（①走 ②坐）電 **tī**，都走 ＿＿＿＿＿（①上去 ②出去），走下來。每天晚上去 **jiàn** 身房 **duànliàn** 三個小時。＿＿＿＿＿（① **chú** 了 ② **lìng** 外）運動以外，小文也吃得很少。兩個月以後，小文 **shòu** ＿＿＿＿＿（①得 ②了）很多，她自己覺得很高興，因為她現在可以穿二號的衣服了。可是她的朋友都說，小文以前一點都 ＿＿＿＿＿（①沒 ②不） **pàng**，現在 **shòu** ＿＿＿＿＿（①是 ②一） **shòu**，可是 ＿＿＿＿＿（①比 ②沒有）以前那麼好看了。＿＿＿＿＿（①不過 ②連）她的男朋友都覺得她看 ＿＿＿＿＿（①起來 ②出來）太 **shòu** 了，＿＿＿＿＿（①讓 ②對）她多吃一點。

Part II.   Read the above paragraph again and decide whether the statements below are true (T) or false (F). If a statement is false, explain why in the space below the statement.

a. (   ) 小文有時候開車，有時候走路去學校。

＿＿＿＿＿＿＿＿＿＿＿＿＿＿＿＿＿＿＿＿＿＿＿＿＿＿＿＿＿＿＿＿＿＿＿＿

b. (   ) 小文每天的運動是去 **jiàn** 身房的兩個小時。

＿＿＿＿＿＿＿＿＿＿＿＿＿＿＿＿＿＿＿＿＿＿＿＿＿＿＿＿＿＿＿＿＿＿＿＿

c. (   ) 小文每天都運動因為她覺得自己太 **pàng** 了。

＿＿＿＿＿＿＿＿＿＿＿＿＿＿＿＿＿＿＿＿＿＿＿＿＿＿＿＿＿＿＿＿＿＿＿＿

d. (   ) 小文以前穿不下二號的衣服。

＿＿＿＿＿＿＿＿＿＿＿＿＿＿＿＿＿＿＿＿＿＿＿＿＿＿＿＿＿＿＿＿＿＿＿＿

e. (   ) 小文的朋友和她的男朋友都覺得她現在 **shòu** 一點，所以比以前好看。

＿＿＿＿＿＿＿＿＿＿＿＿＿＿＿＿＿＿＿＿＿＿＿＿＿＿＿＿＿＿＿＿＿＿＿＿

f. (   ) 小文的男朋友覺得她吃得太少了。

＿＿＿＿＿＿＿＿＿＿＿＿＿＿＿＿＿＿＿＿＿＿＿＿＿＿＿＿＿＿＿＿＿＿＿＿

9.   Talk about your favorite store

Part I.   Answer the following questions truthfully.

a. 你喜歡去哪個 **shāng** 店買東西？

b. 那個 **shāng** 店在哪兒？你怎麼去？

c. 你多 **jiǔ** 去一次那個 **shāng** 店？

d. 你去那個 **shāng** 店都買甚麼？為甚麼？

e. 那個 **shāng** 店跟別的 **shāng** 店有甚麼不同的地方？

f. 你最近是甚麼時候去的？你買了甚麼？

g. 下次你想去買甚麼？

Part II.   Write a paragraph. Use your answers above to write a paragraph about your favorite store. Your paragraph should be at least 120 characters in length.

_____

_____

_____

_____

_____

_____

_____

_____

_____

_____

10.   Writing about shopping

Part I.   Form a cohesive paragraph. Rearrange these sentences so that they form a cohesive paragraph about shopping.

a. 現在我都上 **wǎng** 買東西。上 **wǎng** 比去 **shāng** 店方 **biàn** 得多。

b. 想 **děng** 打 **zhé** 的時候再買嗎？打 **zhé** 的時候 **gù** 客那麼多，你想要的東西，可能早就賣完了。

c. 你走進一個 **shāng** 店去，不一定找得到你想要的東西。

d. 我最不喜歡的事就是 **guàng jiē**，因為 **guàng jiē** 真的太 **huā** 時間了。

e. 我覺得，這樣的 "**guàng jiē**" 特別舒服。

f. 你只要坐在電 **nǎo** 前面，就可以慢慢地找你要的 **yánsè**、大小和式樣。

g. 而且，**xiāng** 同的東西，常常可以找到最 **piányi** 的。

h. 有時候找到了，可是 **yánsè** 或者大小不 **héshì**。有的時候東西好是好，可是太貴了。

Part II.   Write about your own shopping habits. Following the structure of the paragraph above, write a similar paragraph talking about whether you like to shop online or in an actual store. Your paragraph should be at least 120 characters in length.

_____

_____

_____

_____

_____

_____

_____

_____

_____

_____

_____

Lesson 24 Workbook

 Listening and speaking

(audio online)

Structure drills

1. What color clothing? (Use and Structure note 23.7)

You will hear a phrase describing clothing of a certain color. Restate the phrase to say *one* article of that color clothing, as in the example.

Example:
You will hear: **lán kù** 子
You will say: 一條 **lán** 顏色的 **kù** 子
Click "R" to hear the correct response: 一條 **lán** 顏色的 **kù** 子

(a)　　(b)　　(c)　　(d)　　(e)　　(f)　　(g)　　(h)　　(i)

2. I didn't do anything (Use and Structure note 24.1)

You will hear a question asking about something that you did. Reply that you didn't do anything at all, as in the example.

Example:
You will hear: 你買甚麼了？
You will say: 我甚麼都沒買。
Click "R" to hear the correct response: 我甚麼都沒買。

(a)　　(b)　　(c)　　(d)　　(e)　　(f)　　(g)

3.   So AdjV that VP/sentence (Use and Structure note 24.5)

You will hear a statement that includes a description, followed by a result. Restate the information using AdjV 得 VP/sentence, as in the example.

Example:

You will hear: 我很忙，沒時間吃飯。

You will say: 我忙得沒時間吃飯。

Click "R" to hear the correct response: 我忙得沒時間吃飯。

(a)   (b)   (c)   (d)   (e)   (f)   (g)   (h)

4.   Not only this but also that (Use and Structure note 24.7)

You will hear a statement describing some noun. Restate it with 不但 and 而且, as in the example.

Example:

You will hear: 這雙鞋顏色好，也很便宜。

You will say: 這雙鞋不但顏色好，而且很便宜。

Click "R" to hear the correct response: 這雙鞋不但顏色好，而且很便宜。

(a)   (b)   (c)   (d)   (e)   (f)   (g)   (h)   (i)   (j)

5.   If it isn't one thing, it is another (Use and Structure note 24.11)

You will hear a statement presenting two alternatives. Restate the sentence using 不是 A, 就是 B, as in the example.

Example:

You will hear: 這本書是你的，或者是你同屋的。

You will say: 這本書不是你的就是你同屋的。

Click "R" to hear the correct response: 這本書不是你的就是你同屋的。

(a)   (b)   (c)   (d)   (e)   (f)   (g)

6.   Not even one (Use and Structure note 24.12)

You will hear a statement about something that someone did not do or does not have. Restate it, to say *not even one*, as in the example. Be careful to use the right classifier.

Example:

You will hear: 我沒買書。

You will say: 我連一本書都沒買。

Click "R" to hear the correct response: 我連一本書都沒買。

(a)   (b)   (c)   (d)   (e)   (f)   (g)   (h)   (i)   (j)

Listening for information

1.   Let's go shopping

(CD1: 81)   Listen to the five questions and answer them based on the information below.

¥250	¥3.5	¥670	¥390	¥48

a.

b.

c.

d.

e.

2.   What will she wear today?

(CD1: 82)   Chen Fang and Wenwen are discussing what Chen Fang will wear to the party today. Based on Chen Fang's description, draw Chen Fang's outfit and indicate the color of each item.

Draw and color Chen Fang's outfit

3.   A hectic week (Use and Structure note 24.5)

Gao Ming is complaining about her life last week. Complete each description in English **(CD1: 83)** based on her narrative.

a. She had so much homework that...

b. Her stomach was so painful that...

c. She was so tired that...

d. She was so busy that...

4.   Big sale

The following items in a store are on sale. You will hear five questions asking about the **(CD1: 84)** prices of these items. Answer each question in English.

original price	¥50	¥1,200	¥88	¥105
discount	15%	25%	10%	not on sale

a.

b.

c.

d.

e.

5.   An afternoon at Tom's

Tom invited me to his house to watch a football game. Listen to my experience and write in **(CD1: 85)** English the items that Tom does not have in his room.

Tom does not have...

a. _____   b. _____   c. _____   d. _____

6.   A conversation

(CD1: 86)   An exchange student from China just came to your campus. She is asking you some questions about clothing and shopping. Answer her questions in Mandarin, based on your own experience. Use characters where we have learned them.

a.

b.

c.

d.

e.

f.

7.   Phone message

(CD1: 87)   Youmei has just left you a phone message. Listen to her message and write an email to her in Mandarin, responding to each of her questions. Use characters where we have learned them.

8.   Mali's shopping experience

(CD1: 88)   Mali is talking about her shopping experience in China. Based on her narrative, indicate whether the following statements are true (T) or false (F).

a. (   ) Mali spent ￥320 in that store.

b. (   ) The salesperson encouraged Mali to buy more things.

c. (   ) According to Mali, you can bargain in any store in China.

d. (   ) Mali walked out of the store without buying anything.

e. (   ) Mali bought a trendy, brightly colored shirt.

9. Dialogue

Listen to the conversation between a husband and wife, and then select the appropriate **(CD1: 89)** answer to each of the following questions.

a. What will they do after the conversation?
1) They will make a list of the clothing items they need to buy.
2) They will check to see which stores have sales.
3) They will head downtown to go shopping.
4) They will buy some new spring clothes.

b. What did the wife tell her husband?
1) The spring collection is on sale.
2) It is a good time to buy winter clothing.
3) The spring fashions just came out.
4) They need warm clothes for the coming cold front.

c. What does the husband need?
1) shoes
2) a jacket
3) gloves
4) shirts

d. What did they say about style and color?
1) The husband is worried that the new styles and colors will not suit him.
2) The wife promises that the stores have the most recent fashions.
3) The husband does not care about the style or color of his clothes.
4) The wife suggests that men's fashion does not vary much from year to year.

Reading and writing

Focus on Chinese characters

1. Number of strokes

Indicate the number of strokes used in writing each of the following characters.

a. 麻 _____   f. 姐 _____

b. 算 _____   g. 幫 _____

c. 顏 _____   h. 麗 _____

d. 訴 _____   i. 流 _____

e. 折 _____   j. 鞋 _____

2.   Which character?

Circle the character in each line that corresponds to the meaning on the left.

a. **sù** (**gàosu** *inform*)   訴   折

b. **yí** (**piányi** *cheap*)   宜   直

c. **shāng** (**shāngdiàn** *shop*)   尚   商

d. **lìng** (**lìngwài** *in addition, furthermore*)   另   別

e. **sè** (**yánsè** *color*)   爸   色

f. **fēi** (**kāfēi** *coffee*)   非   啡

g. **jī** (**shǒujī** *cell phone*)   機   幾

h. **wǎng** (**shàng wǎng** *use the internet*)   網   細

i. **dàn** (**bùdàn** *not only*)   但   旦

j. **huā** (**huā qián** *spend money*)   花   化

k. **jiù** *old*   崔   舊

l. **qì** (**qìchē** *car*)   汽   氣

3.   First strokes

Write the first two strokes of each of the following characters.

a. 幫 _____   f. 啡 _____

b. 位 _____   g. 顏 _____

c. 告 _____   h. 花 _____

d. 色 _____   i. 姐 _____

e. 宜 _____   j. 煩 _____

4.   Missing strokes

Complete each character by writing in the missing strokes.

a.   氵   **liú** *flow*

b.   隹   **shuāng** *pair*

c.   革   **xié** *shoe*

d.   牛   **gào** (**gàosu** *inform*)

e. 竹   **suàn** *calculate, count*

f. 扌   **zhé** (**dǎ zhé** *give a discount*)

g. 火   **fán** (**máfan** *trouble, bother*)

h. 言   **sù** (**gàosu** *inform*)

i. 亠   **shāng** (**shāngdiàn** *shop*)

j. 亻   **pián** (**piányi** *cheap*)

5.   Total strokes

Rewrite this list of characters, arranging the characters in terms of their total number of strokes. Begin your list with the character with the fewest strokes.

咖	色	幫	商	姐	但	位	宜	麗	網	花	麻	便	鞋	件	百	算	顏

6.   Radicals

Here is a list of characters that we have learned in this lesson. Rewrite each character in the row next to its radical.

訴   流   折   顏   便   宜   啡   另
位   咖   但   告   商   件   員   汽

口	
日	
氵	
亻	
扌	
言	
頁	
宀	

7. Character sleuth: Look for the phonetic

Group the characters below in terms of their rhymes or near-rhymes. Write the characters that rhyme with each other in the column on the right. Write the shared part of each character in the column on the left. For all of these characters, the shared part is the "phonetic," the part of the character that provides a clue to its pronunciation. The first set of rhymes is completed for you. There are twelve additional sets of characters that rhyme or partially rhyme and share a phonetic component among these characters.

馬	現	子	近	非	加	幾	試	見
玩	汽	式	國	機	跟	媽	買	嗎
啡	賣	咖	或	氣	字	新	完	很

phonetic	characters that rhyme or almost rhyme and share a phonetic component
馬	嗎，媽

8. Scrambled sentences

Rewrite these phrases as sentences, putting the words in the correct order to match the English translations.

a. 這 / 貴 / 我 / 不 / 雙 / 一點 / 覺得 / 鞋子 / 都

I think this pair of shoes isn't expensive at all.

b. 衣服 / 紅 / 喜歡 / 姐姐 / 我 / 顏色 / 最 / 穿 /的

My older sister likes to wear red clothes the best.

c. 流行 / 沒 / 打 / 流行 / 折 / 我 / 買 / 只要是 / 不 / 關係 / 就

Whether or not it is stylish isn't important. As long as it's on sale, I'll buy it.

9. Dictionary skills

Following the instructions in Lesson 17 of the Textbook, look up these characters in a Chinese dictionary and provide the requested information.

a. 拿
  pronunciation:
  meaning:
  one two-character word or phrase in which it occurs:

b. 千
  pronunciation:
  meaning:
  one two-character word or phrase in which it occurs:

c. 死
  pronunciation:
  meaning:
  one two-character word or phrase in which it occurs:

10. Find the incorrect characters

Xiao Zhang has written this email to his parents back in the USA telling them about one of his classmates, but he has typed ten characters incorrectly. Read the passage aloud, circle the mistakes, and correct them on the answer sheet below.

昨天我和小張和我的同屋友文到市中心去 **guàng** 商點。因為天汽 **yuè** 來 **yuè** 冷，所以我賣了手 **tào** 和 **ěrzhào**。 也買了心的大衣和一雙紅色的 **pí** 謝。春 **jié** 以前大大小小的商店都在大折，所以我買的東西都很便以。一 **gòng** 化了一 **qiān** 多塊錢。小張甚麼都沒買，只 **péi** 我們去 **guàng jiē**，幫我們 **ná** 東西。到了晚上，我們是在外邊吃了飯才做出 **zū** 車會宿舍的。

---

a. _____   b. _____   c. _____   d. _____   e. _____

f. _____   g. _____   h. _____   i. _____   j. _____

11.   Reading for information I

Read the paragraph for the main ideas and answer the questions that follow in English. You have learned almost all of the characters and words used in this paragraph, so you should be able to answer the questions without looking up any characters we have not learned. If you are stumbling over more than five characters in the passage, you need to review the characters from this and previous lessons.

> 甚麼樣的衣服最流行，我就最不喜歡。流行的衣服很多人都有，很多人都穿，我為甚麼要跟他們穿一樣的衣服呢？不流行沒關係，只要我自己喜歡就好。我不管別人怎麼想。我給我自己穿衣服，不是給別人穿衣服。另外，流行的衣服，很多人都想買，所以也就會比較貴。本來一件衣服不會那麼貴，就是因為很多人都想買才會那麼貴。這就是我為甚麼不喜歡流行的衣服。

a. What is the general topic of this paragraph?

b. What is the narrator's opinion about this topic?

c. What arguments does the narrator give to explain why he holds this opinion?

d. Circle the phrase that the narrator uses to sum up his opinion.

12.   Reading for information II

Read the following from a mother to her son, and answer the questions that follow in English.

> 雖然這件衣服穿在你身上很 **héshì**，但是我覺得你應該買再大一號的。**Dì** 一，穿大一點的衣服，你看起來比 **jiào shòu**。**Dì** 二，衣服大一號，夏天穿你不覺得很 **rè**，**dōng** 天你裏邊還可以再穿別的衣服。**Dì** 三，這件和大一號的一樣貴。最後，如果你以後高了呢，大一號的還可以穿，而現在 **héshì** 的就不能穿了。

a. What is the purpose of this paragraph?

b. How does the mother's opinion differ from the opinion of her son?

c. How many reasons does the mother provide to support her opinion?

d. What is the mother's final argument?

Focus on structure

1.   Anyone, anywhere, any time (Use and Structure note 24.1)

Xiao Zhang is a talented, agreeable person. Here are sentences that describe him. Translate a.–d. into English and e.–g. into Mandarin, using the phrases in parentheses in your translations.

a. 誰都喜歡他。

b. 他覺得甚麼電 **yǐng** 都很有意思。

c. 他甚麼 **gē** 都能 **chàng**。

d. 他比誰都 **pǎo** 得快。

e. He understands everything. (甚麼)

f. He likes to go everywhere. (哪兒)

g. He helps everyone. (誰)

2.   No one, nowhere, never (Use and Structure note 24.1)

Xiao Gao was feeling sick yesterday. Here is how she described her day. Translate a.–c. into English, and d.–f. into Mandarin, using the phrases in parentheses in your translations.

a. 我甚麼東西都沒吃。

b. 我誰都沒看。

c. 我哪兒都沒去。

d. I didn't do any homework. (甚麼)

e. I didn't watch any television. (甚麼)

f. I didn't read any books. (甚麼)

3.   On sale! (Use and Structure note 24.2)

Indicate these discounts as percentages off the price.

a. 打三折   →

b. 打4.5折   →

c. 打九折   →

d. 打四折   →

4.   Do it again! (Use and Structure note 24.3)

Translate these sentences into Mandarin, using 再 ActV or 又 ActV 了 *again*, as appropriate.

a. Can you please help me again?

b. I've forgotten her name again. How embarrassing!

c. It's raining again today. When is it going to get warm?

d. The prices in that store are really cheap. I'm definitely going to shop there again.

e. Don't wear those slacks again. They are too old.

f. He accompanied his girlfriend shopping again.

5.   So AdjV that... Part I (Use and Structure note 24.5, 24.12)

It is the end of the fall semester and everyone is cold, tired, and ready for vacation. This is how some of the students describe how they feel. Translate their descriptions into English.

a. 小王：我忙得連早飯都沒有時間吃。

b. 小馬：我冷得早上都不想起床了。

c. 小高：我累得連自行車也 **qí** 不了。

d. 小葉：我忙得連電 **shì** 都不能看。

e. 小謝：今天冷得我穿了兩雙 **wà** 子。

6.   So AdjV that... Part II (Use and Structure note 24.1, 24.5)

Translate these sentences into Mandarin.

a. The test was so difficult that no one could finish it. (誰)

b. The price of those shoes is so cheap that everyone wants to buy a pair. (誰)

c. My hands are so cold that they are numb.

d. The book was so long that I couldn't finish reading it.

e. There were so many people that I couldn't find him. (Hint: *The people were so numerous that...*)

7.   What are they wearing? (Use and Structure note 24.6)

Translate these descriptions into Mandarin in complete sentences, using characters where we have learned them.

a. Xiao Gao is wearing a new red skirt.

b. Xiao Xie is wearing his old black slacks.

c. Xiao Ye is wearing a pair of white gym shoes.

d. Xiao Lin is wearing a blue coat and a pair of cute blue earmuffs.

e. Xiao Ma is wearing a stylish yellow shirt.

8.   Not only... but also (Use and Structure note 24.7)

Here is a list of nouns and descriptions. Rewrite each line in a complete Mandarin sentence, saying that the noun is *not only* A *but also* B, using 不但 VP₁/sentence 而且 VP₂/sentence.

	noun	A	B
a.	this skirt	stylish	cheap
b.	leather shoes	appropriate	nice looking
c.	my roommate	has diarrhea	has a fever
d.	this fitness center	convenient	clean
e.	today's weather	cold	windy

a.

b.

c.

d.

e.

9. Take it (Use and Structure note 24.8)

Xiao Zhang and Xiao Xie are cleaning up their room again. Translate each of Xiao Xie's directions into Mandarin, using the words in parentheses.

a. Put all of the sneakers under the bed. (把, 放)

b. Bring that pair of slacks over to me. (把, **ná**, 過來)

c. Take all of those books back to the library. (把, **ná**)

d. Take the dirty socks into the bathroom and wash them. (把, **ná**, 把, 洗乾淨)

e. Bring all of the basketballs and soccer balls inside and put them in the closet. (把, **ná**, 放)

10. If it isn't one thing, it's the other thing (Use and Structure note 24.11)

Xiao Gao is very predictable. These sentences describe her behavior. Translate a.–b. into English and c.–e. into Mandarin, using characters where we have learned them.

a. 小高每天不是喝咖啡就是喝 **chá**。

b. 小高每天不是穿紅色的 **qún** 子就是穿紅色的 **chènshān**。

c. When Xiao Gao goes to school, if she doesn't take the bus she takes the subway.

d. After Xiao Gao gets out of class, she either phones her mother or she phones her older sister.

e. On the weekends, Xiao Gao and her friends either go window shopping or they go see a movie.

11.   Scrambled sentences

Rewrite these phrases into sentences, putting them in the right order to match the English translations.

a. **chènshān** / 這 / 那 / 跟 / **huáng** 色 / **qún** 子 / **pèi** / 條 / 的 / 件 / 很

This skirt really matches that yellow blouse.

b. 不 / 家 / 的 / **jià** 錢 / **shāng** 店 / 貴 / 那 / 本來 / 太

The prices in that store were not too expensive to begin with.

c. 便宜 / 算 / 就 / 的 / 是 / 一點 / 意思 / 打折

"Give a discount" means "figure the price a little cheaper."

d. 會 / 位 / 那 / **tǎo jià huán jià** / 小姐 / 真

That young lady certainly knows how to bargain.

e. **rè** / 天氣 / 家 **xiāng** / 不是 / 冷 / 非常 / 的 / 舒服 / 我 / 不 / 太 / 太 / 就是

The weather in my hometown is either too hot or it's too cold, it's extremely uncomfortable.

Focus on communication

1. Dialogue comprehension

Study the Lesson 24 Narrative and Dialogue. Then, read the following statements and indicate whether they are true (T) or false (F).

a. (   ) 小葉和小高買的 **qún** 子，一件三百塊。

b. (   ) 小高買了 **qún** 子、**pí** 鞋、**ěrzhào** 和手 **tào**，可是沒有買 **kù** 子。

c. (   ) 因為地鐵人太多，所以他們坐出 **zū** 車回學校。

d. (   ) 小高想買的 **qún** 子，本來一條一百五十二塊，服務員說可以打八折。

e. (   ) 小高想買 **ěrzhào**，因為北京太冷了，她的 **ěrduǒ** 冷得沒有 **gǎn** 覺了。

f. (   ) 小高喜歡的 **ěrzhào pèi** 她的咖啡色大衣，一定很好看。

g. (   ) 服務員想讓小高試一 **fù** 手 **tào**。

h. (   ) 小葉覺得大為應該買新 **kù** 子，因為他的 **kù** 子看起來太舊了。

i. (   ) 大為甚麼都不買，因為他今天 **wàng** 了 **dài** 錢了。

j. (   ) 今天運動鞋和 **wà** 子都特別便宜。

k. (   ) 他們買的東西太多了，所以小謝來幫小張 **ná**。

l. (   ) 小張、小葉和小高三個人一起回小張的宿舍。

m. (   ) 小張累 **sǐ** 了，因為他買了太多東西。

2. What do you say?

What do you say in each of the following situations? Type your answers, using characters where we have learned them, and email them to your Chinese teacher.

a. Ask the salesperson to bring you that black shirt.

b. Explain to your friend why you absolutely have to go shopping today. (Use the structure 非…不可. Here are some possible reasons: there is a huge sale, you need a jacket because of the cold weather, you are upset over something, etc.)

c. Offer to buy more than one item and ask for a discount.

d. Agree to give the customer a discount, but ask them to keep it quiet and come back next time.

e. Complain that you are tired to death today because you've been cleaning up your room.

f. Comment on how well the skirt matches the blouse that your friend is wearing right now.

g. Ask your friend to go shopping with you.

h. Name three things that you can do with your cell phone.

i. Explain to your friend that you are so tired that you don't feel like eating at all.

j. Persuade your friend to purchase the brown earmuffs because you've never seen any earmuffs cheaper than this pair.

3. Complete the mini-dialogues

Use the structures in parentheses to complete each mini-dialogue.

a. A: 春 **jià** 快到了，你打算做甚麼？

B: _____。（不是…就是…）

b. A: 你看這件大衣怎麼樣？我還沒 **jué** 定我到 **dǐ** 要不要買。

B: _____，你一定要買。（不但…而且…）

c. A: 這麼好的 **cháng** 週末，你上哪兒去了？

B: 週末那麼冷，我 _____。（冷得 VP）

d. A: 你來北京三個月了，去過甚麼地方？

B: 我每天都忙 **zhe** 學習，_____。（QW + 都 NEG VP）

4. Multiple-choice

Using the context as your guide, choose the correct expression to complete each sentence, and then translate the sentences into English.

a. 我 _____ 只想去中國 **lǚyóu**，可是太喜歡那兒，所以 **jué** 定在那兒找工作。
   1) 因為
   2) 本來
   3) 不但

   English:

b. 你 _____ 很累，昨天晚上沒有睡好嗎？
   1) 看起來
   2) 看
   3) 覺得

   English:

c. 我家 **xiāng** 的 **dōng** 天，不但很少下 **xuě** 而且 _____。
   1) 每天都下 **yǔ**
   2) 冷 **sǐ** 了
   3) 比很多地方都 **nuǎn** 和多了

English:

d. 我從昨天晚上開始頭 **téng**，**téng** 得 _____。
   1) 我 **bìng** 了
   2) 大概是因為太冷了
   3) 我甚麼都做不了

English:

5. Reading comprehension

Look at the following two sale flyers and answer the questions.

A)

大減價 SALE	春季服飾 3折起

a. What does "3折起" mean?

b. What season does this sale occur in?

B)

大減價 10 元 任選1件	大減價 15 元 任選2件

This promotion is about a discount. How does the discount work?

6.   Sale promotions

Match each sale promotion sign with its description below, writing the letter of the description above the matching sign. The descriptions include a few words that we have not yet learned, but that should not affect your comprehension of the main points.

A) _____

Buy One Get One **FREE!**

B) _____

Spend $50, **get $20**

Now through December 3ʳᵈ

C) _____

Now through Sunday!

Buy any regular-priced item & take

50% off

any second regular-priced item

D) _____

20% OFF when

purchasing 3 or more items

E) _____

4 DAYS ONLY

TAKE AN EXTRA

30% OFF

ALL SALE ITEMS

F) _____

WINTER CLEARANCE

SALE

Up to **70% OFF**

a. 只有四天！已經打折的東西再打七折。

b. 買一 **sòng** 一。

c. 從現在開始到星期天，買一件，第二件就打五折。

d. 買三件以上就打八折。

e. 冬季大 **jiǎn** 價：三折起。

f. 現在起到十二月三號，你每花五十塊我們就 **sòng** 你二十塊。

7.　Tǎo jià huán jià

Imagine you're the customer. Try your best to bargain with the salesperson to get a discount. Do not use the same tactic twice.

a. 服務員：這條 **kù** 子是今年最流行的，只要六十四塊。

Customer: _____

_____

b. 服務員：這 **fù** 手 **tào** 在我們這兒賣得特別好，跟你的大衣的顏色很 **pèi**。

Customer: _____

_____

c. 服務員：如果你要買這件，我可以給你打八折。

Customer: _____

_____

d. 服務員：　七十塊真的不貴，因為這件 **chènshān pèi qún** 子或者 **kù** 子都好看，甚麼時候都可以穿。

Customer: _____

_____

8.　Writing about the shopping experience

Part I. Form a cohesive paragraph　Rearrange these sentences so that they form a cohesive paragraph that explains how to bargain for the best price. (Note: 謝春美 is a person's name.)

a. 誰都喜歡跟春美一起去買東西，因為不但可以買到便宜的衣服，而且還可以 **rènshi** 不少商店的服務員。

b. 或者，如果衣服的 **jià** 錢太高，但是春美很喜歡，她一定能讓服務員給她打折。

c. 她覺得，**guàng jiē** 不一定每次都要買東西。

d. 謝春美跟每一個女 **hái** 子一樣，很喜歡 **guàng jiē**。

e. **Rènshi** 了以後，下次再去，就可以請他們打折了。

f. 不過，大 **jiǎnjià** 的時候，就非買不可了。

g. 春美很會跟服務員 **tǎojià huánjià**，如果一件衣服已經打折了，她一定會說，買兩件再算她便宜一點。

h. 有的時候雖然不買，看看商店賣的新衣服，可以知道今年流行甚麼，自 **jǐ** 在家穿衣服的時候就知道怎麼 **pèi** 比 **jiào** 好看。

Part II. Shopping: love it or hate it   Following the structure of the paragraph above, write a similar paragraph talking about a shopaholic friend (or yourself), or someone who hates shopping. Your paragraph should be at least 120 characters in length.

_____

_____

_____

_____

_____

_____

_____

_____

_____

_____

_____

Lesson 25 Workbook

Listening and speaking

Structure drills

1. Noun phrases with the main noun omitted (Use and Structure 25.2)

You will hear a sentence in which the subject includes a description and a main noun. Rephrase the sentence, leaving out the main noun, as in the example.

Example:
You will hear: 我買的衣服很便宜。
You will say: 我買的很便宜。
Click "R" to hear the correct response: 我買的很便宜。

(a)　　(b)　　(c)　　(d)　　(e)　　(f)　　(g)　　(h)　　(i)　　(j)

2. I've never done it before (Use and Structure note 25.11)

You will hear a question asking about your general behavior, or whether you have done something before. Answer that you do not have that behavior, or that you have never done that action before, as in the example.

Example:
You will hear: 你吃過這麼好吃的 **yú** 嗎？
You will say: 我從來沒吃過這麼好吃的 **yú**。
Click "R" to hear the correct response: 我從來沒吃過這麼好吃的 **yú**。

(a)　　(b)　　(c)　　(d)　　(e)　　(f)　　(g)　　(h)　　(i)　　(j)

3.   Ongoing situations at a location (Use and Structure note 25.3)

You will hear a sentence about a situation at a location. Restate the sentence, using 著 to indicate that the situation is ongoing, as in the example.

Example:
You will hear: 他 **tǎng** 在地上。
You will say: 他在地上 **tǎng** 著。
Click "R" to hear the correct response: 他在地上 **tǎng** 著。

(a)   (b)   (c)   (d)   (e)   (f)   (g)   (h)   (i)   (j)

4.   Two ways to indicate duration (Use and Structure note 25.5)

You will hear a sentence about the duration of some activity. Restate the sentence, indicating duration with the structure <u>V duration 的 N</u>, as in the example.

Example:
You will hear: 他們坐火車坐了八個鐘頭。
You will say: 他們坐了八個鐘頭的火車。
Click "R" to hear the correct response: 他們坐了八個鐘頭的火車。

(a)   (b)   (c)   (d)   (e)   (f)   (g)   (h)   (i)   (j)

5.   Talking about two actions happening at the same time (Use and Structure note 25.7)

You will hear a sentence talking about two actions that happen at the same time. Restate the sentence with <u>一邊 action₁ 一邊 action₂</u>, as in the example.

Example:
You will hear: 我吃飯的時候看電 **shì**。
You will say: 我一邊吃飯一邊看電 **shì**。
Click "R" to hear the correct response: 我一邊吃飯一邊看電 **shì**。

(a)   (b)   (c)   (d)   (e)   (f)   (g)   (h)   (i)   (j)

6.   Two ways to indicate that situations occur at the same time (Use and Structure notes 25.3, 25.7)

You will hear a sentence saying that two actions occur at the same time. Restate the sentence using V_1 著 V_2, as in the example.

Example:
You will hear: 我們一邊 **liáo** 天，一邊吃飯。
You will say: 我們 **liáo** 著天吃飯。
Click "R" to hear the correct response: 我們 **liáo** 著天吃飯。

(a)   (b)   (c)   (d)   (e)   (f)   (g)   (h)   (i)   (j)

Listening for information

1.　過春節

(CD1: 92) You will hear a short narration about a Chinese family celebrating the New Year. Listen to the passage to find out who is doing each activity and write their name in English under the corresponding activity.

2.   A dorm room scene

You will hear Liu Xun introducing his roommates. Listen to his introduction and identify (CD1: 93) each roommate by name (in Pinyin) in the following picture.

A.

B.

C.

D.

E.

3.   Four sisters

Here is a picture of four sisters: Lanlan, Tingting, Meimei, and Xinxin. Listen to the description (CD1: 94) and identify each sister, writing each person's name under her picture.

4.   Eating out

(CD1: 95) Listen to Wang Shan talking about her experience eating out tonight. Based on her narrative, indicate whether each of the following statements is true (T) or false (F).

a. (   ) 小張沒有來日本飯館。

b. (   ) 小張 **wàng** 了怎麼去那個日本飯館。

c. (   ) 我自己一個人先去那個飯館。

d. (   ) 我打電話給小張的時候，他剛到家。

e. (   ) 這家日本飯館一點也不貴。

5.   An oral quiz

(CD1: 96) Teacher Zhou is asking you several questions about the Chinese New Year. Answer the questions in Mandarin, using characters where we have learned them.

a.

b.

c.

d.

e.

f.

6.   Responding to a phone message

(CD1: 97) Listen to this phone message from Jiajia, an exchange student from China, and prepare an email in Mandarin in reply to her questions.

7.   Preparations for the New Year

Língling is telling her foreign friends about how Chinese people prepare for the New Year. **(CD1: 98)** Based on the information she provides, indicate whether the following statements are true (T) or false (F).

a. (   ) **Niángāo** is easy to make, so it is usually made on New Year's Eve.

b. (   ) Chinese people eat **niángāo** during the Chinese New Year because it is very nutritious.

c. (   ) A lot of house-cleaning has to be done before New Year's Eve.

d. (   ) Dirty clothes need to be washed so that they can be worn on the first day of the New Year.

e. (   ) It is difficult to buy groceries during the Chinese New Year.

8.   Traveling in China

Two foreign students in China are discussing their recent travel experiences. Based on the **(CD2: 1)** information in the conversation, select the appropriate answers to each of the following questions.

a. How does the **ruǎnwò** seat differ from the **yìngwò** seat?
　1) They are about ¥200 different in price on a trip from Beijing to Hankou.
　2 Six people share a **ruǎnwò** room.
　3) **Ruǎnwò** seats have private rooms.
　4) If you travel by **ruǎnwò**, it takes less time to get to the destination.

b. What does the woman think about taking a train in China?
　1) She prefers using other forms of transportation.
　2) She is very excited about it.
　3) She thinks it is uncomfortable traveling by train.
　4) She worries that trains are too crowded.

c. What does the man think about taking a train in China?
　1) It takes a lot of time to travel by train.
　2) One may meet new people on trains.
　3) One has to be cautious when taking trains.
　4) It is better to buy **ruǎnwò** seats when taking trains.

d. How long will it take to go from Beijing to Hankou by train?
　1) eleven hours by express train
　2) one day by regular train
　3) fifteen hours by **ruǎnwò**
　4) twenty hours by **yìngwò**

Reading and writing

Focus on Chinese characters

1.   Number of strokes

Indicate the number of strokes used in writing each of the following characters.

a. 紹 _____   f. 茶 _____

b. 音 _____   g. 假 _____

c. 黃 _____   h. 越 _____

d. 藍 _____   i. 等 _____

e. 弟 _____   j. 樂 _____

2.   Which character?

Circle the character in each line that corresponds to the meaning on the left.

a. **jiǎo (jiǎozi** *dumplings*)   餃   較

b. **huó** *live*   活   話

c. **gèng** *even more*   更   便

d. **lè (kuàilè** *happy*)   樂   東

e. **yuǎn** *far*   園   遠

f. **mǔ** *mother*   母   每

g. **quán** *entire*   全   金

h. **rèn (rènshi** *know*)   忍   認

i. **jiè (jièshào** *introduce*)   介   父

j. **shào (jièshào** *introduce*)   紹   邵

k. **dì (dìdi** *younger brother*)   弟   第

l. **jià (fàng jià** *begin vacation*)   假   佳

3.   First strokes

Write the first two strokes of each of the following characters.

a. 等 _____   f. 著 _____

b. 越 _____   g. 談 _____

c. 藍 _____   h. 較 _____

d. 除 _____   i. 正 _____

e. 極 _____   j. 火 _____

4.   Missing strokes

Complete each character by writing in the missing strokes.

a.   艾   **chá** *tea*

b.   ⺮   **jié** *holiday*

c.   八   **fù** (**fùmǔ** *father and mother*)

d.   言   **shí** (**rènshi** *know, recognize, meet*)

e.   氵   **huó** (**shēnghuó** *life*)

f.   亠   **yè** (**yèlǐ** *in the middle of the night*)

g.   立   **yīn** (**shēngyīn** *sound*)

h.   幺   **lè** (**kuàilè** *happy*), **yuè** (**yīnyuè** *music*)

i.   艹   **huáng** *yellow*

j.   走   **yuè** *more*

5.   Total strokes

Rewrite this list of characters, arranging the characters in terms of their total number of strokes. Begin your list with the character with the fewest strokes.

更	著	父	夜	遠	識	茶	全	較	介	音	弟	假	母	認	等	談	正	除

6.   Radicals

Here is a list of characters that we have learned in this lesson. Rewrite each character in the row next to its radical.

淨	認	看	館	著	談	茶	起	遠	飯	邊
近	話	藍	飽	識	花	越	菜	趣	活	睡

辶	
目	
氵	
飠	
走	
言	
艹	

7.   Character sleuth: Look for the phonetic

Group the characters below in terms of their rhymes or near-rhymes. Write the characters that rhyme with each other in the column on the right. Write the shared part of each character in the column on the left. For all of these characters, the shared part is the "phonetic," the part of the character that provides a clue to its pronunciation. The first set of rhymes is completed for you. There are twelve additional sets of characters that rhyme or partially rhyme and share a phonetic component among these characters.

或	且	新	功	著	氣	餃	紅	遠	房	花
式	放	非	把	加	化	方	咖	汽	校	近
啡	爸	園	活	姐	工	較	試	者	話	國

phonetic	characters that rhyme or almost rhyme and share a phonetic component
工	工紅

8.   Scrambled sentences

Rewrite these phrases as sentences, putting the words in the correct order to match the English translations.

a. 半夜 / 吃 / 十二點 / **bāo** 餃子 / 等到 / 我們 / 以前 / 的時候

We wrap dumplings before midnight, and when it is midnight we eat them.

b. 可以 / 我 / 你 / 弟弟 / 如果 / 我 / 你們 / 認識 / 介紹 / 不 / 給

If you don't know my younger brother, I can introduce you.

c. 可樂 / 茶 / 喝 / 喝 / 你 / 呢 / 想 / 還是

Do you want to drink cola or tea?

d. 一 / 都 / 學生 / 回家 / 放假 / 父母 / 看 / 學校

As soon as the school begins vacation, the students return home to see their parents.

e. 更 / 覺得 / 藍色的 / 黃色的 / 好看 / 我 / 比

I think that the blue one is even nicer looking than the yellow one.

9.   Dictionary skills

Following the instructions in Lesson 17 of the Textbook, look up these characters in a Chinese dictionary and provide the requested information.

a. 準
   pronunciation:
   meaning:
   one two-character word or phrase in which it occurs:

b. 魚
   pronunciation:
   meaning:
   one two-character word or phrase in which it occurs:

c. 熱

pronunciation:

meaning:

one two-character word or phrase in which it occurs:

10. Find the incorrect characters

Zhang Dawei is preparing a short talk that he will give in class tomorrow. His ideas are all set but he has written ten characters incorrectly. (Two of them are written incorrectly twice.) Read the passage aloud, circle the mistakes, and correct them on the answer sheet below.

> 我給你節紹節紹我剛人識的朋友。他 **xìng** 黃。他的父每都是中國人，可是他在美國生活了十多年了。他說 **Yīng** 文說得很好，可是他說中文說得便好，因為方假的時候他常常跟他的父母會中國。跟他談活的時候，我比餃喜黃說中文，因為這羊可以讓我的中文走來走好。

a. ____   b. ____   c. ____   d. ____   e. ____

f. ____   g. ____   h. ____   i. ____   j. ____

11. Reading for information

Read the paragraph for the main ideas and answer the questions that follow in English. You have learned almost all of the characters and words used in this paragraph, so you should be able to answer the questions without looking up any characters we have not learned. If you are stumbling over more than five characters in the passage, you need to review the characters from this and previous lessons.

> 小孩子都非常喜歡過年。過年的時候可以吃很多好吃的東西，穿新衣服，跟別的小朋友一起放鞭炮，還會得到很多紅包。紅包就是紅顏色的信封。信封裏邊是錢。過年的時候，除了父母會給孩子們紅包，家裏來的叔叔阿姨也會給。在短短的幾天裏，有的小孩子可以得到很多錢，所以他們都特別喜歡過年。他們覺得過年是他們一年裏最高興的日子。

a. What is the general topic of this paragraph?

b. The narrator mentions a number of reasons why children like this topic. List them here.

c. What does the narrator present as the most important reason? How can you tell?

Focus on structure

1.   AdjV 不得了 (Use and Structure note 25.1)

Describe each of these people or objects in complete sentences using AdjV 不得了.

a.	小王	
b.	小馬	
c.	**Chén** 先生	
d.	120 mph	
e.	$$$$	

2.   What can you do lying down? (Use and Structure note 25.3)

Here are things that Xiao Zhang likes to do lying down, sitting, and standing. Write a sentence stating each situation using V 著 in each sentence.

Lying down

a. read   →

b. listen to music   →

c. watch television   →

Standing up

d. sing   →

e. make phone calls   →

Sitting down

f. sleep   →

g. drink coffee   →

3.   Don't do these while driving! (Use and Structure note 25.3)

Here are some things that you should not do while driving. Translate them into English, and then add two more of your own (in Mandarin).

a. 別看著電 **shì** 開車。 →

b. 別打著電話開車。   →

c.

d.

4.   How long did she do these activities? (Use and Structure note 25.5)

Here is a list of things that Meili did yesterday and the amount of time she spent on each of them. Write a complete sentence in Mandarin for each activity using the structure V duration 的 O.

a. listened to music (one hour)   →

b. used the internet (one and a half hours) →

c. watched television (a half hour)   →

d. slept (seven hours)   →

e. rode a bicycle (forty-five minutes)   →

5.   Multi-tasking (Use and Structure note 25.7)

Describe what the people are doing in each of the following pictures in complete sentences, using the structure 一邊…一邊….

Example:

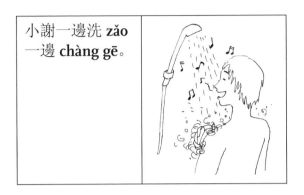

小謝一邊洗 **zǎo** 一邊 **chàng gē**。

a. 張友藍	b. 王剛	c. 謝子真
d. 常學音	e. 高大南	f. 錢家明和她的朋友

a.

b.

c.

d.

e.

f.

6.   Never did it, never do it (Use and Structure note 25.11)

Xiao Wang has invited his roommate home to Xi'an for the New Year and is going over some of the things that they will do. He wants to know if his roommate has ever done these things before. Help him ask these questions by translating them into Mandarin. His roommate has never done any of these things before. Provide his answers here, using 從來 + NEG in each of his replies.

a. Have you been to Xi'an before?

Q:

A:

b. Have you eaten hot and spicy food before?

Q:

A:

c. Have you set off fireworks before?

Q:

A:

d. Have you made dumplings before?

Q:

A:

7.   Translation into English

Translate these sentences into English.

a. 剛才來找你的那個人是誰？

b. 真沒想到用中文跟中國人 **liáo** 天這麼容易。

c. 我剛學 **bāo** 餃子，所以 **bāo** 得不好。

d. 在床上 **tǎng** 著看書是非常不好的習慣。

e. 你怎麼連 **kuài** 子都不會用。你從來沒吃過中國飯吧。

f. 因為你剛學會開車，所以你一定不可以一邊開車一邊打電話。

g. 我的同屋每天晚上都 **fù** 習好幾個鐘頭的中文，常常一直到半夜。

h. 友文把美麗介紹給她的父母以後，美麗就把她 **sòng** 給友文父母的東西 **ná** 出來了。

8. Translation into Mandarin

Translate these sentences into Mandarin, using characters where we have learned them.

a. Yesterday's test was unbelievably difficult.

b. What is that noise outside? Can you hear it?

c. I have never set off fireworks before.

d. I didn't expect that the Spring Festival would be this lively.

e. I found the book that you were just looking for. It was under the bed.

f. You were born in January of 1990. Are you (do you belong to) a snake (**shé**) or a horse?

g. I just got home and I'm dead tired. Help me prepare dinner.

h. I ate until I was full. (Use 吃 and a resultative ending.) I never expected that at midnight we would begin eating dumplings.

9. Scrambled sentences

Rewrite these phrases into sentences, putting them in the right order to match the English translations.

a. 喝 / 一 **píng** / 他 / 回家 / 可樂 / 走路 / **ná** 著 / 一邊/ 一邊

Holding a bottle of cola, he drank and walked home.

b. 穿 / 出去 / 先 / 你 / 等到 / 大衣 / 再 / **ná** 著/ 的時候

Take your coat. Put it on when we go out.

c. **bāo** / **bāo** / 我 / 好 / 你 / 餃子/ 這麼 / 沒想到 / 得

I didn't know that you could wrap dumplings so well.

d. 的時候 / 放 / **hái** 子 / **pǎo** / 看 / 剛才 / **biānpào** / 出來 / 都

Just before when you were setting off the fireworks, the children all ran outside to watch.

e. 火車 / 我 / 人 / 坐 / 會 / 這麼 / 多 / 沒想到 / 回家 / 春節 / 的

I had no idea that there would be this many people taking the train home for the Spring Festival.

Focus on communication

1. Dialogue comprehension

Study the Lesson 25 Narrative and Dialogue. Then, read the following statements and indicate whether they are true (T) or false (F).

a. (　) 今年的春節跟學校放 **hán** 假在 **xiāng** 同的時間。

b. (　) 友文 **dài** 美麗坐火車回家過年。

c. (　) 火車非常 **jǐ**，因為放 **hán** 假的時候，火車 **piào tè** 別便宜。

d. (　) **Shūshu** 就是你爸爸的弟弟。

e. (　) 友文和美麗剛到，年夜飯已經 **zhǔnbèi** 好了。

f. (　) 葉家的年夜飯很 **fēngfù**，有餃子還有很多菜。

g. (　) 全家一起 **bāo** 餃子、吃餃子，是中國人過年的習慣。

h. (　) 友文不知道是誰把她家門口的 "春" 字 **tiē dào** 了。

i. (　) **Tiē dào** 的 "春" 字跟年夜飯的 **yú** 都有特別的意思。

2. What do you say?

What do you say in each of the following situations? Type your answers, using characters where we have learned them, and email them to your Chinese teacher.

a. You want to find out your friend's Chinese zodiac sign.

b. You want to greet people during the Chinese New Year holidays.

c. You want to find out how long it takes your friend to walk from his place to school.

d. You want to learn about your friend's breakfast ritual: does s/he eat standing (by the table), or sitting down.

e. You want to tell your little cousin that he has to wait until the happy birthday song ends before he eats the cake (**dàngāo**).

f. You want to announce your New Year's resolutions (that is, what you definitely will do this year).

g. You want to apologize to your friend that you didn't answer the phone when he called, and you want to explain that you didn't hear the phone ring because you were in the shower just a moment ago.

h. You want to complain about the movie that you just saw. You want to say that it's the worst movie you've ever seen.

i. You want to express your surprise about the subway and say that you did not expect the subway to be this crowded.

3.   Complete the mini-dialogues

Use the structure in parentheses to complete each mini-dialogue.

a. A: 你每天吃飯的時候看電 **shì** 嗎？

   B: 對，_____。（一邊…一邊…）

b. A: 你知道 “好年春” 這個飯館嗎？

   B: _____。（從來 + NEG V…）

c. A: 我媽媽 **bāo** 的餃子怎麼樣？好吃嗎？

   B: _____。（AdjV 得不得了）

d. A: 媽媽，我甚麼時候才能買那雙藍色的 **pí** 鞋？

   B: _____。（等到…）

e. A: 你看起來很累，是不是昨天晚上睡得太少？

   B: _____。（V + duration 的 O）

f. A: 對不起，我剛下課，所以晚了幾分鐘。電 **yǐng** 開始多 **jiǔ** 了？

   B: 沒問 **tí**，_____。（剛剛）

4.   同音字

You have learned how 同音字 can carry symbolic significance in Chinese. Read the following sentences and choose the best answer. Then translate each sentence into English.

a. 過年的時候，除了吃餃子以外，中國人也喜歡吃 “**fā** 菜” (literally "hair weed")，因為吃 **fā** 菜就是說你會 _____。
   1) 吃很多飯
   2) **fā cái**
   3) 有長頭 **fa**

   English:

b. “**Sòng zhōng**” 的意思就是 “**péi** 著快要 **sǐ** 了的父母”。所以中國人過生日的時候最不喜歡 **sòng** 別人 _____。
   1) **zhuō** 子
   2) 鐘 (*clock*)
   3) 床

   English:

c. 在中國，很多 **yī** 院沒有四 **lóu** (*fourth floor*)，因為 “四” 的 **shēng** 音跟 _____ 差不多。
   1) “冷 **sǐ** 了” 的 “**sǐ**”
   2) “有事” 的 “事”
   3) “認識” 的 “識”

   English:

5.   Describe the pictures

Look at the following pictures and write a few sentences to describe each situation.

a. Use V 著 in your sentence.

b. Use 一邊… 一邊…in your sentence.

葉大明

c. Use V 著 in your sentence.

_____

_____

_____

_____

6. Chinese New Year celebration

Match each picture with its description by writing the letter for the description in the line above the appropriate picture.

A. **Bāo** 餃子，等到半夜再吃。

B. 到外邊去放 **biānpào**。

C. 全家人在一起吃 **fēngfù** 的年夜飯，一邊吃飯，一邊 **liáo** 天。

D. 把家裏 **shōushi** 乾淨。

E. 門上的 "春" 字 **dào** 著 **tiē**。不是 **tiē** 得不對，是 "春到了"。

F. 小 **hái** 子最高興的，就是可以 **ná** 到紅 **bāo**。

7.   我最喜歡過春節

Part I.   The following paragraph talks about traditions of the Chinese New Year celebration. Fill in the blanks with the sentences (A.–F.) from Exercise 6.

一年裏我最喜歡的就是春節，因為不但有好吃的，而且有好玩的。中國新年不是在一月就是在二月。每年春節，在別的地方工作、學習的人都一定會回到自己的家 **xiāng** 過節。所以那時候的火車票特別難買 。春節的前幾天，我媽媽就 ＿＿＿，等著大姐回來過節。而爸爸忙著寫春 **lián** (*spring couplets*, matching lines of poetry hung on either side of the door)，**tiē** 在門上。小時候爸爸就告訴我，我家 ＿＿＿。

除 **xī** 的早上，我們就開始做飯，晚上 ＿＿＿，是我最快樂的時候。晚飯以後我和大姐幫 **zhù** 媽媽 ＿＿＿。**Bāo** 好餃子爸爸就 **dài** 著我們 ＿＿＿。半夜除了吃餃子以外，＿＿＿。因為我們可以 **ná** 著爸爸媽媽給我們的紅 **bāo**，去買自 **jǐ** 喜歡的東西。 每年爸爸媽媽給我們 **sòng** 紅 **bāo**，等著買自己喜歡的東西。**Dì** 二天早上是新年，我們不是一家人開車出去玩，就是去看朋友。每個人一看到朋友就說：**Gōng** 喜 **fācái**，新年快樂！過年那幾天，每天我都高興得不得了。

Part II.   Complete the following table in Mandarin. In Column A, provide your answers based on the information in the passage in Part I. In Column B, provide information about your favorite holiday. Here are the names of two holidays in Mandarin that you might want to write about:

Gǎn ēn 節 *Thanksgiving*, **Shèngdàn** 節 *Christmas*.

	A: 中國新年	B: Your favorite holiday _____
time		
significance		
preparation		
things that people do		
favorite part of this holiday as a kid		
why it's my favorite holiday		

8. What is your favorite holiday?

Following the structure of the paragraph in Exercise 7, Part I, and using the information you wrote in Part II, write a paragraph talking about your fondest memories of your favorite holiday. If we have not learned a word in Mandarin, write it in English. Your paragraph should be at least 120 characters in length. When you revise this essay you can look these words up in a dictionary and add them in Mandarin.

_____

_____

_____

_____

_____

_____

_____

_____

_____

_____

_____

Lesson 26 Workbook

Listening and speaking

(audio online)

Structure drills

1. 把 NP (PP) V 一下 (Use and Structure note 26.1)

You will hear a statement asking you to do something. Rephrase the statement with 把 NP V 一下, as in the example.

Example:

You will hear: **Tián** 這張 **biǎo**。

You will say: 請你把這張 **biǎo tián** 一下。

Click "R" to hear the correct response: 請你把這張 **biǎo tián** 一下。

(a)　　(b)　　(c)　　(d)　　(e)　　(f)　　(g)　　(h)　　(i)　　(j)

2. Expressing the passive with **bèi** (Use and Structure note 26.4)

You will hear a sentence stating an action. Rephrase the sentence with **bèi**, as in the example.

Example:

You will hear: 他拿走了我的書。

You will say: 我的書 **bèi** 他給拿走了。

Click "R" to hear the correct response: 我的書 **bèi** 他給拿走了。

(a)　　(b)　　(c)　　(d)　　(e)　　(f)　　(g)

3. Expressing events from different perspectives with 把 and **bèi**
(Use and Structure notes 19.7, 26.1, and 26.4)

You will hear a sentence that includes 把 describing an event. Restate the sentence with **bèi** to change the perspective of the description, as in the example.

Example:
You will hear: 他把我的書拿走了。
You will say: 我的書 **bèi** 他拿走了。
Click "R" to hear the correct response: 我的書 **bèi** 他拿走了。

(a)　　(b)　　(c)　　(d)　　(e)

4. Talking about hypothetical situations involving the same subject in
both clauses: 要是...就 (Use and Structure note 26.7)

You will hear a statement about two situations in which the subject is the same for both situations. Restate it to say that if the first situation occurs, the second one should or will follow, using 要是...就, as in the example.

Example:
You will hear: 你把 **hù** 照 **diū** 了很麻煩。
You will say: 你要是把 **hù** 照 **diū** 了，就很麻煩。
Click "R" to hear the correct response: 你要是把 **hù** 照 **diū** 了，就很麻煩。

(a)　　(b)　　(c)　　(d)　　(e)　　(f)　　(g)　　(h)

5. Talking about hypothetical situations involving two different subjects:
要是...就 (Use and Structure note 26.7)

You will hear a statement about two situations in which there is a different subject for each situation. Restate it to say that if the first situation occurs, the second one should or will follow, using 要是...就, as in the example.

Example:
You will hear: 你不喜歡吃中國飯，我們去吃日本飯。
You will say: 你要是不喜歡吃中國飯，我們就去吃日本飯。
Click "R" to hear the correct response: 你要是不喜歡吃中國飯，我們就去吃日本飯。

(a)　　(b)　　(c)　　(d)　　(e)　　(f)　　(g)　　(h)　　(i)　　(j)

6. 從 time 起 *from this time on* (Use and Structure note 26.12)

You will hear a statement about some action that you do, followed by a time phrase. Say that beginning with that time, you will do or have done the action.

Example:
You will hear: 我要看好自己的東西。（現在）
You will say: 從現在起，我要看好自己的東西。
Click "R" to hear the correct response: 從現在起，我要看好自己的東西。

(a)   (b)   (c)   (d)   (e)   (f)   (g)   (h)

Listening for information

1. What to do?

(CD2: 5) You will hear four different situations. Respond to each situation in a complete Mandarin sentence, using Pinyin or a mix of characters and Pinyin, as instructed by your teacher.

a.

b.

c.

d.

2. Equal to

(CD2: 6) Listen to the five questions and provide appropriate responses. You may want to have your calculator handy!

(¥1 = US$0.17, US$1 = ¥6.8)

a. _____   d. _____

b. _____   e. _____

c. _____

3.   The population of major cities

You will hear five announcements stating the current population of five cities in China, the **(CD2: 7)** United States, and Taiwan. Listen to the announcement and write the population of each city on the following form.

city	population (人口)
Shanghai	
New York	
Beijing	
Taipei	
Houston	

4.   Mother's instructions

Yòuwén is reporting what her mother has told her to do. Listen to her report and fill in the **(CD2: 8)** tasks in the order in which her mother wants her to do them.

first task   →   second task   →   third task   →   last task

_____   _____   _____   _____

5.   Test information

Zhang Ping needs to take the Chinese placement test. However, he left the information **(CD2: 9)** sheet on his desk at home. He called his mother to check the information. Based on the details stated by his mother, fill in the information in the following form.

中文考試	
date	
time	
location	
address	

6.   Where is the purse?

(CD2: 10–11) Listen to Wang Lili tell us what happened to her purse. Then, listen to each of the questions that follow, and answer them in English.

a.

b.

c.

d.

e.

7.   Train station announcement

(CD2: 12) Listen to the announcement at a train station and choose an appropriate answer for each of the two questions below.

a. When does this train leave for Xi'an?
   1) 11:00 p.m.
   2) 2:00 p.m.
   3) 3:00 p.m.
   4) 4:00 p.m.

b. What should the passengers do after hearing the announcement?
   1) check their luggage
   2) get off the train in five minutes
   3) turn off any electronic devices
   4) show their tickets

8.   Listen and write

(CD2: 13) Chen Wen left a phone message for Maliya, an exchange student from Spain who is going on a trip soon. Listen to Chen Wen's message and write down the main points in English.

The main points of Chen Wen's phone message:

9.   Dialogue

Shibo is telling his friend about his computer. Listen to the conversation and answer the (CD2: 14) following questions.

a. What did the library administrators do when Shibo told them about his computer?
   1) They called the school policemen.
   2) They checked the students sitting around Shibo.
   3) They searched the library.
   4) They did not do anything.

b. Who stole Shibo's computer, according to a female student?
   1) someone who said that he was Shibo's friend
   2) a man with black hair
   3) a tall, thin man
   4) a student wearing a pair of shorts

c. What was Shibo doing when his computer got stolen?
   1) talking to a girl
   2) checking out some books
   3) drinking water
   4) going to the restroom

 # Reading and writing

Focus on Chinese characters

1.   Number of strokes

Indicate the number of strokes used in writing each of the following characters.

a. 哥 _____   f. 椅 _____

b. 旁 _____   g. 妹 _____

c. 爬 _____   h. 碼 _____

d. 廁 _____   i. 拿 _____

e. 寒 _____   j. 長 _____

2. Which character?

Circle the character in each line that corresponds to the meaning on the left.

a. **qíng** (**shìqing** *situation, matter*)   請   情

b. **xìng** *family name*   姓   虹

c. **xiāng** (**xiāngjī** *camera*)   相   想

d. **jǐ** (**zìjǐ** *self*)   己   已

e. **xuě** *snow*   雷   雪

f. **yòu** *right*   右   友

g. **míng** (**míngzì** *name*)   各   名

h. **gē** (**gēge** *older brother*)   哥   歌

i. **lǚ** (**lǚxíng** *travel, journey*)   放   旅

j. **sòng** *give as a gift*   述   送

k. **qiān** *thousand*   壬   千

l. **dì** (**dì'yī** *first*)   弟   第

3. First strokes

Write the first two strokes of each of the following characters.

a. 包 _____   f. 元 _____

b. 妹 _____   g. 爬 _____

c. 照 _____   h. 名 _____

d. 第 _____   i. 送 _____

e. 長 _____   j. 情 _____

4. Missing strokes

Complete each character by writing in the missing strokes.

a. **ná** *take*

b. **zhù** (**bāngzhù** *help*)

c. **qíng** (**shìqing** *situation, matter*)

d. **cè** (**cèsuǒ** *toilet*)

e. **zuǒ** *left*

f. **xìng** (**xìngmíng** *family name and given name*)

g. **dì** (**dì'yī** *first*)

h. **bāo** *bag*

i. **yòu** *right*

j. **páng** (**pángbiān** *beside*)

5. Total strokes

Rewrite this list of characters, arranging the characters in terms of their total number of strokes. Begin your list with the character with the fewest strokes.

第	旅	寒	姓	己	名	爬	助	碼	情	右	拿	送	妹	照	長	哥	於	椅	英	旁	雪	包

6. Radicals

Here is a list of characters that we have learned through this lesson. Rewrite each character in the row next to its radical.

名　旁　另　哥　相　慣　旅　姐　妹　右　運
椅　機　情　連　功　送　員　遠　忙　極　動

方	
女	
口	
木	
辶	
忄	
力	

7.   Character sleuth: Look for the phonetic

Group the characters below in terms of their rhymes or near-rhymes. Write the characters that rhyme with each other in the column on the right. Write the shared part of each character in the column on the left. For all of these characters, the shared part is the "phonetic," the part of the character that provides a clue to its pronunciation. The first set of rhymes is completed for you. There are fourteen additional sets of characters that rhyme or partially rhyme and share a phonetic component among these characters.

紅	又	右	請	馬	星	爸	完	旁	餃	放	元
相	爬	姓	張	口	情	工	友	弟	媽	生	校
碼	長	第	較	房	嗎	院	吧	想	方	功	把

phonetic	characters that rhyme or almost rhyme and share a phonetic component
工	工，紅，功

8.   Scrambled sentences

Rewrite these phrases as sentences, putting the words in the correct order to match the English translations.

a. 長 **chéng** / 爬 / 從來 / 我 / 過 / 沒

I have never climbed the Great Wall.

b. 選 / 老師 / 的 / 東西 / 送 / 我 / 幫助 / 妹妹/ 請 / 我 / 給

Please help me select something to give as a gift to my younger sister's teacher.

c. 椅子 / 的 / 書包 / 別 / 上 / 在 / 你 / 把 / 放

Don't put your book bag on the chair.

d. 你 / 左邊 / 房間 /房間 / 廁所 / 的 / 的 / 在 / 在 / 你 / 右邊 / 還是

Is the bathroom to the right of your room or to the left of your room?

9.   Dictionary skills

Following the instructions in Lesson 17 of the Textbook, look up these characters in a Chinese dictionary and provide the requested information.

a. 被
   pronunciation:
   meaning:
   one two-character word or phrase in which it occurs:

b. 丟
   pronunciation:
   meaning:
   one two-character word or phrase in which it occurs:

c. 城
   pronunciation:
   meaning:
   one two-character word or phrase in which it occurs:

10.   Find the incorrect characters

Zhang Dawei has written an email to his friends back home about a trip that he took recently, but he has written ten characters incorrectly. Read the passage aloud, circle the mistakes, and correct them on the answer sheet below.

放寒假的時後，我跟幾個同學做火車到中國男方去旅行。我的一個同學弟一天在火車站就把照想機給 **diū** 了。本來以為出去玩是一件很讓人高行的事請，可是他當然很生汽也很難過，我們也不高興，但是我們學會了出去旅行一定要小心看好自己的東四。你幫助我拿書包，我幫助你看東西。我們旅行了一個星期左友，沒有再讓人生氣的事情。

a. _____   b. _____   c. _____   d. _____   e. _____

f. _____   g. _____   h. _____   i. _____   j. _____

11.   Reading for the main ideas

You have not learned all of the characters in the following paragraph, but you have learned all of the structures and much of the vocabulary. Read the paragraph for the main ideas and answer the questions that follow in English.

我想選音樂的專業，但是我父母勸我不要學音樂，他們希望我學醫。他們認為喜歡唱歌，喜歡聽音樂跟選專業是兩件很不相同的事情。學音樂，畢業以後不容易找工作。找到工作，掙的錢也不會多。我問他們為甚麼一談到選專業，他們就會想到錢。我跟他們說我覺得錢一點都不要重要。他們說我現在覺得錢不重要，因為我一沒錢就給家裏打電話要錢。我真跟他們說不清楚。

a. This paragraph reports a conversation between three people. Who are they?

b. What were they discussing?

c. There was a disagreement among them. What was it about?

12.   A conversation between Dawei and Guoqiang

Read this conversation and answer the questions that follow in English. (You have learned all of the characters so if you find any that you don't recognize, look them up in the textbook and learn them.) Then, translate lines F.–K. into English.

A. 國強：你知道嗎？你的老師有名。

B. 大為：我當然知道我的老師有名。你有名，我也有名，我們都有名字。

C. 國強：我的意思是你的老師很有名。

D. 大為：有名不是有名字嗎？

E. 國強：不是，有名是很多人都知道你、很多人都知道你的名字的意思。你跟我都有名字，但是我們沒有名。

F. 大為：那麼有名，他一定有很多錢了。

G. 國強：對，他很有錢。

H. 大為：他很有名，很有錢，一定也很有學生了。

I. 國強：你不可以說很有學生，只能說有很多學生。

J. 大為：為甚麼有很多錢可以說很有錢，而有很多學生不能說很有學生呢？

K. 國強：我也不知道。我是中國人。我只知道你不可以這樣說，可是我不知道你為甚麼不可以這樣說。

a. This conversation is about similar phrases with very different meanings. What are the phrases?

b. What do the phrases mean?

13.   Some good advice

Rewrite this advice in Chinese characters. Write the word **diū** in Pinyin.

Chūqu lǚxíng de shíhou, zuì hǎo bǎ nǐ de xìngmíng、diànhuà hàomǎ hé zhù de dìfang dōu xiě zài yī zhāng zhǐ shàng, fàng zài nǐ de shūbāo lǐ.

Yàoshi nǐ de shūbāo (diū) le, bié de rén zhǎodào yǐhòu, kànjian nǐ de míngzì hé diànhuà hàomǎ, kěyǐ gěi nǐ dǎ diànhuà.

Focus on structure

1.   Practice with 把 (Use and Structure note 26.1)

a. 請把這張 **biǎo tián** 一下。

- 把你的中文名字寫下來。
- 把你的英文名字寫下來。

b. "出生日期"是甚麼意思? 英文怎麼說? 請把你的出生日期寫一下。

c. 你是男的還是女的? 請你寫一下。

d. **Tián** 完以後請把這個 **biǎo** 給老師看看。

中文姓名（請一正楷填寫）	□ 1 男 □ 2 女	□ 1 境內居民 □ 2 港澳居民 □ 3 台籍人士 □ 4 外籍人士	出生日期 　年　　月　　日
pīnyīn /英文姓名（請按護照 "大寫" 填寫，姓與名之間以空格分開）			

2.   Big numbers (Use and Structure note 26.3)

Here are numbers involving 10,000 and multiples of 10,000, written in Arabic numerals. Rewrite them in Chinese numerals, as in the example. Use characters for everything except **wàn** *10,000*.

Example:
27,460   →   兩 **wàn** 七千四百六

a. 12,385   →

b. 61,222   →

c. 150,500   →

d. 478,606   →

e. 5,478,000   →

f. 9,999,999   →

g. 12,345,678   →

3.   International currency conversion (Use and Structure notes 26.2, 26.3)

How much is the US dollar worth in other currencies? Here are the conversion rates as of when this book was written, rounded off to the nearest dollar. The international abbreviations of the currency names are provided.

- Rewrite them in Mandarin, using characters for everything except **wàn** *10,000* and **yuán** *dollar*, as in the example.
- Then, go online and look up the most current conversion rates and add a sentence stating the rate. You can use a website such as the Universal Currency Converter website (http://www.xe.com/ucc/) to find the most current rates.

Example:
1,000 USD = 6,782 CNY (Chinese Yuan) (also abbreviated as RMB 人 **mín bì**)
一千美 **yuán** 等於六千七百八十二 CNY

现在 _____

a. 10,000 USD = 13,960 SGD (Singapore Dollars)

现在 _____

b. 500 USD = 16,100 TWD (New Taiwan Dollars)

现在 _____

c. 99,000 USD = 105,290 CAD (Canadian Dollars)

现在 _____

d. 1,500 USD = 131,143 JPY (Japanese Yen)

现在 _____

e. 189,000 USD = 151,738 EUR (Euro)

现在 _____

4.   More or less this amount (Use and Structure note 26.10)

Provide a short answer to each question in Mandarin, using 左右 or 差不多 in each answer.

a. How many students are in each Chinese class? _____

section 1	section 2	section 3
19	20	21

b. What is the age of these students? _____

student 1	student 2	student 3	student 4	student 5	student 6
18	$17^{1}/_{2}$	$17^{1}/_{2}$	$18^{1}/_{2}$	18	$18^{1}/_{2}$

c. What is the price of computer model number 0335? _____

store A	store B	store C
$790	$810	$805

d. How long did students take to complete the test? _____

student 1	student 2	student 3
45 minutes	50 minutes	40 minutes

5.   Almost that amount (Use and Structure note 26.10)

Provide a short answer to each question in Mandarin based on the information in parentheses, using 差不多 in each answer.

a. How long has Xiao Zhang studied Chinese? (one year and eleven months)

b. How much money does Xiao Ye get paid each month for her summer job? (￥1995)

c. How long did Xiao Wang sleep last night? (nine hours fifty minutes)

d. How much is the annual tuition fee at Xiao Zhang's college in the United States? ($39,500)

6.   Get people to do things (Use and Structure note 26.6)

Translate these sentences into Mandarin, using 請, 叫, or 讓 in each sentence.

a. Let's invite our teachers to dinner, okay?

b. You should tell your roommate to study Chinese.

c. My mom makes me wear socks when the weather is cold.

d. If your friends don't want to drink beer, you shouldn't make them drink it.

e. I want to ask your older brother to help me study Chinese.

f. Mom told the children to clean up the room. (There are two correct choices.)

g. The doctor told me to take this medicine. (There are two correct choices.)

7.   Passive (Use and Structure note 26.4)

Translate these sentences into English.

a. 這件事 **bèi** 他知道了。

b. 他還不到二十歲就喝酒，**bèi** 他的爸爸看見了。

c. 我的手機 **bèi** 我弟弟用壞了。

Translate these sentences into Mandarin, using **bèi** in each sentence, and writing characters where we have learned them.

d. While I was studying in the library, my computer was stolen by someone.

e. Sorry, the dumplings we made today were all eaten up by the teachers.

8. Hypothetical situations with 要是 (Use and Structure note 26.7)

Answer the questions in complete Mandarin sentences.

a. 要是有人給你一百 **wàn** 塊錢你會做甚麼？

b. 要是你的中文課沒有考試，你還會 **fù** 習功課嗎？

c. 要是你的同屋身體不舒服，你會做甚麼？

d. 要是你的同屋把你的可樂喝完了，你會不會生氣？為甚麼？

e. 要是你把電 **nǎo** 給 **diū** 了，你會怎麼樣？

9. Translate into English

Translate these sentences into English.

a. 聽說北京現在有 1,700 **wàn** 人左右。

b. 我的同屋把我昨天剛買的可樂給喝了。

c. 我寫的功課 **diū** 了。不能給老師，等於我昨天晚上甚麼都沒做。

d. 明天會下 **yǔ**。**Kǒng** 怕我們不能去爬山了。

e. 今天下雪下得這麼大，我以為沒有課了呢。

f. 我以為今天的考試會很難。沒想到容易得不得了。

g. 我昨天晚上把我的經 **jì** 課的課本給 **wàng** 在圖書館了。

h. 你這樣說就等於你不 **xīwàng** 我們跟你一起去。

10.   Translate into Mandarin

Translate these sentences into Mandarin, using characters where we have learned them.

a. I thought (mistakenly) that I wouldn't be able to buy American food in China.

b. From today on, I will practice writing a few characters every day.

c. My mom said that if I can't come home this weekend, she can come to school to see me.

d. (1) We asked Xiao Xie's mom to teach us how to make dumplings.

   (2) She is having us come to her house this weekend to learn.

e. That child is really afraid of his father, but he isn't afraid of his mother.

f. I'm afraid I might be too busy to go to the cafeteria to eat, so I have a lot of food in my room.

g. If you are going to go to the bathroom in the train station, you should ask your friends to watch your things.

11.   Scrambled sentences

Rewrite these phrases into sentences, putting them in the right order to match the English translations.

a. 說/ 你 / 你 / 父母 / 你 / 把 / 想 / **zhuānyè** / 應該 / 跟 / 一下 / 選 / 的 / 的

   You should discuss which major you want to choose with your mother and father.

b. 早就 / **yán** / 了/ 不 / 要是 / 我 / 老師 / 選 / 課 /那個 / 那門

   If that teacher weren't strict I would have taken his course long ago.

c. 功課 / 看/ 你 /把 / 然後 / 去 / 請 / 電 **yǐng** / 做完 / 先 / 再

   First finish your homework and then go see a movie.

d. 了 / 考試 / 漢字 / 要是 / 沒有 / 就 / 好 / 明天

   It would be good if there wasn't a Chinese-character test tomorrow.

e. 時候 / 在 / 書 / 的 / 誰 / 你 / 考試 / 看 / 讓

   Who told you to look at the book while taking the test?

Focus on communication

1. Dialogue comprehension

Study the Lesson 26 Narrative and Dialogue. Then, read the following statements and indicate whether they are true (T) or false (F).

a. ( ) 大為的 **biǎo** 妹以前沒來過中國。

b. ( ) 大為有時間 **dài biǎo** 妹跟同學去爬長 **chéng**，因為現在是寒假。

c. ( ) 他們去爬長 **chéng** 的那天下雪，所以人很少。

d. ( ) 大為的照相機是他哥哥買的。

e. ( ) 那個相機要一 **wàn** 多塊美 **yuán**。

f. ( ) 大為的同學覺得，一定有人把相機 **tōu** 走了。

g. ( ) 除了相機以外，大為還 **diū** 了 **hù** 照。

h. ( ) 大為的相機是在廁所裏 **diū** 的。

i. ( ) 大為覺得不用請 **biǎo** 妹看著相機，因為他一會兒就回來。

j. ( ) 工作人員跟大為說，以後一定要 **zhù** 意自己 **dài** 的東西。

k. ( ) 大為 **tián** 了一張 **biǎo**，**xīwàng** 如果相機找到了，工作人員可以告訴他。

2. What do you say?

What do you say in each of the following situations? Type your answers, using characters where we have learned them, and email them to your Chinese teacher.

a. You lost your cell phone and you ask the staff person to help.

b. You want to know how much $1,000 USD is in RMB.

c. You apologize to your friend because you accidentally left her coat in the subway station, and now you can't find it.

d. When the teacher announces that the exam will begin in five minutes, you wonder what to do because you thought the exam was next week and you did not prepare for it.

e. You explain to your friends that you still live with your parents because you don't want to leave them.

f. You are talking to your father about job hunting: You have applied for five jobs so far. Google is your first choice, but you think it's a long shot.

g. Your friend looks very agitated. Ask him not to be mad and tell you what happened. Also offer to help.

h. Tell your roommate you are very upset because you accidentally lost the gift that your boyfriend just gave you.

i. You volunteer as a receptionist in a clinic. Tell a patient to fill out the form first, and then sit in a nearby chair and wait for a few minutes.

j. As a librarian, instruct a visitor on how to apply for a library card. (Tell him to fill out the form with his name, address, and phone number.)

k. Advise your friend not to wear leather shoes today. You're afraid that if he wears leather shoes, he won't be able to climb the Great Wall.

3. Complete the mini-dialogues

Use the structure in parentheses to complete each mini-dialogue.

a. A: 你怎麼沒穿你最喜歡的那件大衣？

B: _____。（**bèi**）

b. A: 你為甚麼不早一點買火車 **piào**？你不知道春節的火車 **piào** 最難買嗎？

B: _____，沒想到 **piào** 已經賣完了。（以為）

c. A: 這個照相機我沒看過，是從哪兒來的？

B: 是我 _____ 從美國 **dài** 回來的。（讓）

A: 多少錢？

B: 不貴。_____。（左右；等於）

d. Teacher:"己"這個字跟"已經"的"已"差不多。

Student: 好，我 _____。（**zhù** 意）

e. A: 我已經三個星期沒有看見你了，這個週末你有時間嗎？

B: 對不起，_____。（**kǒng** 怕）

f. A: 你離開了這麼 **jiǔ**，也不給我打電話，真難過！

B: 別生氣，現在我回來了，_____，我不會離開你了。（從…起）

4. Complete and translate

Using the context as your guide, choose the correct expression to complete each sentence, and then translate the sentences into English.

a. 我以為你明天才會來，＿＿＿＿＿。
  1) 我已經把房間 **shōushi** 乾淨了
  2) 所以我放假了，可以 **dài** 你出去玩
  3) 沒想到你今天就到了

  English:

b. 昨天早上我送朋友去火車站，＿＿＿＿ 去 **guàng** 商店，很晚才回家。
  1) 然後
  2) 以前
  3) 再說

  English:

c. 今年 **shǔ** 假我大概不會去中國。八月的天氣太 **rè** 了，**bìng** 且，＿＿＿＿＿＿＿。
  1) 我沒有去過北京
  2) 我早就想去爬長 **chéng** 了
  3) **fēi** 機 **piào** 貴得不得了

  English:

5. Who is he?

a. 這個人可以幫助你做甚麼？

b. 甚麼地方會有這 **zhǒng** 人？

c. 你去找這 **zhǒng** 人的時候，他會怎麼幫你？

6. All about emotions

Answer each of the following questions in complete Mandarin sentences, based on the information in the illustration, as in the example.

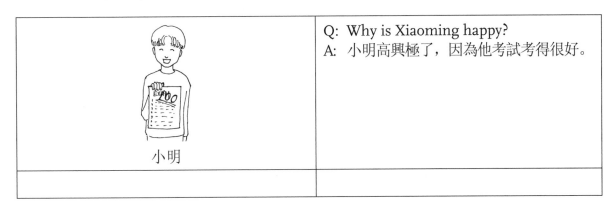

小明	Q: Why is Xiaoming happy? A: 小明高興極了，因為他考試考得很好。

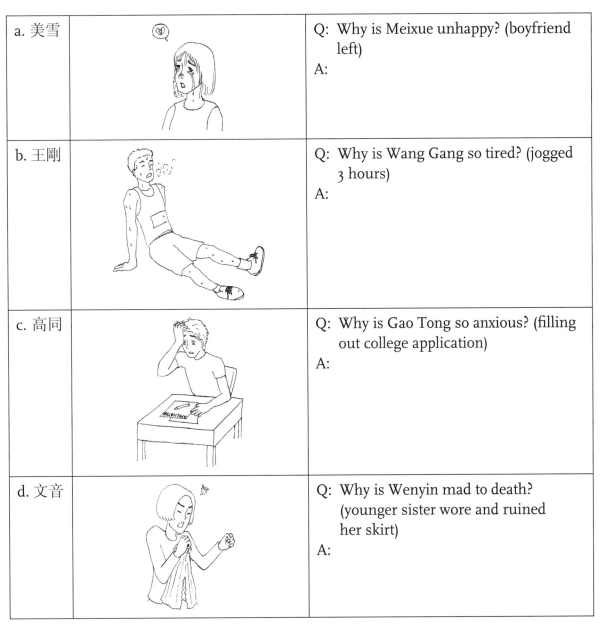

a. 美雪		Q: Why is Meixue unhappy? (boyfriend left) A:
b. 王剛		Q: Why is Wang Gang so tired? (jogged 3 hours) A:
c. 高同		Q: Why is Gao Tong so anxious? (filling out college application) A:
d. 文音		Q: Why is Wenyin mad to death? (younger sister wore and ruined her skirt) A:

7. I lost my favorite... Part I

Think about one item that was special to you but got lost (maybe returned later). Answer the following questions about that particular experience in complete Mandarin sentences.

a. 你 **diū** 的東西是甚麼？

b. 你是甚麼時候拿到這個東西的？

c. 這個東西是誰送給你的？你知道那是在哪兒買的嗎？多少錢？

d. 這個東西為甚麼很 **zhòng** 要？

e. 這個東西是甚麼時候 **diū** 的？

f. 這個東西是在哪兒 **diū** 的？你為甚麼會去那兒？

g. 請你說一下那天 **diū** 東西的經過。

h. 東西 **diū** 了以後，你覺得怎麼樣？(*For Example:* 為甚麼特別難過，或者特別生氣？)

i. 你發現東西 **diū** 了以後，請別人幫忙了嗎？

j. 東西最後找到了嗎？如果找到了，是怎麼找到的？

k. 這件事情以後，你會特別 **zhù** 意甚麼？

8. I lost my favorite... Part II

Use your answers from Exercise 7 to write a paragraph about an "I lost..." experience. Your paragraph should be at least 150 characters in length.

_____

_____

_____

_____

_____

_____

_____

_____

Lesson 27 Workbook

 Listening and speaking

Structure drills

(audio online)

1. NP V 起來 AdjV *NP is AdjV to V* (Use and Structure note 27.1)

You will hear a phrase describing an action and a noun phrase. Rephrase the sentence using <u>NP V 起來 AdjV</u>, saying that *the noun phrase is AdjV to V*, as in the example. Translations of the example sentences are provided.

Example:
You will hear: 聽那個很有意思的 **gù** 事。 *Listen to that very interesting story.*
You will say: 那個 **gù** 事聽起來很有意思。 *That story is interesting to listen to.*
Click "R" to hear the correct response: 那個 **gù** 事聽起來很有意思。

(a)　　(b)　　(c)　　(d)　　(e)　　(f)　　(g)　　(h)

2. Expressing *both…and* with **jì**…又 (Use and Structure note 27.5)

You will hear a statement describing a noun phrase with two qualities. Rephrase the statement with **jì**…又, as in the example.

Example:
You will hear: 這個學生很 **cōng** 明也很用功。
You will say: 這個學生 **jì cōng** 明又用功。
Click "R" to hear the correct response: 這個學生 **jì cōng** 明又用功。

(a)　　(b)　　(c)　　(d)　　(e)　　(f)　　(g)　　(h)　　(i)　　(j)

3.   V₁ 起來 AdjV₁, V₂ 起來 AdjV₂ (Use and Structure note 27.7)

You will hear a statement describing an action in two different ways. Rephrase the statement with V₁ 起來 AdjV₁ V₂ 起來 AdjV₂, as in the example.

Example:
You will hear: 包餃子，很容易說，很難做。
You will say: 包餃子，說起來容易，做起來難。
Click "R" to hear the correct response: 包餃子，說起來容易，做起來難。

(a)   (b)   (c)   (d)   (e)   (f)   (g)   (h)

4.   把…V-**chéng** *taking something and turning it into something else* (Use and Structure note 27.9)

You will hear two noun phrases followed by a verb. Use them to form a sentence saying that you took the first noun phrase and turned it into the second one, as in the example.

Example:
You will hear: 七點、一點、聽
You will say: 我把七點聽 **chéng** 一點了。
Click "R" to hear the correct response: 我把七點聽 **chéng** 一點了。

(a)   (b)   (c)   (d)   (e)   (f)   (g)   (h)   (i)   (j)

5.   In fact it is not at all like that (Use and Structure notes 27.8, 27.12)

You will hear a statement about what someone believes. Reply that, in fact, the situation is not like that, using **shíjì** 上 and 並 + NEG, as in the example.

Example:
You will hear: 我以為中文很難學。
You will say: **Shíjì** 上，中文並不難。
Click "R" to hear the correct response: **Shíjì** 上，中文並不難學。

(a)   (b)   (c)   (d)   (e)   (f)   (g)   (h)   (i)   (j)

Listening for information

1.   Cooking ingredients

(CD2: 18) Chef Liu is talking about the ingredients for two dishes. Listen to her and circle the ingredients used in each dish.

a. First dish: ginger, tofu, sugar, soy sauce, green onion, fish, vinegar, pork, garlic

b. Second dish: ginger, tofu, sugar, soy sauce, green onion, fish, vinegar, pork, garlic

2.   A dinner party

Aimei and several of her friends had dinner together in a Chinese restaurant. Each of them (CD2: 19) ordered some dishes. Listen to Aimei's description of the dinner and complete the table with the names of the dishes that each person ordered (in Pinyin).

姓名	中國菜
Àiměi	
Zhāng Xīn	
Liào Tiānmíng	
Páng Yàoguāng	

3.   Stinky tofu

Listen to the story of the dish "stinky tofu," and answer the questions that follow in (CD2: 20–21) complete Mandarin sentences, using characters where we have learned them. The story includes two words that we have not learned, but you should be able to follow the story without knowing precisely what these two words mean.

a.

b.

c.

4.   Chicken with green onions

Listen to the recipe for **cōngyóu jī** *chicken with green onions*, and answer the questions that (CD2: 22–23) follow in complete Mandarin sentences. Use characters where we have learned them. The word **zhēng** means *steam*.

a.

b.

c.

d.

e.

5.   Doctor's instructions

(CD2: 24) Chongwen hurt his leg (**tuǐ**) while playing ball. His doctor is telling him what he should do every day to recover. Write down the doctor's instructions about exercising and taking medicine in English. The narrative contains one word that you have not yet learned. It refers to something that Chongwen should do. Write that word in Pinyin in the appropriate place in the table, paying attention to tones.

exercise	medicine
I.	I.
2.	2.
3.	

6.   A conversation

(CD2: 25) You are chatting with a Chinese friend about cooking. Answer her questions in Mandarin, based on your own experience. Use characters where we have learned them.

a.

b.

c.

d.

e.

f.

7.   In the library

(CD2: 26–27) Listen to the librarian's instructions to Mike about applying for a library card (**jiè** 書 **zhèng**), and then provide a short answer in Mandarin to each question.

a.

b.

c.

d.

e.

8. Telephone message

Zhiqiang has left you a phone message about tonight's dinner plans. Write an email to him **(CD2: 28)** in Chinese responding to each of his questions.

> Your email responding to each of Zhiqiang's questions:

9. Dialogue I

Listen to the conversation between Tom and his friend Huiru about Beijing. Answer the **(CD2: 29)** questions based on the dialogue.

a. What is Tom's summer plan?
1) travel
2) do research
3) work
4) study

b. What is Tom specifically asking about?
1) the road situation
2) finding a suitable apartment
3) transportation in the city
4) safety in the community

c. What does Huiru say about riding a bicycle?
1) Bicycles are often stolen.
2) Bicycle riding is convenient.
3) Bicycle riding is not cheap.
4) Bicycle riding saves time.

10. Dialogue II

Kathy is asking Jianmin to teach her how to cook Chinese food. Listen to their conversation **(CD2: 30)** and answer the following questions. The conversation includes a few words that you have not learned, but you should still be able to follow the main points and answer all of the questions.

a. What does Kathy say about the difference between American and Chinese food?
1) It is harder to cook American food.
2) It is easier to eat Chinese food.
3) It is common to have shredded meat in Chinese dishes.
4) It is difficult to use chopsticks when eating meat.

b. What should be added when marinating the meat mentioned in the dialogue?
  1) garlic
  2) cooking wine
  3) green onion
  4) hot oil

c. What does Kathy want to learn?
  1) how to cut meat
  2) how to choose the right meat
  3) how to cook meat in various ways
  4) how to marinate meat

 # Reading and writing

Focus on Chinese characters

1. Number of strokes

Indicate the number of strokes used in writing each of the following characters.

a. 懂 ____   f. 備 ____

b. 客 ____   g. 熱 ____

c. 魚 ____   h. 練 ____

d. 準 ____   i. 筷 ____

e. 雞 ____   j. 久 ____

2. Which character?

Circle the character in each line that corresponds to the meaning on the left.

a. **bìng** (**bìngqiě** *moreover*)   半   並

b. **ròu** *meat*   肉   內

c. **rù** *enter*   入   八

d. **wǔ** (**zhōngwǔ** *noon*)   牛   午

e. **zhòng** (**zhòngyào** *important*)   種   重

f. **zhǒng** *type of*   種   懂

g. **qié** (**qiézi** *eggplant*)   茄   加

h. **liàn** (**liànxí** *practice*)   凍   練

i. **fā** (**fā shāo** *have a fever*)   癸   發

j. **zhǔn** *accurate*   淮   準

k. **kè** *guest*   客   宮

l. **bèi** (**zhǔnbèi** *prepare*)   佣   備

3. First strokes

Write the first two strokes of each of the following characters.

a. 久 _____   f. 備 _____

b. 筷 _____   g. 共 _____

c. 發 _____   h. 午 _____

d. 肉 _____   i. 茄 _____

e. 種 _____   j. 魚 _____

4. Missing strokes

Complete each character by writing in the missing strokes.

a.   **rè** *hot*

b.   **jī** *chicken*

c.   **bìng** *(not) at all*

d.   **zhǔn** *accurate*

e.   **dǒng** *understand*

f.   **liàn** (**liànxí** *practice*)

g.   **rù** *enter*

h.   **kè** *guest*

i.   **chǎo** *stir-fry*

j.   **bèi** (**zhǔnbèi** *prepare*)

5. Total strokes

Rewrite this list of characters, arranging the characters in terms of their total number of strokes. Begin your list with the character with the fewest strokes.

懂	練	發	久	客	備	熱	茄	入	午	種	共	重	準	魚	雞	並	炒	肉	筷

6. Radicals

Here is a list of characters that we have learned through this lesson. Rewrite each character in the row next to its radical.

懂　第　熱　茄　寒　練　情　等　穿　英　算
藍　茶　冷　然　客　級　慣　花　次　紹　筷

忄	
灬	
艹	
冫	
宀	
糹	
竹	

7. Character sleuth: Look for the phonetic

Group the characters below in terms of their rhymes or near-rhymes. Write the characters that rhyme with each other in the column on the right. Write the shared part of each character in the column on the left. For all of these characters, the shared part is the "phonetic," the part of the character that provides a clue to its pronunciation. The first set of rhymes is completed for you. There are fourteen additional sets of characters that rhyme or partially rhyme and share a phonetic component among these characters.

嗎	塊	懂	中	練	極	識	筷
想	種	連	炒	請	較	媽	放
認	碼	級	人	話	餃	快	重
少	活	方	鐘	相	情	只	房

phonetic	characters that rhyme or almost rhyme and share a phonetic component
重	重，懂

8.   Scrambled sentences

Rewrite these phrases as sentences, putting the words in the correct order to match the English translations.

a. 容易 / 我 / 不 / 筷子 / 發現 / 用 / 並

I realized that it is not at all easy to use chopsticks.

b. 以前 / 得 / 課 / 你 / / 功課 / 上 / 準備

Before going to class, you have to prepare the lesson.

c. 想 **fǎ** / 我們 / 的 / 說 / 你 / 你 / 跟 / 請 / 說 / 一 / 把

Please tell me your opinion.

d. 不 / 我 / 我 / 認識 / 你 / 哥哥 / 以為 / 你 / 的

I assumed you didn't know my older brother.

9. Dictionary skills

Following the instructions in Lesson 17 of the Textbook, look up these characters in a Chinese dictionary and provide the requested information:

a. 簡

pronunciation:

meaning:

one two-character word or phrase in which it occurs:

b. 費

pronunciation:

meaning:

one two-character word or phrase in which it occurs:

c. 借

pronunciation:

meaning:

one two-character word or phrase in which it occurs:

10. Find the incorrect characters

Ye Youwen has dashed off this email to one of her friends as she waits for guests to arrive. She is in such a hurry that she has written ten characters incorrectly. (One is written incorrectly twice.) Read the passage aloud, circle the mistakes, and correct them on the answer sheet below.

> 客人很塊就要道了。一共來五個，都是我的同學。我爸爸媽媽請他們來我家吃五飯。來以前他們說不要客氣，不用誰備很多吃的東西。吃甚麼不種要。種要的是在一氣談談話，認只一下我的父母。因為我父母不會說英文，所以他們來我家吃反可以跟我父母連習說中文，並且可以練習用快子吃飯。

a. ____   b. ____   c. ____   d. ____   e. ____

f. ____   g. ____   h. ____   i. ____   j. ____

11. Reading for the main ideas

The following paragraph contains a few characters that we have not yet learned, but you should be able to "read around them" and understand the main points of the passage. Read the paragraph for the main ideas and answer the questions that follow in English.

> 自助餐
>
> 中文有的時候很麻煩。比方說，有一個說法是從英文借來的，但是你不可以把借來的英文都說出來，都說清楚。說清楚就不對了。"自助餐"就是這樣。自是自己。助是幫助。餐在這裏就是飯的意思。自助餐實際上就是自己幫助自己的飯。但是你不可以這樣說。中國人不懂甚麼是自己幫助自己的飯。你只能說自助餐。

a. 自助餐是甚麼？

b. 你認為甚麼時候吃自助餐很方便？

c. 寫這個 **gù** 事的人為甚麼說"中文有的時候很麻煩"？

12.　Translation into English

Translate the following conversation into English.

國強：大為，你最喜歡的中國菜是甚麼？

大為：我喜歡吃肉，所以我最喜歡的是做兩次的肉。

國強：做兩次的肉？我怎麼沒聽說過？

大為：你怎麼沒聽說過。上個週末我們一起去吃飯我就要的這個菜。你吃了很多。

國強：那是回 **guō** 肉，不是做兩次的肉。

大為：為甚麼叫回 **guō** 肉？

國強：回 **guō** 肉就是把肉先做一次，再讓肉回到 **guō** 裏一次，一共做兩次。

大為：請你再說一次。肉，一共做幾次？

國強：做兩次。

大為：所以是做兩次的肉。

Focus on structure

1. Both this and that (Use and Structure note 27.5)

Translate these sentences into Mandarin using the structure **jì AdjV₁ 又 AdjV₂**.

a. Stir-fried eggs with tomatoes is both cheap and simple.

b. Eggplant with yuxiang sauce is both fragrant and delicious.

c. Those dishes are both beautiful and expensive.

d. The ingredients for cooking fish are both simple and inexpensive.

2. Describing things in terms of two qualities (Use and Structure note 27.7)

Translate these sentences into Mandarin using the structure **V₁ 起來 AdjV₁ V₂ 起來 AdjV₂**.

a. Dumplings are easy to make and delicious to eat.

b. Chinese characters are beautiful to look at but hard to write.

c. This kind of clothing is comfortable to wear and easy to wash.

d. This kind of song is beautiful to listen to but difficult to sing.

3. More practice with V-chéng (Use and Structure note 27.9)

These sentences all include resultative verbs in which the ending is **chéng**. Translate them into English.

a. 他常常把 "問老師" 說成 "**wěn** (*kiss*) 老師"。

b. 炒菜以前，你得先把肉 **qiē chéng** 塊兒。

c. **Zāogāo**，我不小心把 "人" 寫 **chéng** "入" 了。

d. 我把她看 **chéng** 她妹妹了。

e. 二十塊錢常常寫 **chéng** ¥20。

4.   Borrow and loan (Use and Structure note 27.13)

Translate these sentences into English.

a. 請把你的 **bǐ** 借給我。

b. 你最好別跟別人 **jiè** 東西。

c. 要是你想買車你可以從 **yín** 行 **jiè** 錢。

d. 他跟我 **jiè** 了好幾本書。

e. 你 **yuàn** 意不 **yuàn** 意把你的電 **nǎo jiè** 給別人？

5.   Scrambled sentences

Rewrite these phrases into sentences, putting them in the right order to match the English translations.

a. **wèi** 道 / 貴 / 很好 / 飯館 / 並 / 菜 / 那家 / 而且 / 的 / 不

The dishes in that restaurant taste good, moreover they aren't at all expensive.

b. **tiáoliào** / 菜 / 放了 / **xiāng** 吧 / 這個 / 不少 / **wén** 起來 / 一定 / 真

This dish is very fragrant to smell. They certainly put in a lot of seasoning.

c. 以外 / 有 / 筷子 / **wǎn** / 我 / **pán** 子 / 除了 / 和 / 也

Besides chopsticks, I also have bowls and plates.

d. 的 / 不 / 了 / 我 / 我 / 發現 / **gòu** / 剛 / 錢

I just realized I don't have enough money.

e. **yán** / 這 / 關心 / 個 / **jì** / 又 / 很 / 學生 / 老師 / 很

This teacher is both very strict and also cares about her students.

6.   Translation into English

Translate these sentences into English.

a. 我去圖書館 **jiè** 書。圖書館沒有這本書。老師把他的 **jiè** 給我了。

b. **Shíjì** 上，說中文並不難。難的是寫漢字。

c. 現在的經 **jì** 不太好。大學 **bìyè** 生找工作，說起來容易做起來難。

d. 今天的中文功課是想一個你小的時候聽的 **gù** 事，明天用中文給老師和同學 **jiǎng**。

e. 快過春節了。**Shāng** 店的東西都在打折。比方說，有的打九折，有的打八五折，還有的打七折。

f. 這個人在吃的方 **miàn** 一點都不 **jiǎngjiu**，可是在穿的方 **miàn** 非常 **jiǎngjiu**。

g. 這個週末是大為的生日。我們請他來我們的宿舍喝酒。我們 **shǒu** 先 **shōushi** 房間，然後把髒衣服洗乾淨，最後去買 **pí** 酒和吃的東西。

h. 下個星期六我們一起去長 **chéng** 玩，你 **dài** 吃的，我 **dài** 喝的，早上六點學校門口見。一 **yán** 為定。

7.   Translation into Mandarin

Translate these sentences into Mandarin, using characters where we have learned them.

a. I don't like to go on the web and chat with other people. I think it is too much of a waste of time.

b. This weekend we are going to go climb the Great Wall. Do you want to (are you willing to) come with us?

c. Before returning to my home country, I definitely want to learn how to cook a few authentic Chinese dishes.

d. I study Chinese together with Xiao Wang. We study Chinese together with Professor Zhang.

e. He lived in China for several years, so the Chinese that he speaks is very authentic.

f. I think your way of doing things is not correct. Let's try another method, okay?

g. Actually, there is no problem with this method. (Use 並.) The problem is that you don't understand it.

h. I don't have enough time. I definitely won't be able to finish the homework tonight.

Focus on communication

1.   Dialogue comprehension

Study the Lesson 27 Narrative and Dialogue. Then, read the following statements and indicate whether they are true (T) or false (F).

a. (   ) 中國菜 **jiǎngjiu** 看起來漂亮、**wén** 起來 **xiāng**，吃起來有 **wèi** 道。

b. (   ) 美麗最會做的中國菜就是雞 **dàn** 炒西紅 **shì** 和魚 **xiāng** 茄子。

c. (   ) 魚 **xiāng** 茄子有 **cōng**，**jiāng**，**suàn**，**táng** 等等的 **tiáoliào**，可是沒有魚。

d. (   ) 美麗想請國強的媽媽教她做魚 **xiāng** 茄子。

e. (   ) 謝太太認為，中國菜不一定都很難做。有的家常菜又好吃又容易做。

f. (   ) 雞 **dàn** 炒西紅 **shì** 要放 **táng**、**yán** 和 **cōng**。

g. (   ) 做雞 **dàn** 炒西紅 **shì** 的時候，雞 **dàn** 別 **wàng** 了多炒幾分鐘。

h. (   ) 做雞 **dàn** 炒西紅 **shì** 的時候，把西紅 **shì** **qiēchéng** 塊兒，不要放進 **guō** 裏炒，放在炒好的雞 **dàn** 上就可以了。

i. (   ) 美麗跟謝媽媽 **jiè** 了一個 **guō**，回家練習做中國菜。

2.   What do you say?

What do you say in each of the following situations? Type your answers, using characters where we have learned them, and email them to your Chinese teacher.

a.   You want to start a story with "Once upon a time…".

b.   You are making eggplant with yuxiang sauce. Ask your sister to wash the eggplants and cut them into small pieces.

c.   You want to ask your Chinese friend to teach you a simple yet delicious Chinese dish.

d.   You promise your little brother that if he goes to bed early you will tell him a story.

e.   Apologize to your grandma that you can't go visit her this weekend because there's not enough time. You thought next Monday was still a holiday (a day off), but later you realized that it's not.

f.   Imagine saying "I do" (I'm willing to!) when you marry someone in China.

g. Your friend insists on taking you out to the movies. Make a deal with your friend that the movie tickets are his treat, but dinner is on you.

h. Say a few nice words to compliment a dish that your mom cooked that is on the dinner table. (For example, what it smells like, what it looks like, etc.)

i. You have just taken a bite of a wonderful dish. It's so tasty that you want the hostess to tell you what seasonings are (put) in it.

j. Name one dish that you like the best and provide at least two reasons for your choice.

k. You try to convince your parents to learn how to use the internet. Name a few advantages. (Use the phrase "for example.")

l. You need to borrow a wok and some ginger from your neighbor because you want to practice making scallion-ginger chicken. Explain to your neighbor that you found the recipe (way of making it) online.

m. Instruct your kitchen helper to cut the meat into strips (條) that are not too long and not too short.

3. Complete the mini-dialogues

Use the structure in parentheses to complete each mini-dialogue.

a. A: 給 **hái** 子選名字甚麼最重要？

   B: 給 **hái** 子選名字 _____。 (**jiǎngjiu**)

b. A: 你給我 **jiǎng jiǎng**，一雙好的鞋子應該怎麼樣？

   B: _____。 (V起來)

c. A: **Dōng** 天去爬長 **chéng** 怎麼樣？

   B: 很多人認為 _____。 (**shíjì**上)

d. A: 你明天幾點鐘回來？

   B: 大概 _____ 吧。 (use two numbers in a row)

e. Wife: 你怎麼會穿黃色的 **chènshān**？黃 **chènshān** 跟這條 **kù** 子一點也不 **pèi**。

   Husband: 真的嗎？那我去 _____。 (V-**chéng**)

f. A: 沒想到北京這麼冷，這次旅 **yóu** 我只 **dài** 了 **chènshān** 來，這幾天怎麼 **bàn** 呢？

   B: _____ 沒關係，我可以 **jiè** 給你一件大衣。 (**gòu**)

g. A: 你教我做一個地道的美國菜，怎麼樣？

   B: 沒問 **tí**。就做 _____ 好了。_____ (**jì**…又)

4.   Complete and translate

Using the context as your guide, choose the correct expression to complete each sentence, and then translate the sentence into English.

a. 大家都以為中國菜裏的 **yóu** 特別多，**shíjì** 上 ＿＿＿＿＿。
   1) 地道的中國菜並不是這樣。
   2) 大家都喜歡吃，因為 **jì** 方便又便宜
   3) 炒菜的時候我不喜歡放那麼多 **yóu**。

   English:

b. 買衣服最重要是大小 **héshì**，也就是說，＿＿＿＿＿
   1) 打折的時候去買衣服正好。
   2) 買衣服的時候一定要試穿。
   3) 有沒有大一號的？

   English:

c. 炒雞 **dàn** 一點兒也不難。你看，＿＿＿＿＿＿＿。
   1) 下次我做給你吃
   2) 兩三分鐘就炒好了
   3) 一定要用筷子打 **yún**

   English:

5.   Goldilocks and the Three Bears

Here is the story *Goldilocks and the Three Bears* in Chinese. Look at the illustrations and fill in the blanks to complete the story. Research online if you are not familiar with the story.

a. 很久很久以前，＿＿＿＿＿＿＿＿叫 Goldilocks。有一天，她＿＿＿＿＿＿一個房子裏。

b. 她看到 **zhuō** 上有＿＿＿＿＿＿ **zhōu** (*porridge*)。第一 **wǎn** 太＿＿＿＿＿＿＿＿，

＿＿＿＿＿＿＿＿＿＿，＿＿＿＿＿＿＿＿＿＿＿＿＿，所以 Goldilocks 就

把＿＿＿＿＿＿＿＿＿＿。

c. 然後，Goldilocks 看到三把椅子。第一把太＿＿＿＿＿＿＿＿＿＿＿＿，

＿＿＿＿＿＿＿＿＿＿＿＿＿，＿＿＿＿＿＿＿＿＿＿＿＿＿＿，

所以 Goldilocks 就坐下來，可是，她不小心把＿＿＿＿＿＿＿＿＿＿＿。

d. 後來，Goldilocks 走進房間裏，看到＿＿＿＿＿＿＿＿＿＿＿＿。她太累了，

就在＿＿＿＿＿＿＿＿＿＿＿＿。

e. **Xióng** (*bear*) 爸爸、**xióng** 媽媽和小 **xióng** 回到家，＿＿＿＿＿＿（i. **shǒu** 先，ii. 然後，

iii. 後來），小 **xióng** 看到他的 **zhōu** 不見了，說：是誰＿＿＿＿＿＿＿＿＿＿？

＿＿＿＿＿＿（i. **shǒu** 先，ii. 然後，iii. 後來）小 **xióng** 看到他的椅子壞了，就更生氣

了，他說：我的椅子 **bèi** ＿＿＿＿＿＿＿＿＿？

f. ＿＿＿＿＿＿＿＿（i. **shǒu** 先，ii. 然後，iii. 後來）他們走進房間裏，看到 Goldilocks

＿＿＿＿＿＿＿＿＿＿＿＿。小 **xióng** 生氣得不得了。＿＿＿＿＿＿＿＿＿

＿＿＿＿＿＿＿＿＿＿＿＿＿＿＿＿＿＿＿＿＿＿＿＿＿＿＿＿＿＿＿＿＿

＿＿＿＿＿＿＿＿。 (*So scared that she jumped out of the bed and ran out.*)

6. Cinderella (**Huī Gūniang** *Dust Girl*)

Part I. Describe each scene, using the words provided in parentheses. Here are the words and phrases we have not yet learned that you will need to tell the story: 後母 *stepmother*, 王子 *prince*, **xiān** 女 *fairy godmother*, A 跟 B **jiéhūn** *A gets married to B*, **zhī** (*classifier for one shoe*).

a.	(打 **sǎo**) ＿＿＿＿＿＿＿＿＿＿＿＿＿＿＿ ＿＿＿＿＿＿＿＿＿＿＿＿＿＿＿ ＿＿＿＿＿＿＿＿＿＿＿＿＿＿＿

b.	(難過、幫助、送給) _____ _____ _____
c.	(cān 加、wǔ 會) _____ _____ _____
d.	(離開、跑、diū) _____ _____ _____
e.	(試穿、V 不下) _____ _____ _____
f.	_____ _____ _____

Part II. The complete story   Working with a partner, compare each other's sentences from Part I and work together to write the story of Cinderella in Mandarin, starting with "Once upon a time…" Your story should be at least 150 characters in length.

_____

_____

_____

_____

_____

_____

_____

_____

7.   A recipe for 西紅 **shì dàn huā tāng** (*soup*) *tomato egg drop soup*

Part I.   The following is a recipe for 西紅 **shì dàn huā tāng** *tomato egg drop soup*. The recipe is divided into three sections, and each section includes illustrations of the process.

For each section:

- Complete the sentences.
- Put the sentences in the correct order so that they form a cohesive set of instructions for making tomato egg drop soup.
- Translate the recipe into English.

The additional vocabulary items that you need for this recipe are: **tāng** *soup*, **huā** *flower*, **gǔn** *boil*, and **jiǎo** *stir*. Translations are also provided in the recipe.

a.	A. 先準備好 _____、_____ 和一個雞 **dàn**。
	B. 再加兩 **wǎn** 水。
	C. 然後，放一點 **yóu** 在 **guō** 裏，**yóu** 熱了以後，把 _____ 一起放 _____ **fān** 炒一下。
	D. **Shǒu** 先，把西紅 **shì** **qiē** _____，把 **cōng** **qiē** _____。
Order:	
English translation:	

b.	A. 最後放一點 **yán**，試試 **wèi** 道。
	B. 把 **dòufu qiē** _____，等水 **gǔn** (*boil*) 了以後，
	放 _____。
	C. 水 **gǔn** (*boil*) 了，再把 **dàn** _____。一邊放，一邊
	用筷子 **jiǎo** (*stir*) 一下。
	D. **Dòufu** 放進去以後，把雞 **dàn** 打開，放 _____，
	用筷子 _____。
Order:	
English translation:	
c.	A. 因為 **dàn** 打在 **tāng** 裏看起來跟 **huā** (*flower*) 差不多，
	B. 一兩分鐘以後，西紅 **shì dàn huā tāng** _____。
	C. 所以叫 **dàn huā tāng**。
Order:	
English translation:	

Part II.   Imagine you are teaching a novice in the kitchen how to make tomato egg drop soup. Using the descriptions above, follow the style of the Lesson 27 Narrative in the Textbook and write a paragraph. Make it clear and encouraging for this person that you are teaching. You can throw in some tips along the way.

_____

_____

_____

_____

_____

_____

8.   A recipe

Think about your favorite simple dish (a pasta dish, pizza, sandwiches, dessert, etc.). Follow the steps in Exercise 7 and write the recipe below. Use the supplementary vocabulary in this Lesson or consult a dictionary for words you don't know. Work with your classmates to type all of your recipes in Chinese (using Pinyin for characters we have not learned) and prepare a cookbook of simple Western dishes in Chinese.

_____

_____

_____

_____

_____

_____

_____

_____

_____

_____

_____

9.   How-to: Describing a process in Chinese

Write step-by-step instructions explaining how to do one of the processes on the following list, or select your own topic to write about.

Step I: Pick a topic.

Sample processes:

- How to compare and shop for the cheapest airfare online.
- How to prepare for a job interview.
- How to prepare for a big annual sale of your favorite produce or store. (For example, what you can do ahead of time to get ready for the sale.)
- How to lose weight in a healthy way (both dieting and exercise tips).
- How to be a good host/hostess at a party.
- How to choose the right major for you.
- How to comfort a friend who just had an accident/lost something/broke up with someone/got fired, etc.
- Your topic: _____

Step II.   Brainstorm your idea in English.

1. _____

2. _____

3. _____

4. _____

Things to avoid: _____

Things to pay special attention to: _____

_____

Other tips: _____

Step III.   Use the above ideas to write step-by-step instructions in Chinese. In your instructions, use the expressions **shǒu** 先、然後、再、一邊…一邊…、**zhù** 意、別…、把…, and 最後.

_____

_____

_____

_____

_____

_____

_____

_____

_____

_____

_____

Lesson 28 Workbook

 Listening and speaking

(audio online)

Structure drills

1. Chèn X 的時候 *taking advantage of a time when X*, Part I
(Use and Structure note 28.3)

You will hear a statement saying what someone is doing, followed by a location phrase. Say that the person is taking advantage of the time when he is at that location to do the action, as in the example.

Example:
You will hear: 小葉學做中國菜，在北京
You will say: 小葉 **chèn** 在北京的時候學做中國菜。
Click "R" to hear the correct response: 小葉 **chèn** 在北京的時候學做中國菜。

(a)   (b)   (c)   (d)   (e)   (f)   (g)   (h)

2. Chèn X 時候 *taking advantage of a time when X*, Part II
(Use and Structure note 28.3)

You will hear a statement saying what someone is doing, followed by a statement saying that someone else is doing a different action. Say that the second person is taking advantage of the time the first person does some action to do a different action, as in the example.

Example:
You will hear: 他寫 **xìn**，我去打電話。
You will say: **Chèn** 他寫 **xìn** 的時候，我去打電話。
Click "R" to hear the correct response: **Chèn** 他寫 **xìn** 的時候，我去打電話。

(a)   (b)   (c)   (d)   (e)   (f)   (g)   (h)

3.   Not as good as (Use and Structure note 28.5)

You will hear a statement saying that some situation is better than another in some way. Summarize the information using 不如 to say that one situation is not as good as the other, as in the example.

Example:
You will hear: 學中文比學日文有用。
You will say: 我覺得學日文不如學中文。
Click "R" to hear the correct response: 我覺得學日文不如學中文。

(a)   (b)   (c)   (d)   (e)   (f)   (g)   (h)

4.   It can't get any better than this (Use and Structure note 28.6)

You will hear a statement describing the quality of person or thing. Say that the person or thing has as much of that quality as is possible, as in the example.

Example:
You will hear: 非常便宜的書
You will say: 這本書再便宜不過了。
Click "R" to hear the correct response: 這本書再便宜不過了。

(a)   (b)   (c)   (d)   (e)   (f)   (g)   (h)   (i)   (j)

5.   Done for this reason (Use and Structure note 28.9)

You will hear a statement saying that someone has done some action for some reason. Use the structure 為了 NP 而 VP to say that the action was done for that reason, as in the example.

Example:
You will hear: 因為我想去中國，所以我在學中文。
You will say: 我為了去中國而學中文。
Click "R" to hear the correct response: 我為了去中國而學中文。

(a)   (b)   (c)   (d)   (e)   (f)   (g)   (h)

Listening for information

1.   Beijing one-day tour

Miss Huang at Shanghao Travel Agency is describing the itinerary and fee for a one-day (CD2: 34) tour in Beijing. Listen to her description and provide the information in English for the following form.

Beijing One-Day Tour		
Tour time schedule	Start time: _____ End Time: _____	
Scenic spots visited		places
	morning	_____
	afternoon	_____
Meals included:	_____	

Fee per person:
    individual
    groups of five or more
	_____
	
	_____	

2.   Math questions

(CD2: 35)   You will hear three math word problems. Answer each question in English.

a.

b.

c.

3.   Studying Chinese

(CD2: 36)   This is the first meeting of Teacher Ye's Chinese class. Several students explain why they are studying Chinese. Listen to each student's statement and fill in the reason in English for each student.

student	reason
#1	
#2	
#3	
#4	

4. Change of plans

Mr. Zhao, a travel agent, has left a message for you. Listen to the message and write an (CD2: 37) instant message to him in Mandarin, answering his questions.

Instant message to Mr. Zhao:

5. Ma Rong's trip

Ma Rong is talking about his summer trip. Based on his narration, indicate whether the (CD2: 38) following statements are true (T) or false (F).

a. (   ) Ma Rong traveled in three countries.

b. (   ) Ma Rong saved a lot of money because of the help from the travel agency.

c. (   ) Ma Rong is fluent in French, so it is easy for him to travel in France.

d. (   ) The trip lasted three weeks.

e. (   ) They found Italy to be the most fun country, so they stayed there the longest time.

6. On the airplane

You will hear an announcement from a flight attendant on a flight to Guangzhou. Answer (CD2: 39–40) the questions that follow in Mandarin, based on the announcement.

a.

b.

c.

d.

e.

f.

7.   Check-in at a hotel

(CD2: 41–42) Yang Tianren is checking in at a hotel. Listen to the dialogue between him and the hotel receptionist. Then, answer the questions that follow in Mandarin based on their conversation.

a.

b.

c.

d.

e.

8.   A conversation

(CD2: 43) You are studying in China. Your Chinese roommate wants to know about traveling in the USA. Answer her questions in Mandarin based on your own experience. Use characters where we have learned them.

a.

b.

c.

d.

e.

f.

9.   Listen and write

(CD2: 44–45) You will hear an announcement from Mr. Wang, a tourist guide. Listen to what he is telling his group and answer the questions that follow in Mandarin, based on his announcement.

a.

b.

c.

d.

e.

f.

10.   Dialogue

Miss Chen is calling the front desk from her hotel room. Listen to the dialogue between her **(CD2: 46)** and the hotel clerk. Choose appropriate answers, based on the dialogue.

a. What is the problem with Miss Chen's room?
   1) There is no internet connection.
   2) The TV is broken.
   3) The bathroom is dirty.
   4) The room is too small.

b. What was the hotel clerk's first response to Miss Chen's request?
   1) He will send someone to check the room.
   2) He will find another single room for her.
   3) He will find a bigger room for her.
   4) He will give her free internet connection.

c. What will Miss Chen do after the conversation with the clerk?
   1) go to another hotel
   2) pay less for the room
   3) get one night free for the room
   4) move to a bigger room

Reading and writing

Focus on Chinese characters

1.   Number of strokes

Indicate the number of strokes used in writing each of the following characters.

   a. 唱 _____   f. 復 _____

   b. 街 _____   g. 飛 _____

   c. 影 _____   h. 址 _____

   d. 單 _____   i. 歌 _____

   e. 遊 _____   j. 故 _____

2. Which character?

Circle the character in each line that corresponds to the meaning on the left.

a. **gē** *song*   歌   哥

b. **gù** (**gùshi** *story*)   古   故

c. **jì** (**jīngjì** *economics*)   濟   齊

d. **jià** (**jiàqian** *price*)   價   賣

e. **jiē** *street*   行   街

f. **lā** (**kǎlā OK** *karaoke*)   立   拉

g. **piào** *ticket*   漂   票

h. **dān** (**jiǎndān** *simple*)   單   草

i. **jì** (**jìhuà** *plan*)   討   計

j. **yóu** (**lǚyóu** *travel*)   遊   游

k. **yè** (**shāngyè** *business*)   並   業

l. **shì** (**diànshì** *television*) 視   規

3. First strokes

Write the first two strokes of each of the following characters.

a. 帶 ____   f. 址 ____

b. 飛 ____   g. 單 ____

c. 卡 ____   h. 歌 ____

d. 影 ____   i. 餐 ____

e. 劃 ____   j. 故 ____

4. Missing strokes

Complete each character by writing in the missing strokes.

a.   癶   **cān** (**zǎocān** *breakfast*)

b.   亻   **jià** (**jiàqian** *price*)

c.   方   **yóu** (**lǚyóu** *travel*)

d.   西   **piào** *ticket*

e.　礻　**shì** (**diànshì** *television*)

f.　業　**yè** (**shāngyè** *business*)

g.　彳　**fù** (**fùxí** *review*)

h.　阝　**jì** (**guójì** *international*)

i.　宀　**shí** (**shíjìshàng** *actually, in reality*)

j.　彳　**jiē** *street*

5.　Total strokes

Rewrite this list of characters, arranging the characters in terms of their total number of strokes. Begin your list with the character with the fewest strokes.

拉	票	際	影	實	帶	視	價	址	遊	劃	街	濟	故	單	計	復	卡	餐	唱

6.　Radicals

Here is a list of characters that we have learned through this lesson. Rewrite each character in the row next to its radical.

午　客　濟　地　認　千　流　寒　別　客　識
劃　活　坐　實　到　歌　訴　容　歡　壞　計

氵	
欠	
十	
言	
宀	
土	
刂	

7.   Character sleuth: Look for the phonetic

Group the characters below in terms of their rhymes or near-rhymes. Write the characters that rhyme with each other in the column on the right. Write the "phonetic," the shared part of each character, in the column on the left. There are at least eleven sets of characters that rhyme or partially rhyme and share a phonetic component among these characters.

工　相　筷　買　少　漂　功　快
機　炒　著　請　歌　懂　種　哥
者　賣　重　紅　幾　票　想　情

phonetic	characters that rhyme or almost rhyme and share a phonetic component

8.   Scrambled sentences

Rewrite these phrases as sentences, putting the words in the correct order to match the English translations.

a. 中國 / 中文 / 為 / 來 / 他 / 學 / 而 / 到 / 是 / 了 / 的

It was in order to study Chinese that he came to China.

b. 好做 / 好吃 / 不 / 可是 / 我 / 中國 / 認為 / 飯

I figure Chinese food is delicious but not easy to cook.

c. 手機 / 好用 / 上網 / 太 / 個 / 可以 / 但是 / 這 / 不

This cell phone can access the internet but it is not easy to use.

d. 你 / 買 / 為 / 酒 / 的 / 些 / 是 / 這

This alcohol was bought for you.

9. Dictionary skills

Following the instructions in Lesson 17 of the Textbook, look up these characters in a Chinese dictionary and provide the requested information.

a. 信
   pronunciation:
   meaning:
   one two-character word or phrase in which it occurs:

b. 交
   pronunciation:
   meaning:
   one two-character word or phrase in which it occurs:

c. 剩
   pronunciation:
   meaning:
   one two-character word or phrase in which it occurs:

10. Find the incorrect characters

Zhang Dawei has written an email home explaining how people buy tickets in China, but he has written ten characters incorrectly. Read the passage aloud, circle the mistakes, and correct them on the answer sheet below. Then, translate the passage into English.

> 在美國賣飛機漂，如果你買來回票，飛幾票的家錢會更宜一些。可是實濟上在中國不是這樣，所以有的人到一個地房去旅行，去的時後坐飛機，會來的時候坐火車。火車票北飛機票好買。

a. ____   b. ____   c. ____   d. ____   e. ____

f. ____   g. ____   h. ____   i. ____   j. ____

English:

11. Reading for the main ideas

The following paragraph contains a few characters that we have not yet learned, but you should be able to "read around them" and understand the main points of the passage. Read the paragraph for the main ideas and answer the questions that follow in English.

> 很多青年人喜歡跟朋友一起去酒吧。在那裏他們可以聊天、看球賽或認識新的朋友。可是旅館為甚麼要有酒吧呢？住旅館的人，家一定不在附近。如果你的家不在附近，可能在旅館的附近你也沒有朋友。那麼，你跟誰一起喝酒呢？如果你想在酒吧認識一些新的朋友，可是因為你的家不在附近，所以你馬上又要離開這個地方。你要離開這個地方，為甚麼還要在這兒認識新朋友呢？我不知道甚麼樣的人會去旅館的酒吧喝酒。

a. What is the main topic of this paragraph?

b. Which two groups of people does the author compare in this paragraph?

c. What is the paradox (the contradiction) that the author presents in this paragraph?

12. Add the punctuation

Add punctuation to the following paragraph, and then translate it into English. You should add a total of six commas, three periods, and one question mark to the passage.

書店是賣書的商店但是酒店不是賣酒的商店有的旅館的名字叫酒店有的飯館的名字也叫酒店旅館一定可以睡覺而且常常有飯館和酒吧而飯館一定不能睡覺有的賣酒有的不賣你可以告訴我酒店真正的意思是甚麼嗎

English:

Focus on structure

1. Good to do (Use and Structure note 28.1)

Answer each of the following questions in complete Mandarin sentences, using the structure 好 + ActV and the verb provided in parentheses. Then, translate your responses into English.

a. 你的同屋唱歌唱得怎麼樣？ （聽）
   A:

   English:

b. 你覺得這個手機怎麼樣？ （用）
   A:

   English:

c. "學生 **zhī** 友" 卡拉 **OK** 在哪兒？你知道嗎？（找）

A:

English:

d. 小王的女朋友怎麼樣？（看）

A:

English:

e. 學校旁邊的餐廳的菜怎麼樣？（吃）

A:

English:

2.   Take advantage (Use and Structure note 28.3)

Here is a list of places that Xiao Zhang's cousin hopes to visit while she is in Asia, along with something she hopes to do in each place. Write a sentence in Mandarin for each situation, saying that she wants to *take advantage of the time that she is in that place* to do each thing.

a. travel in Shanghai: see the Bund

b. see her older brother in Beijing: eat famous Beijing Roast Duck

c. in Japan: eat Japanese food

d. in Sichuan: eat spicy food

e. in Beijing: climb the Great Wall

f. visit friends in Taiwan: drink tea

3.   Do the math! Fractions and percentages (Use and Structure note 28.4)

Rewrite a.–d. as numerical fractions, as in the example.

Example:

三分 **zhī** 二   →   2/3

a. 七分 **zhī** 五   →

b. 十分 **zhī** 一   →

c. 十五分 **zhī** 八   →

d. 六分 **zhī** 五   →

Rewrite e.–h. in Mandarin, as in the example.

Example:

2/3   →   三分 **zhī** 二

e. 9/10   →

f. 8/9   →

g. 1/4   →

h. 1/20   →

Rewrite i.–l. as numerical percentages %.

i. 百分 **zhī** 二   →

j. 百分 **zhī** 一   →

k. 百分 **zhī** 二十五   →

l. 百分 **zhī** 四十   →

4. Not as good (Use and Structure note 28.5)

Answer each question with 不如, saying that the first choice is not as good as the second, and then translate your answers into English.

a. 你覺得藍色的 **kù** 子和 **hēi** 色的 **kù** 子一樣嗎?
   A:

   English:

b. 在中國學中文和在美國學中文一樣嗎?
   A:

   English:

c. 中國電影和美國電影一樣嗎?
   A:

   English:

d. 你覺得 **duànliàn** 身體，**pǎo bù** 和打球一樣嗎?
   A:

   English:

e. 坐汽車去學校和自己開車去學校一樣嗎?
   A:

   English:

5.   Focus on the purpose or beneficiary (Use and Structure note 28.9)

Translate the following sentences into English.

a. 你應該為了你的 **jiāng** 來而用功學習。

b. 他為了 **duànliàn** 身體而 **cān** 加 **jiàn** 身房，可是 **cān** 加了以後，只去過兩、三次。

c. 為了你的身體好，做飯的時候少放一點 **yán** 吧。

d. 為了去中國旅遊，我現在在圖書館工作 **zhèng** 錢。

e. 為了上一個好大學，很多中學生週末去上課，準備考試。

6.   Scrambled sentences

Rewrite these phrases into sentences, putting them in the right order to match the English translations.

a. 朋友 / 我 / 中國 / 個 / 要 / 一 / **chèn** / 機會 / 認識/ 些 / 這 / 多

   I want to take advantage of this opportunity to make a few more Chinese friends.

b. 功課 / 做完 / 要 / 你 / 嗎 / 明天 / 的 / **jiāo** / 了

   Have you finished doing the homework that we have to hand in tomorrow?

c. 吃 / 沒 / 想 / **kǎoyā** / 有 / 早餐 / 我 / 人

   I think no one eats roast duck for breakfast.

d. 時間 / 又 / 錢 / 地鐵 / **shěng** / **shěng** / 坐 / **jì**

   Taking the subway saves both time and money.

e. 坐 / **miǎnfèi** / 北京 / 公共/ 在 / 老人 / 汽車

   In Beijing old people ride the bus for free.

7. Translation into English

Translate these sentences into English.

a. 這種手機最近很流行，百分 **zhī** 八十的學生都有。

b. 今年的工作很好找。百分 **zhī** 六十五的 **bì** 業生在 **bì** 業以前就找到了工作。

c. 有這樣一個難得的好朋友帶你在中國旅行是一個非常難得的機會。

d. 很多人喜歡運動只是喜歡看比 **sài**。

   我認為看比 **sài** 不如 **cān** 加比 **sài**。

   Cān 加比 **sài** 可以 **duànliàn** 身體。

e. 友文 **chèn** 在中國學習的時候學會了幾個地道的中國菜。

f. 我們學的中文是 **biāo** 準的中文。你的說法不 **biāo** 準。

8. Translate into Mandarin

Translate these sentences into Mandarin, using characters where we have learned them.

a. Xiao Xie wants to use the time during spring break to prepare (for) a very big exam.

b. Teacher, I didn't understand what you said. Please go over it again.

c. Because you don't have credit, (so) the bank didn't give you a credit card.

d. Economic conditions in the USA this year are very good.

e. When I am traveling, I am not interested in famous sites and historic places.

f. If the room rate in that hotel does not include breakfast, and the internet is not free, please do not make a reservation in (reserve) that hotel.

g. Nowadays a lot of college students recognize that studying Japanese is not as good as studying Chinese.

h. Some tourist sites sound really good but actually aren't that good.

Focus on communication

1.   Dialogue comprehension

Study the Lesson 28 Narrative and Dialogue. Then, read the following statements and indicate whether they are true (T) or false (F).

a.   (   ) 大為和他 **biǎo** 妹這幾天都在北京。

b.   (   ) 大為和他 **biǎo** 妹新的、舊的旅遊 **jǐng** 點都去了。

c.   (   ) 大為去 **Xiù** 水街 **guàng** 得很高興。

d.   (   ) 大為的 **biǎo** 妹常常來中國看他。

e.   (   ) 大為打算開車帶著 **biǎo** 妹去上海看看。

f.   (   ) 大為給旅行社打電話的那天是星期六。

g.   (   ) 他打算去上海玩五天。

h.   (   ) 大為想 **dìng jiāotōng** 方便而且比較便宜的酒店。

i.   (   ) 打八五折的機票就是 **jiǎn** 價八塊五。

j.   (   ) 從北京到上海坐飛機要坐一天。

k.   (   ) 星期五沒有打折的機票，所以坐火車比飛機好。

l.   (   ) 坐火車回北京 **jì** 便宜又可以 **shěng** 旅館錢。

m.   (   ) 大為想知道有沒有比坐火車 **gèng** 好的方法。

n.   (   ) 大為和 **biǎo** 妹會在上海睡三個晚上。

o.   (   ) 旅行社 **dìng** 的酒店離甚麼都很近，還可以 **miǎn fèi** 上網。可是早餐得出去吃。

p.   (   ) 大為要 **fù** 現金，因為旅行社不讓他用 **xìn** 用卡。

2.   What do you say?

What do you say in each of the following situations? Type your answers, using characters where we have learned them, and email them to your Chinese teacher.

a.   You call the travel agent and ask him to book a round-trip plane ticket to Shanghai.

b.   You call the travel agent to inquire about the cheapest round-trip plane ticket to China.

c.   As a travel agent, ask your client if she can leave on Thursday instead of Friday because flight tickets are much more expensive on weekends.

d.   As a travel agent, convince your client to book a double room, rather than reserving two single rooms, because it saves a lot of money.

e.   Apologize to your client that you don't take credit cards. It's cash only.

f.   As a clerk at the lost and found counter, ask the customer to briefly describe his lost cell phone.

g.   Tell your travel agent the ideal hotel you would like to book (including room type, location and price).

h.   Ask for the address of the travel agency so that you can pick up the tickets tomorrow afternoon yourself.

i.   Explain to your out-of-town guests that they have to go to _____ (a place of your choice) because their visit is a rare (hard to obtain) event.

j.   Tell the salesperson that if she can give you 50% off, nothing would be better than that.

k.   You complain that from yesterday until now, you've only completed one-third of your homework. There are still two-thirds unfinished.

l.   Persuade your friend to go to the party with you by telling him that he should grab this opportunity to meet more girls.

m. Ask your Chinese friend what's the most trendy and famous restaurant in Beijing.

n.   Warn your friend not to drag you to karaoke because you sing worse than anyone.

o.   Discuss with your friend the pros and cons of purchasing a soft-sleeper train ticket.

p.   Ask the person on the other end of the phone to repeat what he just said because you didn't hear it clearly a moment ago.

3.   Complete the mini-dialogues

Use the structure in parentheses to complete each mini-dialogue.

a. A: 這個週末很多商店打折，有的店打三折、有的打五折。

   B: 真的嗎？那 _____。（**chèn**…機會）

b. A: 你那麼會做菜，做幾個好菜請我吃吧！

   B: _____。（A 不如 B）

c. A: 這個旅館怎麼樣：離車站十分鐘，單人間，可是加床不要錢。

   B: 聽起來很好，如果 _____。（再好不過了）

d. A: 這麼大的 pizza 你一個人吃得完嗎？

   B: 當然吃不完。_____。（X分 **zhī** Y）

e. A: 你不是不喜歡運動嗎？怎麼開始上 **jiàn** 身房了呢？

   B: _____。（為了…而）

f. A: 我女朋友的父母請我去她家吃飯，你覺得我應該帶甚麼好呢？

   B: _____（最好）

g. A: 每次我帶朋友回來我爸爸就不高興。他說我們的 **shēng** 音太大了。

   B: 很 **jiǎn** 單。你就_____（**chèn**…的時候）

4.   Multiple choice

Using the context as your guide, choose the correct expression to complete each sentence, and then translate the sentences into English.

a. 星期一的機票比週末的便宜得多，如果 _____ 就再好不過了。
   1) 坐火車比坐飛機便宜
   2) 你能星期一走
   3) 星期六下午有機票

   English:

b. 你難得 _____，一定要 **chèn** 這個機會去 **fù** 近的旅遊 **jǐng** 點。
   1) 來一次加 **zhǒu**
   2) 給我打電話
   3) 喜歡旅遊

   English:

c. 這個房間一個晚上三百二十塊，房間裏有兩張單人床，另外，＿＿＿＿＿＿＿。

   1) 打電話和上網都 **miǎn fèi**

   2) 請幫我 **dìng** 兩間旅館

   3) 一共 **dāi** 幾天？

English:

5. For rent

Below are two rental advertisements. Fill in the blanks with the words given, according to the context. Each word may be used more than once.

fù 近	張	又	另外
jiāotōng	離	**hán**	左右

Advertisement #1:

單人房出 **zū**。一個月四百五十塊。＿＿＿＿＿＿學校很近，走路五分鐘。就在地鐵站旁邊，＿＿＿＿＿＿ 方便。＿＿＿＿＿＿ 有商店、書店和電影院。房間裏 **miān** 有 **zhuō** 子、椅子和 一 ＿＿＿＿＿＿ 單人床，**kuān** 帶 **miǎn fèi**，不 ＿＿＿＿＿＿ 水电 (*water and electricity: utility*)，跟同屋一起用一間廁所。

Advertisement #2:

房間出 **zū**。一個月五百六十塊。房間 ＿＿＿＿＿＿大又乾淨。裏 **miān** 有雙人床，電視、書 **jià** 和 **guì** 子。＿＿＿＿＿＿，還有自己的廁所。＿＿＿＿＿＿ 水电，**kuān** 帶 **miǎn fèi**。到學校開車十五分鐘 ＿＿＿＿＿＿，＿＿＿＿＿＿ 最近的地鐵站差不多十分鐘。

---

6. Reading comprehension

Read the above two rental advertisements again, and then answer the following questions in Mandarin.

a. 甚麼人會喜歡第一個房間？為甚麼？

b. 甚麼人會喜歡第二個房間？為甚麼？

c. 如果是你，你會選哪一個房間，為甚麼？

7.   Form a cohesive paragraph

Rewrite these sentences, putting them in the correct order to form a cohesive paragraph about making reservations by phone in China.

a. 他們幫你找到旅館以後，你可以問一問房間裏有沒有 **kuān** 帶上網。

b. 這樣你的旅館就 **dìng** 好了。

c. 你先告訴他們你打算住幾天，和你想住甚麼樣的房間。

d. 最後你還可以問一下住旅館的錢 **hán** 不 **hán** 早飯。

e. 在中國打電話 **dìng** 旅館很方便也很容易。

f. 你覺得都可以了以後，你再把你的 **xìn** 用卡的號碼告訴他們。

g. 如果有，**kuān** 帶是不是 **miǎn fèi**。

h. 另外你可以跟他們說你想住在城市的甚麼地方。

8.   Travel package jargon

Below are two very common expressions you will see in travel advertisements. Read the expressions, and then answer the questions below each one.

a. 機加酒兩人同行一人半價
   1) 你覺得甚麼是 "機加酒" ？

   2) "兩人同行一人半價" 是甚麼意思？

b. **Xìn** 用卡機 **chǎng miǎn fèi jiē** 送。
   1) 甚麼是 "**jiē** 送" ？

   2) **Shēn** 請這張 **xìn** 用卡有甚麼好的地方？

9. Write a travel advertisement

Write a short paragraph to promote this travel package. Your advertisement should be at least 100 characters in length.

(Vocabulary note: **Xiānggǎng** *Hong Kong*)

---

3 days/2 nights

HONG KONG Holiday Package

From March 01–31, [this year]

Book 2 weeks in advance to get US$10 discount!

US$280 per person

Package includes:

Round-trip air ticket via Hong Kong Express

Round-trip airport–hotel pickup

2 nights hotel accommodation at *Mountain View* or *Riverside Hotel*

Daily breakfast, free internet

Half-day city tour

AA STAR TRAVEL (681-2375/ Reserv_AAstar@yahoo.com)

_____

_____

_____

_____

_____

_____

10. Reading

Read the following paragraph, and then answer the questions.

坐火車、飛機和汽車哪個最方便？

春節到了，每個人都想回家跟家人過年。到 **dǐ** 坐火車、飛機和汽車哪個最 **héshì**？別以為坐飛機一定是最貴的。我為大家看了一下今年的情 **kuàng**：比方說你在西 **ān** 工作，要回上海過年。從西 **ān** 到上海的飛機票，除 **xī** 夜那天下午打三折，只要三百八十元，時間不到兩個鍾頭。而西 **ān** 到上海的火車票，**yìngwò** 兩百九十，**ruǎnwò** 四百元，要花二十個鍾頭。汽車票價是三百五十元，要坐十七個鍾頭左右。所以，大家在買票以前，上網或者是給旅行社打電話，選一個 **jì shěng** 錢又方便的方法回家過年。

a. 你覺得，誰會 **yuàn** 意坐火車回上海？

b. 如果是你，你會選哪個？飛機、火車還是汽車？為甚麼？

11. Planning your spring break

You and your friends are going on a four-day trip to _____ (a destination of your choice) during spring break. Work in pairs to do a little research online about the expense (flight/train/rental car/lodging). Follow the style of Exercise 10 and write a paragraph to compare these choices.

Part I. Planning   In the following table, note your travel plans in English.

Destination: _____

Choice of transportation: (at least two options)

	option one	option two	(option three)
cost			
time			
pros			
cons			

Choice of lodging: (at least two options)

	option one	option two	(option three)
cost			
location			
pros			
cons			

Part II.   Write a paragraph in Mandarin comparing these choices and explaining your final choices of transportation and lodging. Your paragraph should be at least 120 characters in length.

_____

_____

_____

_____

_____

_____

_____

Lesson 29 Workbook

 Listening and speaking

Structure drills

(audio online)

1. To each his own (Use and Structure note 29.1)

You will hear a statement saying that two people will do similar actions. Rephrase the information, saying that *each will do her own thing,* as in the example.

Example:
You will hear: 你回你的宿舍，我回我的宿舍。
You will say: 我們 **gè** 回 **gè** 的宿舍。
Click "R" to hear the correct response: 我們 **gè** 回 **gè** 的宿舍。

(a)   (b)   (c)   (d)   (e)   (f)   (g)   (h)

2. Every which way (Use and Structure note 29.2)

You will hear a statement saying that someone has done some action but has not reached the result that they wanted. Rephrase the information, saying that the person has done the action *every which way* and has not reached the desired result, as in the example.

Example:
You will hear: 我沒找到我的手機。
You will say: 我找來找去，還是沒找到我的手機。
Click "R" to hear the correct response: 我找來找去，還是沒找到我的手機。

(a)   (b)   (c)   (d)   (e)   (f)   (g)   (h)

3.   Not unless (Use and Structure note 29.4)

You will hear a statement saying that if you don't do something, something else will not happen. Restate the information, saying that *unless* you do something, something else will not happen, as in the example.

Example:

You will hear: 如果你不幫助我，我不能寫完讀書報告。

You will say: 除非你幫助我，要不然我寫不完讀書報告。

Click "R" to hear the correct response: 除非你幫助我，要不然我寫不完讀書報告。

(a)   (b)   (c)   (d)   (e)   (f)   (g)   (h)   (i)   (j)

4.   More and more, Part I (Use and Structure note 29.7)

You will hear a statement saying that an action is happening *more and more* in a certain way. Restate the information, saying that *the more* something happens, *the more* of some quality it has, as in the example.

Example:

You will hear: 雨下得越來越大。

You will say: 雨越下越大。

Click "R" to hear the correct response: 雨越下越大。

(a)   (b)   (c)   (d)   (e)   (f)   (g)   (h)

5.   More and more, Part II (Use and Structure note 29.7)

You will hear a statement about doing something with some object. Restate the information, saying that *as for that object, the more* you do it *the more* some quality results, as in the example.

Example:

You will hear: 我 **ài** 吃 **là** 的菜。

You will say: **Là** 的菜，我越吃越 **ài** 吃。

Click "R" to hear the correct response: **Là** 的菜，我越吃越 **ài** 吃。

(a)   (b)   (c)   (d)   (e)   (f)

6.   More and more, Part III (Use and Structure note 29.7)

You will hear a statement about two situations. Restate the information, saying that *the more* the first action happens, *the more* true the second situation is, as in the example.

Example:

You will hear: 老師 **jiǎng yǔ** 法，我不懂。

You will say: 老師越 **jiǎng yǔ** 法，我越不懂。

Click "R" to hear the correct response: 老師越 **jiǎng yǔ** 法，我越不懂。

(a)   (b)   (c)   (d)   (e)   (f)   (g)   (h)

7.   Whatever you do (Use and Structure note 29.8)

You will hear a question asking what you are going to do. Reply that you will do whatever the other person does, as in the example.

Example:
You will hear: 你選甚麼課？
You will say: 你選甚麼課，我就選甚麼課。
Click "R" to hear the correct response: 你選甚麼課，我就選甚麼課。

(a)   (b)   (c)   (d)   (e)   (f)   (g)   (h)   (i)   (j)

8.   I'll do whatever I want (Use and Structure note 29.8)

You will hear a question asking what you are going to do. Reply that you will do whatever you want, as in the example.

Example:
You will hear: 你選甚麼課？
You will say: 我想選甚麼課就選甚麼課。
Click "R" to hear the correct response: 我想選甚麼課就選甚麼課。

(a)   (b)   (c)   (d)   (e)   (f)   (g)   (h)   (i)   (j)

Listening for information

1.   What do they need?

You will hear five statements about five people's physical states. Based on the statements, choose the item that each person needs most.   **(CD2: 51)**

Items   A   B   C   D   E

a.   b.   c.   d.   e.

2.   More and more

(CD2: 52) You will hear four statements about Xiao Wang's daily life. Write down (in English) the reason and result that each statement describes.

statement	reason	result
1		
2		
3		
4		

3.   Ordering dinner

(CD2: 53) You will hear three customers ordering food and drink in a restaurant. Write their orders in English on the following form.

customer	dish	drink
1		
2		
3		

4.   Food delivery

(CD2: 54–55) Peiru is placing a telephone order at a nearby restaurant. Listen to her talking with the service person. Then, listen to the questions that follow, and answer them in Mandarin.

a.

b.

c.

d.

e.

f.

5. McDonald's in China

You will hear a radio commercial for McDonald's Restaurants (**màidāngláo**) in China. **(CD2: 56)**
Listen to the commercial and write down the main points in English.

Main points in the commercial:

6. Birthday celebration

You and Zhang Xin are planning a birthday celebration for your good friend Cai Wen. **(CD2: 57)**
Zhang Xin left a voice message for you. Listen to the message and write an email in
Mandarin responding to her questions.

Your response:

7. A conversation

Your friend from China is asking you about dining in the USA. Listen to each question and **(CD2: 58)**
answer it in Mandarin.

a.

b.

c.

d.

e.

f.

8. Study-abroad experience

(CD2: 59) Jackie is talking about her experience studying in China. Listen to her talk, and then indicate whether each of the following statements is true (T) or false (F). We have not learned the word she uses for 'study abroad' but you should be able to identify it within the context of her talk.

a. (   ) Jackie thinks it is best to live in a university dormitory.

b. (   ) Jackie recommended the Chinese Program in Yunnan to everyone.

c. (   ) Jackie learned a lot about the daily life of Chinese people during her study abroad.

d. (   ) Jackie's Chinese improved by talking with her Chinese roommate.

 9. Travel plans

(CD2: 60) He Xiang is telling her friends about her trip. Answer the following questions, based on her description.

a. How did they arrange the trip?
  1) with a travel agency
  2) by themselves
  3) via the college student center
  4) through a traveler's hotline

b. Which fact about Hainan is true?
  1) Hainan is larger than Taiwan.
  2) The weather there is always warm.
  3) The mountain area on the island is cool.
  4) Not many tourists are on the island.

c. Which of the following facts about their trip is true, based on He Xiang's description?
  1) They spent more than four hours on the plane to Hainan.
  2) They stayed in Hainan for a week.
  3) They ate special local food every day.
  4) They enjoyed all kinds of fruit.

 10. Dialogue

(CD2: 61) Mr. and Mrs. Wang are talking about their Friday dinner plans. Answer the following questions, based on their conversation.

a. What fact correctly describes Mr. Wang's reservation?
  1) He reserved a table for twelve people.
  2) He ordered a meal of ten dishes.
  3) He reserved a private room.
  4) He made the reservation at a Cantonese restaurant.

b. What did Mr. and Mrs. Wang say about Mr. and Mrs. Zhang?
   1) They may not come for dinner.
   2) They will come later due to another event.
   3) They do not eat meat or fish.
   4) They like that restaurant very much.

c. What food or drink will they likely order?
   1) roast duck
   2) a pork dish
   3) beer
   4) soft drinks

Reading and writing

Focus on Chinese characters

1. Number of strokes

Indicate the number of strokes used in writing each of the following characters.

a. 報 _____   f. 健 _____

b. 肚 _____   g. 迎 _____

c. 忘 _____   h. 費 _____

d. 預 _____   i. 像 _____

e. 換 _____   j. 緊 _____

2. Which character?

Circle the character in each line that corresponds to the meaning on the left.

a. **jué** (**juédìng** *decide*)   決   快

b. **qīng** *green-blue*   情   青

c. **tīng** (**cāntīng** *cafeteria*)   聽   廳

d. **gòu** *enough*   句   夠

e. **bǎo** *full*   飽   抱

f. **fù** (**fùjìn** *vicinity*)   附   府

g. **fèi** *expense, fee*   費   筫

h. **yù** (**yùdìng** *make a reservation*)   順   預

i. **wèi** *flavor, aroma*   末   味

j. **yíng** (**huānyíng** *welcome*)   迎   卯

k. **xiàng** *resemble*   像   象

l. **jiàn** (**jiàn shēn** *exercise, work out*)   建   健

3. First strokes

Write the first two strokes of each of the following characters.

a. 香 ____   f. 預 ____

b. 風 ____   g. 緊 ____

c. 瓶 ____   h. 附 ____

d. 線 ____   i. 費 ____

e. 換 ____   j. 糖 ____

4. Missing strokes

Complete each character by writing in the missing strokes.

a.   千   **xiāng** *fragrant*

b.   幺   **xiàn** *thread, line*

c.   彳   **yíng** (**huānyíng** *welcome*)

d.   口   **wèi** *flavor, aroma*

e.   亡   **wàng** *forget*

f.   广   **tīng** (**cāntīng** *cafeteria*)

g.   并   **píng** *bottle*

h.   氵   **jué** (**juédìng** *decide*)

i.   幸   **bào** *report*

j.   夕   **gòu** *enough*

5. Total strokes

Rewrite this list of characters, arranging the characters in terms of their total number of strokes. Begin your list with the character with the fewest strokes.

肚	醋	瓶	費	川	預	忘	香	決	附	像	訂	緊	換	風	報	飽	青	夠	線

6. Radicals

Here is a list of characters that we have learned through this lesson. Rewrite each character in the row next to its radical.

廁　酒　換　緊　忘　像　淨　預　決　紹　練
線　思　打　準　級　醋　廳　顏　想　濟　價

心	
西	
冫	
纟(糸)	
厂	
扌	
亻	
頁	

7. Character sleuth: Look for the phonetic

Group the characters below in terms of their rhymes or near-rhymes. Write the characters that rhyme with each other in the column on the right. Write the "phonetic," the shared part of each character, in the column on the left. There are at least twelve sets of characters that rhyme or partially rhyme and share a phonetic component among these characters.

房　飽　並　聽　想　土　請　情　旁
廳　少　重　汽　肚　種　炒　瓶　長
張　青　相　園　包　遠　懂　氣　放

phonetic	characters that rhyme or almost rhyme and share a phonetic component

8.   Scrambled sentences

Rewrite these phrases as sentences, putting the words in the correct order to match the English translations.

a. 茄子 / 覺得 / 魚 / 糖醋 / 魚香 / 不如 / 我

I think that sweet and sour fish is not as good as eggplant in yuxiang sauce.

b. 準備 / 菜 / 的 / 做 / 住 / 學 / 中國 / 中國 / 她 / 幾年 / 為了 / 地道 / 去

In order to learn how to cook authentic Chinese food, she is preparing to go and live in China for a year.

c. 為 / 菜 / 的 / 這 / 特別 / 你 / 個 / 是 / 做

This dish was made especially for you.

d. 特別 / 川菜 / 很 / 味道 / 的

The flavor of Sichuan cuisine is unique.

9.   Dictionary skills

Following the instructions in Lesson 17 of the Textbook, look up these characters in a Chinese dictionary and provide the requested information:

a. 讀
pronunciation:
meaning:
one two-character word or phrase in which it occurs:

b. 餓
   pronunciation:
   meaning:
   one two-character word or phrase in which it occurs:

c. 各
   pronunciation:
   meaning:
   one two-character word or phrase in which it occurs:

10.   Find the incorrect characters

Xiao Zhang has written an email to one of his friends from the Chinese class back in the USA, but he has written ten characters incorrectly. Circle his mistakes and write the correct characters in the answer sheet below. Then, translate the paragraph into English.

學交附近新開了一家四川風味的餐聽。我作天給他們的丁餐熱線打電話訂了一個糖醋魚、一個魚相茄子和一瓶可口可樂，讓他們把菜關到我的宿舍。菜很塊就送到了。味到很好，我吃得很包。飽得我都快走不動了。看來我得多去幾次建身房了。

a. ____   b. ____   c. ____   d. ____   e. ____

f. ____   g. ____   h. ____   i. ____   j. ____

English:

11.   Reading for the main ideas

The following paragraph contains a few characters that we have not yet learned, but you should be able to "read around them" and understand the main points of the passage. Read the paragraph for the main ideas and answer the questions that follow in English.

飲食和文化

有的人認為從吃的東西的樣子上，就能看出來中國文化和美國文化很不相同。中國人都喜歡吃餃子。從外邊看，看不出來餃子裏邊有甚麼，可能是雞肉的，也可能是牛肉的。可能是茄子的，也可能是西紅柿的。這些東西都包在餃子裏邊了。只有吃的時候才能知道。而美國的"三明治"和"漢堡包"呢，是肉的還是魚的，有沒有西紅柿，從外邊可以看得清清楚楚。有的人說中國的文化和美國的文化也是這樣。中國人做一件事情，你從外邊看不出來為甚麼，而美國人做一件事情你就可以看出來。你覺得這種說法對嗎？

---

a. What is the author comparing in this paragraph?

b. 三明治 and 漢堡包 are foods commonly eaten in the USA. Based on the pronunciation of the characters that you know in each food name, and *without* looking up the words online or in a dictionary or asking your teacher, identify each of these foods.

c. What is the author's theory about the difference between the things that he is comparing? Do you agree? Why or why not?

Focus on structure

1.   Unless you do this (Use and Structure note 29.4)

Meili and Youwen are talking about a trip that Meili is planning to Sichuan. Youwen is giving Meili advice. Translate a.–c. into English, and d.–e. into Mandarin.

a. 除非你早一點訂票，要不然你可能買不到 **ruǎnwò** 票。

b. 除非你訂商業區的飯店，要不然 **jiāotōng** 不會方便。

c. 四川很多地方不用 **xìn** 用卡。除非你帶現金，要不然你買不了東西。

d. I have heard that hotels have broadband internet connections but the rooms don't have computers. Unless you bring your own computer you won't be able to use the internet.

e. Unless you are used to hearing Sichuan people speak, you may not understand what they say.

2. The more you do it (Use and Structure note 29.7)

Guoqiang is asking Dawei about a number of things. Translate Dawei's responses into Mandarin.

a. Q: 你覺得川菜怎麼樣？

   A: _____

   (I think it's really spicy. But it's strange. The more I eat it, the more I like it.)

b. Q: 經濟課怎麼樣？

   A: _____

   (The more I study, the harder it gets.)

c. Q: 你喜歡喝茶還是喝可樂？

   A: _____

   (I prefer tea. The more cola I drink, the thirstier I get.)

d. Q: 我們今天吃餃子，好不好？

   A: _____

   (I don't want to eat dumplings again. The more I eat them, the fatter I get.)

3. As you please, Part I (Use and Structure note 29.8)

Translate a.–d. to English, and translate e.–h. into Mandarin, using the pattern <u>QW</u> 就 <u>QW</u>.

a. 哪個旅行 **shè** 便宜我們就跟哪個旅行社訂。

b. 你把相機 **jiè** 給誰了我就去跟誰要回來。

c. 哪件事重要我們就先做哪件事。

d. 你說甚麼地方好玩我們就去甚麼地方。

e. I'll go wherever you go.

f. We'll select whatever method saves money.

g. We'll stay (live) at whatever hotel you make reservations for.

h. We'll go whenever it is convenient.

4. As you please, Part II (Use and Structure note 29.8)

Youwen and Meili are both in a good mood as they finish a day of shopping and are discussing plans for the rest of the day. Write the responses to each of these suggestions in complete Mandarin sentences, using the pattern <u>QW 就 QW</u>, and using the question word in parentheses after each suggestion.

a. 這雙鞋很不 **cuò**。你看，我買不買？（甚麼）

b. 我們去咖啡館喝一點咖啡吧。（哪兒）

c. 我們晚上吃中國飯，行嗎？（甚麼）

d. 我們請那個新的學生跟我們一起吃飯吧。（誰）

e. 吃飯以後，我們去看那個日本電影，好不好？（哪）

5. Scrambled sentences

Rewrite these phrases in sentences, putting them in the right order to match the English translations.

a. 穿 / 應該 / **pí** 鞋 / 好的 / 要 / 一雙 / 舒服 /越 / 越

With an expensive pair of shoes, it should be that the more you wear them the more comfortable they are.

b. 四川菜 / 有 / 的 / 吃飯 / 哪兒 / 上 / 好吃 / 就 / 哪兒 / 我們

Wherever there is delicious Sichuan food, let's go there to eat. (Let's go eat wherever there is delicious Sichuan food.)

c. 看 / 特別 / 開開 / 新車 / 舒服 / 你 / 開起來

Drive it and see. New cars are very comfortable to drive.

d. 會 / 不 / 下 **yǔ** / 明天 / 一定

It won't necessarily rain tomorrow. (It may not rain tomorrow.)

e. 做 / **ài** / 吃去 / 媽媽 / 菜 / 吃 / 吃來 / 還是 / 最 / 的 / 我

I've eaten everywhere, and I think that the food that mom cooks is the best.

f. 那麼 / 不 / 一 **bān** / 少 / 中國 / 讓 / 穿得 / 父母 / **hái** 子

Chinese parents generally don't let their children wear so little.

6. Translate into English

Translate these sentences into English.

a. 青菜、水果會讓你越吃越年 **qīng**。

b. 這個照相機我越看越喜歡，如果便宜一點就再好不過了。

c. 你試試看這個手機用起來容易不容易。

d. 雖然商店都在打折，但是我看來看去也沒有看到一件喜歡的衣服。

e. 我每天 **dú** 書 **dú** 累了，就出去走一走，放 **sōng** 一下。

f. 自己做飯不一定比去外邊買麻煩。

g. 做作業可以大家在一起做，但是考試只能 **gè** 寫 **gè** 的。

h. 我為了幫他找書包，已經在車站裏外跑來跑去跑了半個鐘頭了。

7. Translate into Mandarin

Translate these sentences into Mandarin, using characters where we have learned them.

a. His story made us feel like the more we listened the sadder we were.

b. Try it and see. I think that this pen may be broken.

c. Ask and see whether she wants to go traveling with us.

d. The most expensive restaurants are not necessarily the most delicious.

e. Listen. Is that Xiao Wang's voice?

f. Let's have a little talk. Why did you decide to change majors?

g. There aren't any good restaurants in the vicinity. We've eaten all around and every time we go to that Cantonese restaurant.

h. This is the time when the roads are most crowded. Unless you take a subway, you won't be able to get to the airport in an hour.

Focus on communication

1. Dialogue comprehension

Study the Lesson 29 Narrative and Dialogue. Then, read the following statements and indicate whether they are true (T) or false (F).

a. (　) 春假 **jiéshù** 以後，大家又忙著學習。

b. (　) 學校附近的中國餐館多極了，可是國強連想都沒想就決定要吃四川菜。

c. (　) 他們沒有訂位子就去餐廳了，所以服務員要他們等三十分鐘。

d. (　) 大為又 **kě** 又 **è** 不想等，所以他們決定換一家餐廳。

e. (　) 他們先點了 **pí** 酒和可樂。

f. (　) 餐廳裏沒有 **bīng** 茶。

g. (　) 大為 **ài** 吃四川菜，可是他覺得四川菜太 **là** 了。

h. (　) 上次大為來這家飯館吃四川菜，後來吃壞肚子了。

i. (　) 他們一共點了六個菜，都是 **là** 的。

j. (　) 服務員上 **cuò** 菜，所以送了他們一個燒茄子。

k. (　) 美麗最 **ài** 吃茄子，她一高興就多給了一些小費。

l. (　) 他們把菜都吃完了，還打包了一個魚香茄子帶走。

m. (　) 你可以預先打電話給這家餐館訂餐。

2. What do you say?

What do you say in each of the following situations? Type your answers, using characters where we have learned them, and email them to your Chinese teacher.

a. Ask your mom to teach you a couple of her specialty dishes.

b. Ask the waiter to bring you a glass of water without ice. Explain to your friend that in general you do not drink iced water.

c. Invite everyone to come to your house for a karaoke party this Saturday because you want everyone to relax after the exam.

d. You just made a dish. Ask your friend to have a taste of your authentic _____ (dish of your choice).

e. You have just arrived at the restaurant. Tell the waiter your last name, and say that you have a reservation for 6:30 for a party of seven.

f. As a waiter, apologize to your customer that the restaurant is very crowded right now, and tell him that the possible wait time is an hour and a half. Ask the customer for his last name and ask him how many people are in his party.

g. You refuse to go shopping with your friend now (V 不了) because you are thirsty and hungry and tired.

h. Tell the waiter you don't drink hot tea. Ask what other drinks they have.

i. Tell your mom you'll eat whatever she has because you are starving.

j. Ask the waiter to switch the chicken cubes in *gongbao chicken* to tofu because you don't eat meat.

k. As a waiter, ask the customers if they want to take the leftover dishes home.

l. As a waiter, thank your customers for coming and invite them to come back again next time.

m. You are wondering (thought it was really strange) where you placed the beer and juice that you just bought.

3. Complete the mini-dialogues

Use the structure in parentheses to complete each mini-dialogue.

a. A: 你這麼喜歡看電影，那你說說看，哪國的電影最好看？

   B: 這很難說，＿＿＿＿＿＿＿＿＿＿＿＿＿＿＿＿＿＿＿。（**gè** 有 **gè** 的）

b. A: 你怎麼 ＿＿＿＿＿＿＿＿＿＿＿＿＿＿＿＿＿＿＿？（V 來 V 去）

   B: 因為我穿這件 **chènshān** 看起來最 **shòu**！

c. A: 真 **zāogāo**，我怎麼忘了帶錢了？

   B: ＿＿＿＿＿＿＿＿＿＿＿＿＿＿＿＿，要不然我們就回不了家了。
   （**Xìngkuī**）

d. Patient (calling): 請問，我可以跟葉 **Yī** 生 **yuē** 今天下午看 **bìng** 嗎？

   Receptionist: 對不起，今天下午人特別多，＿＿＿＿＿＿＿＿＿＿＿＿＿＿。
   （除非 … 要不然 …）

e. A: 怎麼樣，這家飯館的川味 **niú** 肉 **miàn** 做得地道吧？

   B: 真不 **cuò**，＿＿＿＿＿＿＿＿＿＿＿＿＿＿＿。（越 V 越）

f. A: 這雙鞋看起來這麼小，我怎麼可能穿得了？

   B: ＿＿＿＿＿＿＿＿＿＿＿＿＿＿＿＿＿（VV看）

g. A: 今天這麼熱，你想去哪兒？

   B: ＿＿＿＿＿＿＿＿＿＿＿＿＿＿＿＿＿（QW 就 QW）

4.   Complete and translate

Using the context as your guide, choose the correct expression to complete each sentence, and then translate the sentences into English.

a. 在商店 **diū** 了錢包 (*wallet*) 很難找回來。除非 _____，要不然大概沒有 **xīwàng**。
   1) 你找到了
   2) 你把地址和電話給服務員
   3) 你剛走出來就發現，馬上回去找

   English:

b. 這個旅行 **shè guǎng** 告的 **jǐng** 點我都沒有興趣，看來看去 _____。
   1) 我覺得我還是跟朋友自己出去旅行吧
   2) 貴極了
   3) 我甚麼地方都想去

   English:

c. 對不起，那本書已經賣完了，我們剛跟商店訂了書。這樣吧，_____
   1) 這兩本書 **miǎn** 費送給你。
   2) 給我你的電話號碼，書送來了我就給你打電話。
   3) 你為甚麼一定要買那本書？

   English:

5.   Ordering in a restaurant

Part I.   Read the following passage about Xiao Zhang's birthday celebration dinner, using the context to help you choose the correct word or phrase to complete each sentence.

　　這個週末是我的生日。小謝上星期開始就 _____（a. 用 b. **chèn** c. 拿）我不 **zhù** 意的時候，_____（a. **yuē** b. 帶 c. 訂）了小高，小葉和小王、在最近新開的四川飯館 _____（a. 點 b. 帶 c. 訂）了位子。昨天下課，他來學校 **jiē** 我，路上甚麼也沒有說，我覺得 _____（a. 累 b. 麻煩 c. **qíguài**）極了。等我 _____（a. 認為 b. 以為 c. 發現）大家都在飯館門口等我，我高興得不得了，沒想到他們這麼早就幫我 _____（a. 過 b. 吃 c. **yuē**）生日。小高說，_____（a. 只要 b. **yuàn** 意 c. 為了）給我一個 *surprise*，小謝計劃了很久呢。

　　這家飯館的拿手菜 _____（a. 可能 b. 當然 c. **kǒng** 怕）是四川菜。我最 **ài** 吃 **là** 的，所以我 _____（a. 馬上 b. 事先 c. 決定）點了 **là** 子雞 **dīng** 和 **gōngbǎo niú** 肉。小高喜歡吃青菜，她點了 **bái** 菜和魚香茄子。小謝說我們點甚麼他 _____（a. 都 b. 也 c. 就）吃甚麼，不過他一定要點青 **dǎo pí** 酒。還幫我們都點了可樂和 **bīng** 茶。小王說他不能吃 **là** 的，_____（a. 另外 b. **xìngkuī** c. 再說）這家餐廳也有不 **là** 的菜。他怕吃 **là** _____（a. 可是 b. 而且 c. 所以）最喜歡吃 **dòufu**，就要了一個燒 **dòufu**，還點了一個糖醋魚。小葉覺得這些菜已經 _____（a. 不夠 b. 很地道 c. 夠了），所以她只點了麻 **là** 餃子，因為她說 _____（a. 從來 b. 到 **dǐ** c. 的 **què**）沒吃過 **là** 餃子，想 **cháng cháng** 看。小謝點了 **mǐ** 飯，不過服務員說他們的炒飯特別有名，所以我們又把

mǐ 飯 _____（a. 換成 b. 炒成 c. 加）炒飯，還特別請他們別放 **là** 的，這樣小王就可以吃了。

等服務員 _____（a. 點菜 b. 上菜 c. 打包）的時候，我們一邊喝 **yǐnliào** 一邊 **liáo** 天。這家飯館上菜上得很快，一下子 _____（a. 除非 b. 除了 c. 並且）燒 **dòufu** 以外，別的菜都來了。_____（a. 然後 b. 後來 c. 以後）服務員發現他忘了幫我們點燒 **dòufu**，馬上說這個菜送給我們，另外，再送了一個 西紅 **shì** 炒雞 **dàn**。

這些菜 _____（a. **jì** b. 雖然 c. 而且）好吃又地道，我們都吃得飽得不得了。開學以後大家忙著學習，_____（a. 難過 b. 難得 c. 最好）有機會在一起吃飯，我覺得這是最好的生日 **lǐ wù**！

Part II.   Answer the following questions about the passage in Part I in Mandarin.

a. 為甚麼他們昨天吃飯？ 昨天到 **dǐ** 是不是小張的生日？

b. 這個生日晚會是誰計劃的？誰來 **cān** 加了？

c. 他們點的菜，哪些是 **là** 的？哪些不 **là**？

d. 為甚麼他們點了炒飯？炒飯 **là** 不 **là**？

e. 請你 **tián** 一下這個 **biǎo**:

	小張	小謝	小高	小葉	小王
喜歡吃甚麼/不能吃甚麼					
點了甚麼菜					

f. 西紅 **shì** 炒雞 **dàn** 為甚麼不算錢？

g. 小張的生日 **lǐ wù** 是甚麼？

6.   What did they say?

You are a participant at the dinner party described in Exercise 5. Write (or type) in Mandarin what each person said in the following situations.

a. Xiao Zhang was eager to find out where Xiao Xie was taking him in the car. So he kept asking Xiao Xie where exactly ("after all") they were going.

b. Xiao Xie explained why he picked this particular restaurant for Xiao Zhang.

c. Xiao Xie insisted that they order beer because Xiao Zhang was turning twenty-one!

d. Xiao Gao knows Xiao Wang does not eat spicy food. She suggested some non-spicy dishes to Xiao Wang.

e. Xiao Ye was very excited when she discovered "spicy dumplings" and decided to give them a try.

f. The waiter recommended that they order fried rice instead of white rice.

g. Xiao Wang asked the waiter about the missing simmered tofu. The waiter apologized for it and made amends immediately.

h. Xiao Xie asked the waiter to bring the bill. The waiter asked if they wanted to take the leftovers with them.

i. Xiao Zhang expressed his gratitude to everyone after dinner.

j. The waiter saw them off at the door.

7. Restaurant jargon

This exercise includes very common expressions used in Chinese restaurants. You have not learned all of them, but you should be able to figure out the meanings from the context. Read each sentence and answer the questions that follow about its meaning.

a. 這邊吃還是外帶？
  1) 你覺得"外帶"的意思是甚麼？

  2) 你覺得這句話是甚麼時候說的？
    A. 在飯館門口的時候
    B. 要點菜的時候
    C. 吃飽的時候

  3) 你覺得"外帶"和"外送"有甚麼不一樣？

b. 對不起，我們不 **jiēshòu** 訂位，也不 **shōu xìn** 用卡。
  1) 你覺得甚麼是"**jiēshòu**"？

  2) 請問去這個飯館一定得帶甚麼？

c. 你覺得"加 **miàn** 不加價"是甚麼意思？

d. 如果要把 **bái miàn** 換 **chéng** 黃 **miàn**，請先告知。
  1) 你覺得"請先告知"是甚麼意思？

  2) 這家飯館的 **miàn** 一 **bān** 都是 **bái miàn** 還是黃 **miàn**？

e. 一家紅茶店的門口 **tiē** 著一張 **guǎng** 告："買大送小"。你覺得，"大"和"小"是甚麼？

f. 你覺得"今日特餐"是甚麼意思？

8. Give me some advice

Xiao Mei always has trouble making decisions. Luckily she has good friends who are always there for her. Read the situations below involving Xiao Mei and her friends. Use the two structures that express condition: 如果…就 and 除非…要不然, to complete everyone's reply. For each situation, come up with your own suggestion at the end as well, using either of the structures.

Situation 1:

小美：我現在有兩個工作機會。一個在學校餐廳，一個在離學校半個鐘頭的書店。餐廳的工作沒有意思，但是時間很不 **cuò**。書店的工作我比較喜歡，可是離學校太遠了。怎麼 **bàn**？

青青：別去書店。除非＿＿＿＿＿＿＿＿＿＿＿＿＿＿，要不然我覺得去書店太麻煩了。

天明：我覺得書店的工作比較好。一個星期工作幾天？如果＿＿＿＿＿＿＿＿＿＿，我可以送你去。

心宜：你還是去書店吧。書店可以學到很多事。除非這個工作跟你以後的工作沒有關係，要不然 ＿＿＿＿＿＿＿＿＿＿＿＿＿＿。

Your suggestion: ＿＿＿＿＿＿＿＿＿＿＿＿＿＿＿＿＿＿＿＿＿

＿＿＿＿＿＿＿＿＿＿＿＿＿＿＿＿＿＿＿＿＿＿＿＿＿＿＿

Situation 2:

小美：快幫我決定，買這條紅色的 **qún** 子好，還是買那件 **bái** 色的 **chènshān** 好？

青青：這個紅色穿在你身上有點 **qíguài**。除非這條 **qún** 子正在打折，＿＿＿＿＿＿＿＿

＿＿＿＿＿＿＿＿＿＿＿＿＿＿＿。

天明：當然買 **bái** 色的 **chènshān**！＿＿＿＿＿＿＿＿＿＿＿＿＿，**pèi** 甚麼都好看。紅 **qún** 子也不 **cuò**，如果 ＿＿＿＿＿＿＿＿＿＿＿＿＿＿，就兩件都買吧。

心宜：你先想一想你有幾件 **bái chènshān**。＿＿＿＿＿＿＿＿＿＿＿＿＿＿＿＿，要不然我覺得你應該買紅 **qún** 子，有時候也得換個不一樣衣服的吧！

Your suggestion: ＿＿＿＿＿＿＿＿＿＿＿＿＿＿＿＿＿＿＿＿＿

＿＿＿＿＿＿＿＿＿＿＿＿＿＿＿＿＿＿＿＿＿＿＿＿＿＿＿

Lesson 30 Workbook

Listening and speaking

Structure drills

1. S 把NP₁ V 作 NP₂ *S sees/calls NP₁ NP₂* (Use and Structure note 30.5)

You will hear three noun phrases, followed by either 看作 or 叫作. Use the information to say the subject considers/calls NP₁ NP₂, as in the example.

Example:
You will hear: 中國人，漢語的標準語，**pǔ** 通話，叫作
You will say: 中國人把漢語的標準語叫作 **pǔ** 通話。
Click "R" to hear the correct response: 中國人把漢語的標準語叫作 **pǔ** 通話。

(a)　　(b)　　(c)　　(d)　　(e)　　(f)

2. Marking the verb in a noun description: 所 V 的, Part I
　　(Use and Structure note 30.6)

You will hear a statement involving a noun phrase in which the description involves a verb. Restate the information, adding 所 before the verb, as in the example. Notice that in many of these sentences, the main noun (the noun that follows the description + 的) is omitted.

Example:
You will hear: 這就是他問的問題。
You will say: 這就是他所問的問題。
Click "R" to hear the correct response: 這就是他所問的問題。

(a)　　(b)　　(c)　　(d)　　(e)　　(f)　　(g)

3. Marking the verb in a noun description: 所 V 的, Part II
(Use and Structure note 30.6)

You will hear a sentence involving a subject, verb, and object. Restate the information as a description of the object, placing 所 before the verb, as in the example. Translations are provided for the example to help you understand the structure.

Example:
You will hear: 他學方言。 *He studies dialects.*
You will say: 他所學的方言 *the dialects that he studies*
Click "R" to hear the correct response: 他所學的方言 *the dialects that he studies*

(a)   (b)   (c)   (d)   (e)   (f)   (g)   (h)   (i)   (j)

4. **Wúlùn + QW** *no matter (who, what, when, where, how, what quality)*
(Use and Structure note 30.8)

You will hear a sentence followed by a question phrase. Restate the sentence using **wúlùn** and the question phrase to say *no matter (who, what, when, where, how, what quality)*, as in the example.

Example:
You will hear: 學生都得 **cān** 加考試。（誰）
You will say: **Wúlùn** 誰都得 **cān** 加考試。
Click "R" to hear the correct response: **Wúlùn** 誰都得 **cān** 加考試。

(a)   (b)   (c)   (d)   (e)   (f)   (g)   (h)   (i)

5. **Jíshǐ** S₁ 也 VP/S₂ *even if/even though S₁, VP/S₂*
(Use and Structure note 30.10).

You will hear two actions. Restate these using **jíshǐ**… 也 to say that *even if/even though* the first action occurs, the second will not occur.

Example:
You will hear: 我知道，我不告訴你
You will say: **Jíshǐ** 我知道，我也不告訴你。
Click "R" to hear the correct response: **Jíshǐ** 我知道，我也不告訴你。

(a)   (b)   (c)   (d)   (e)   (f)   (g)   (h)   (i)   (j)

6. A 跟 B 沒有直接的關係 *There isn't a direct connection between A and B*

You will hear two phrases. Say that there isn't any direct relationship between the two phrases, as in the example.

Example:

You will hear: 書寫，發音
You will say: 書寫跟發音沒有直接的關係。
Click "R" to hear the correct response: 書寫跟發音沒有直接的關係。

(a)   (b)   (c)   (d)   (e)   (f)   (g)

7. Influencing others: 影 **xiǎng**

You will hear a statement saying that doing something influences other people or other things. Restate the sentence, saying that doing something *has an influence on* others, as in the example.

Example:

You will hear: 你大 **shēng** 說話影 **xiǎng** 別人學習。
You will say: 你大 **shēng** 說話對別人學習有影 **xiǎng**。
Click "R" to hear the correct response: 你大 **shēng** 說話對別人學習有影 **xiǎng**。

(a)   (b)   (c)   (d)   (e)   (f)   (g)

Listening for information

(CD2: 65)

1. The Tower of Babel

You will hear five students talking about the dialects they speak. Based on their statements, fill out the form.

student	hometown	dialect spoken	alternative name for the dialect
#1			
#2			
#3			
#4			
#5			

2.   Learning Chinese

Mali is describing her experience learning different aspects of Chinese. Listen to her (CD2: 66) description and write down her comments in English.

aspects	experience
characters	
pronunciation	
tones	
grammar	

3.   Two cuisines

Mark is asking his roommate Wang An, an exchange student from China, about Hunan (CD2: 67–68) and Sichuan cuisines. Answer the questions that follow in Chinese characters, based on Wang An's reply. His reply includes one word that you have not learned, but you should be able to "listen around" that word and understand his remarks.

a.

b.

c.

d.

4. Self-reflection

(CD2: 69–71) Wen Ding, Baojia, and Xiao'ai are taking turns talking about their strengths and weaknesses. Listen to their remarks, and write down their self-evaluations in English, using the form below.

person	strengths	weaknesses
1. Wen Ding		
2. Baojia		
3. Xiao'ai		

5. Language study commercial

(CD2: 72) You will hear a radio commercial for a language-study program. Listen to the commercial and write (in English) the three main points stated in the commercial.

> Three main points of the commercial:
>
> 1.
>
> 2.
>
> 3.

6. A conversation

(CD2: 73) Your Chinese friend is asking you some questions about your experience learning Chinese. Listen to each question and answer it in Mandarin.

a.

b.

c.

d.

e.

f.

7. Class presentation

You will hear a phone message from Shuting about the class presentation. Listen to her **(CD2: 74)** message and write an email responding to her questions. The message includes two words that you have not learned, but you should be able to "listen around" the words and guess their meanings.

Your email responding to Shuting's phone message:

8. Dialogue I

Nike is telling Zufang about the Chinese linguistics course that he is taking this semester. **(CD2: 75)** Answer the questions, based on their conversation.

a. What is the focus of the Chinese linguistics course taken by the male student?
 1) history
 2) characters
 3) grammar
 4) dialects

b. What led him to take this Chinese linguistics course?
 1) He is a linguistics major.
 2) He is studying Chinese.
 3) He is not clear about Chinese grammar.
 4) The professor is excellent.

c. What other course is he taking?
 1) Introduction to Linguistics
 2) Phonology
 3) American Dialects
 4) English Grammar

9. Dialogue II

Yaru and Weisi are discussing where to live while in college.   **(CD2: 76)**

a. Why does the male student want to move out of his home?
 1) His home is far from the university.
 2) He wants to be away from his parents.
 3) He would like to try campus life.
 4) He and his good friend want to share a place.

b. What does the female student say about living in a dorm?

   1) It is close to the classrooms.
   2) You need to get used to living with other people.
   3) You will meet many interesting people.
   4) It is much more expensive.

c. According to the woman, what is it like living off campus?

   1) It is inexpensive.
   2) It is convenient.
   3) It is lonely.
   4) It is far from the school.

 # Reading and writing

Focus on Chinese characters

1. Number of strokes

Indicate the number of strokes used in writing each of the following characters.

a. 錯 _____   f. 怪 _____

b. 題 _____   g. 之 _____

c. 灣 _____   h. 德 _____

d. 底 _____   i. 標 _____

e. 筆 _____   j. 既 _____

2. Which character?

Circle the character in each line that corresponds to the meaning on the left.

a. **jiè** *borrow, loan*   借   錯

b. **hái** *child*   該   孩

c. **chéng** *become, turn into*   城   成

d. **dǐ** (**dàodǐ** *in fact, after all*)   低   底

e. **gè** *each*   各   名

f. **jiǎn** (**jiǎndān** *simple*)   簡   間

g. **bǐ** *pen*   書   筆

h. **tōng** (**pǔtōng** *ordinary*)　　通　桶

i. **shěng** *save*　　省　眚

j. **jiǎng** *speak*　　讓　講

k. **jiē** *pick up a guest*　　椄　接

l. **tí** (**wèntí** *question, problem*)　　提　題

3.　First strokes

Write the first two strokes of each of the following characters.

a. 各 _____　　f. 通 _____

b. 既 _____　　g. 灣 _____

c. 之 _____　　h. 台 _____

d. 簡 _____　　i. 孩 _____

e. 成 _____　　j. 錯 _____

4.　Missing strokes

Complete each character by writing in the missing strokes.

a.　亠　**yán** (**yǔyán** *language*)

b.　彳　**dé** (**Déguó** *Germany*)

c.　忄　**guài** (**nánguài** *no wonder*)

d.　小　**shěng** *save*

e.　夕　**gè** *each, every*

f.　亻　**jiè** *borrow, loan*

g.　竹　**bǐ** *pen*

h.　言　**yǔ** (**yǔyán** *language*)

i.　目　**jì** *both*

j.　广　**dǐ** (**dàodǐ** *in the end, after all*)

5. Total strokes

Rewrite this list of characters, arranging the characters in terms of their total number of strokes. Begin your list with the character with the fewest strokes.

題	省	簡	灣	既	怪	底	成	言	德	各	之	借	錯	通	孩	台	講	接	語	筆

6. Radicals

Here is a list of characters that we have learned through this lesson. Rewrite each character in the row next to its radical.

通	題	遊	拉	錯	極	流	鐘	借	怪	訂
語	計	迎	情	灣	像	講	健	預	標	接

忄	
亻	
扌	
頁	
言	
氵	
木	
辶	
金	

7. Character sleuth: Look for the phonetic

Group the characters below in terms of their rhymes or near-rhymes. Write the characters that rhyme with each other in the column on the right. Write the "phonetic," the shared part of each character, in the column on the left. There are eleven sets of characters that rhyme or partially rhyme and share a phonetic component among these characters.

五	遠	爬	間	完	玩	瓶	把	廳	簡	客	忘
校	妹	漂	各	少	標	懂	小	重	京	味	忙
中	炒	爸	聽	並	餃	園	語	影	種	較	吧

phonetic	characters that rhyme or almost rhyme and share a phonetic component

8.   Scrambled sentences

Rewrite these phrases as sentences, putting the words in the correct order to match the English translations.

a. 的 / 特點 / 方言 / 各 / 各 / 中國 / 有

As for Chinese dialects, each has its own characteristics.

b. 子 / 的 / 孩 / 錯 / 那 / 菜 / 真 / 個 / 做 / 不

The food that the child cooked is really not bad.

c. 會 / 會 / 德 / 講 / 底 / 語 / 你 / 不 / 到

Can you really speak German?

d. 筆 / 把 / 我 / 你 / 借 / 請 / 的 / 給

Please lend me your pen.

9.   Dictionary skills

Following the instructions in Lesson 17 of the Textbook, look up these characters in a Chinese dictionary and provide the requested information.

a. 處

   pronunciation:

   meaning:

   one two-character word or phrase in which it occurs:

b. 猜

   pronunciation:

   meaning:

   one two-character word or phrase in which it occurs:

c. 使

   pronunciation:

   meaning:

   one two-character word or phrase in which it occurs:

10.   Find the incorrect characters

Xiao Zhang has written this essay for his Chinese class, but he has written eight characters incorrectly. Circle his mistakes and write the correct characters in the answer sheet below. Then, translate the paragraph into English.

> 我覺得漢語非常難學。弟一，漢語裏有 **shēngdiào**，但是英語裏沒有 **shēngdiào**。如國你的語言裏沒有 **shēngdiào**，讓你去學一個有 **shēngdiào** 的語言，你相能容易嗎？第二，學漢語，就得學漢字。歲然很多語言不月漢字，但是有的語言，北方說日語，就用漢字。日木人學漢語就會覺得容易得多，因為他們沒有漢字的門題。第三，英語和法語，或者別的一些西方的語言裏邊有的字在以前是一樣的，現在的寫法和說法也茶不多。但是英語和中文沒有這樣的關係。所以我覺得中文比法文難學。

a. ____   b. ____   c. ____   d. ____

e. ____   f. ____   g. ____   h. ____

English:

11.   Reading for the main ideas I

The following paragraph contains a few characters that we have not yet learned, but you should be able to "read around them" and understand the main points of the passage. Read the paragraph for the main ideas, and then respond to the requests and questions that follow in English.

> 其實，方言不一定都是哪個地方的語言。在同一個地方，不同的人說話也不一樣，這也是方言。比方說，讀過很多年書的人，跟沒有上過學的人說話就不一樣。他們之間的這種語言上的差別也是方言之間的差別。

a. State the main topic of this paragraph in one word.

b. How would the author define this word?

c. Give an example from English that supports the author's definition of this word.

12.   Reading for the main ideas II

Read the following paragraph for the main ideas, and then respond to the requests and questions that follow in English.

> 方言就是一個地方的語言。在很早很早以前，交通不方便，不同地方的人來往很少，人們只說自己那個地方的語言，這樣就有了很多方言。在英國的英語裏和美國的英語裏都有方言。**Lúndūn** 人說的話就跟英國其他地方的話不一樣。在美國南方話和北方話也有很大的差別。就是在北方，**Niǔyuē** 人和 **Bōshìdùn** 的人說話也不一樣。這些方言的差別都比較小，而中國的方言差別比較大。

a. According to the author, what is one reason why a language has different dialects?

b. The author says that there can be dialects within dialects. Give some examples of this, based on the information in the paragraph.

c. What does the author say about the difference between the dialects of English and the dialects of Chinese?

Focus on structure

1.   Definitions (Use and Structure note 30.1)

Here is a list of items and their descriptions. Write a sentence for each, saying that an item with this description is called [name of item], as in the example. Then translate your sentences into English.

Example:

在中國大 **lù**，標準語言，**Pǔ** 通話　　　→　　　在中國大 **lù**，標準語言叫作 **Pǔ** 通話。

a. 一個地方說的語言，方言　　　→

English:

b. 兩個東西不同的地方，差別　　　→

English:

c. 飯館最有名的菜，拿手菜　　　→

English:

d. **lìshǐ** 上有名的地方，名 **shèng gǔjì**　　　→

English:

e. 中國人吃飯用的東西，筷子　　　→

English:

2.   Strengths and weaknesses (Use and Structure note 30.7)

Answer each of the following questions in complete Mandarin sentences, using characters where we have learned them.

a. 你自己的長 **chu** 是甚麼？

b. 你覺得坐飛機的 **duǎnchu** 是甚麼？

c. 手機的用 **chu** 是甚麼？

d. 你覺得中文的難 **chu** 是甚麼？

e. 喝酒的壞 **chu** 是甚麼？

3.   No matter what (Use and Structure note 30.8)

Complete these sentences by adding a clause that begins with **wúlùn** to match the English translations.

a. _____ , **jiāo** 通都很方便。

No matter where you want to go, the transportation is very convenient.

b. 謝媽媽很會做菜，_____。

Mama Xie is a very good cook. Whatever you want to eat, she can cook it.

c. 中文作業你非做不可。_____。

You have to do the Chinese homework. No matter whether you are busy or not, you still have to do it.

d. 這個菜是我女朋友做的。_____。

This dish was made by my girlfriend. Whether it tastes good or not, I have to eat it.

e. 我父母今天從美國來看我。_____。

My parents are coming from the USA to see me. No matter what time they arrive, I have to go to the airport to pick them up.

4.   Even if, even though (Use and Structure note 30.10)

Complete these sentences by adding a clause that begins with **jíshǐ** to match the English translations.

a. 這裏的 **jiāo** 通很方便。_____。

The transportation here is very convenient. Even if you don't have a car, you can go anywhere.

b. 謝媽媽很會做菜，_____。

Mama Xie is a very good cook. Even if she has never cooked a dish before, she can cook it.

c. 中文作業你非做不可。_____。

You have to do the Chinese homework. Even if you are very busy, you still have to do it.

d. 這個菜是我女朋友做的。_____。

This dish was made by my girlfriend. Even though it doesn't look very delicious, I still have to eat it.

e. **Pǔ** 通話的四 **shēng** 不難學。_____。

The four tones of Putonghua are not too difficult to learn. Even if the language that you speak does not have tones, you will still be able to learn them.

5.   She did it this way (Use and Structure note 30.11)

Translate each sentence into Mandarin, using <u>AdjV AdjV 地 +VP</u> to express the way that Xiao Gao performed each action.

a. Xiao Gao listened carefully to what the teacher said.

b. Xiao Gao slowly completed all of her homework.

c. Xiao Gao quickly straightened up her room.

d. Xiao Gao reviewed the characters well. (She worked hard on this task.)

6.   Scrambled sentences

Rewrite these phrases into sentences, putting them in the right order to match the English translations.

a. 就 / 話 / 的 / 是 / **pǔ** 通人 / 說 / **pǔ** 通話

Putonghua is the language that ordinary people speak.

b. 事 / 是 / 的 / 的 / 就 / 今天 / 今天 / 做完 / 長 **chu** / 我

My strength is that I finish today's work today.

c. 甚麼 / 打 / 問 / 你 / 問題 / 可以 / 電話 / **wúlùn** / 來 / 我 / 有 / 都

Whatever questions you have, you can phone me and ask.

d. 來 / **chèn** / 是 / 人 / 打折 / 到 **chu** / 東西 / 商店 / 的 / 裏 / 都 / 買

The store is full of people taking advantage of the sale to buy things.

e. 的/ 喜歡 / 是 / 是 / 而 / 所 / 經濟 / 音樂 / 我 / 不

What I like isn't economics but music.

7.   Translate into English

Translate these sentences into English.

a. 他去過很多地方，會說好幾種不同的方言。

b. 我 **cāi** 你完全沒有聽懂老師在課上所說的話。

c. 我連有四個 **shēngdiào** 的 **pǔ** 通話都說不好，怎麼能學有九個 **shēngdiào** 的 **Guǎng** 東話呢？

d. 他們之間的事情，我所知道的不多。

e. 對我來說，漢字最難學。我可以只學說話，不學書寫嗎？

f. **Pǔ** 通話和北京話在語法、發音和 **cíhuì** 上的差別都不大。

g. 在中國大 **lù** 的中國人只用簡體字，在台灣的中國人只用 **fán** 體字，而在美國學漢語的學生有的既要學簡體字，又要學 **fán** 體字。

h. 這門課 **jī** 本上沒有考試，但是有很多功課和 **dú** 書報告。

i. 你把這個功課分成三天做，就不會覺得那麼多了。

j. 你既不運動又吃得多，難怪會 **pàng**。

8. Translate into Mandarin

Translate these sentences into Mandarin, using characters where we have learned them.

a. No wonder he didn't come to class today. It turns out he was sick.

b. Whether I study Chinese or not next semester depends upon whether or not I have time.

c. My roommate makes loud phone calls (loudly makes phone calls) every night and interferes with (influences) my studying.

d. Simplified characters, from the perspective of foreign students, are not at all easy.

e. I've already asked you many times. Is this teacher in fact difficult or not?

f. Everyone has her own strengths and weaknesses.

g. Today is the last test of this semester. Even though I am sick, I have to go take (participate in) the test.

h. I've always considered you a good friend.

i. Actually, how much you sleep and what your grade is on tests have a direct relationship.

1.   Dialogue comprehension

Study the Lesson 30 Narrative and Dialogue. Then, read the following statements and indicate whether they are true (T) or false (F).

a. (   ) **Pǔ** 通話和國語是現 **dài** 漢語的標準語。

b. (   ) 漢語的方言 **jī** 本上有七種。只說漢語的人，甚麼方言都聽不懂。

c. (   ) 方言和方言之間的差別，有的大，有的小。

d. (   ) 雖然說不同方言的人可能 **hù** 相聽不懂，但是寫出來的文字，一定看得懂。

e. (   ) 外國學生學漢語難 **chu** 是，書寫和發音沒有直接的關係。

f. (   ) 大為昨天去吃飯的餐廳裏，服務員跟他們說 **Pǔ** 通話，可是服務員之間說的是方言。

g. (   ) 方言和方言之間，除了發音是最 **zhǔ** 要的不同以外，**cíhuì** 和語法一 **bān** 差別不大。

h. (   ) 小張的老師說學漢語的學生如果不離開北京，就不 **xū** 要學方言。

i. (   ) 在中國，全國的小孩子上學以後都要學 **Pǔ** 通話。

j. (   ) 台灣跟大 **lù** 一樣，也用簡體字。

k. (   ) 學簡體字還是 **fán** 體字，**jī** 本上你應該自己決定，沒有好或者不好。

2.   What do you say?

What do you say in each of the following situations? Type your answers, using characters where we have learned them, and email them to your Chinese teacher.

a.   Answer your friend's question about studying in China or in Taiwan. Explain to her that each has its own advantages and it's hard to tell which one is better.

b.   As a travel agent, explain to your client that after the discount and the $80 off, if you pay with cash, this train ticket is basically 50% off.

c.   Tell your friend the main differences between American English and British English.

d.   As a fruit vendor, advertise your promotion: every day after 9:30, no matter what fruit they purchase, it's 50 cents apiece.

e.   After you have taken one bite, tell your friend that the "la zi ji ding" is in fact <u>not</u> as spicy as he thought and urge him to give it a try.

f.   As a teacher, tell your students that they should ask you directly if they have questions instead of asking other classmates.

g. When your friend thanks you for your help, tell him there's no need to say thank you between you and him because of course friends should help each other!

h. Ask your friend to guess how many languages you speak.

i. Tell your friends about at least one of your strengths and weaknesses.

j. Complain about how crowded this place is—there are people everywhere.

k. Tell your friends whether you are learning traditional or simplified characters. Briefly explain the advantages and disadvantages of the type of characters you are learning, and explain the main reason why you are learning that form of characters.

l. Tell your classmates the person who influenced you the most.

m. After your boyfriend explained that the girl you saw with him the other day was his cousin, you are relieved and say "that explains it." You also joke that no wonder he's not afraid of you getting mad at all.

n. Ask your friend to divide the cake (**dàngāo**) into six pieces.

3. Complete the mini-dialogues

Use the structure in parentheses to complete each mini-dialogue.

a. A: 大家都說美國人不講 **jiu** 做菜，你覺得呢？

　　B: ＿＿＿＿＿＿＿＿＿＿＿＿＿＿＿＿＿＿＿＿＿＿＿。（**Qí** 實…）

b. A: 我昨天剛從中國回來。去了一個月，玩得高興極了。

　　B: 我怎麼不知道你去中國了？＿＿＿＿＿＿＿＿＿＿＿＿＿。（難怪…）

c. A: 你覺得這麼晚了我們還找得到東西吃嗎？

　　B: 當然！＿＿＿＿＿＿＿＿＿＿＿＿＿＿＿＿＿。（到 **chù** 都是）

d. A: 我已經每天去上課了，為甚麼我的成 **jì** 還是沒有進 **bù**？

　　B: 如果 ＿＿＿＿＿＿＿＿＿＿＿＿＿＿＿，**jíshǐ** ＿＿＿＿＿＿＿

　　＿＿＿＿＿＿＿＿＿＿＿＿＿，成 **jì** 還是不會進 **bù**。（**jíshǐ**…）

e. A: 你的老師怎麼這麼關心你們？真難得。

　　B: 王老師 ＿＿＿＿＿＿＿＿＿＿＿＿＿＿＿，所以他非常關心我們。（看作…）

4. Complete and translate

Using the context as your guide, choose the correct expression to complete each sentence, and then translate the sentences into English.

a. 我現在才知道，中國人一 **bān** 不喝 **bīng** 的。難怪 _____
　　1) 餐廳裏不賣 **bīng yǐnliào**。
　　2) **suān là tāng** 這麼有名。
　　3) 吃得太 **là** 的時候喝甚麼呢？

English:

b. 很多人不知道，四川菜 _____ 不都是 **là** 的。
　　1) 到底
　　2) **qí** 實
　　3) **jíshǐ**

English:

c. 老師：因為"筷子"聽起來跟"快子"一樣，所以，送別人筷子意思就是 **xīwàng** 別人"快一點有孩子"。

　　學生： _____。
　　1) **Yuàn** 者上 **gōu**
　　2) **Yuán** 來如 **cǐ**
　　3) 一言為定

English:

d. 最近的天氣越來越冷，晚上出去 **jíshǐ** _____ 還是冷得不得了。
　　1) 穿了大衣、**dài** 了 **ěrzhào**，手 **tào**，
　　2) 不穿大衣
　　3) 事先訂位

English:

e. A: 我要去上海工作一年，到底我 **xū** 要不 **xū** 要學上海話？

　　B: 完全不 **xū** 要， _____ 你自己有興趣。
　　1) 難怪
　　2) **xìngkuī**
　　3) 除非

English:

5.   Cantonese and Mandarin

Part I.   Using the context as your guide, complete this paragraph by filling in the blanks with the appropriate words below.

發現	當然	比方說	聽起來
另外	**jī** 本上	有名	而

說到漢語的方言，最 _____ 的大概就是 **Guǎng** 東話了。如果你去中國 **chéng** *(China-town)*，你會 _____，很多人只說 **Guǎng** 東話，不說 **Pǔ** 通話。**Guǎng** 東話和 **Pǔ** 通話所用的 **cíhuì** 差不多，可是因為發音不同，_____ 完全不一樣。**Guǎng** 東話有八個 **shēngdiào**，_____ **Pǔ** 通話只有四個。在語法上，**Guǎng** 東話和 **Pǔ** 通話 _____ 差不多，可是有些字放的地方跟 **Pǔ** 通話不太一樣。_____，**Pǔ** 通話裏的“多吃點兒”，在 **Guǎng** 東話裏說“吃多點兒”。_____，**Gǔ** 漢語 *(Classical Chinese)* 對 **Guǎng** 東話的影 **xiǎng** 很大。**Pǔ** 通話裏的“多少”，**Guǎng** 東話說“幾多”。“幾多”就是從 **Gǔ** 漢語裏頭來的。雖然有這些不同，但是兩個語言所用的書寫文字是一樣的。所以，說 **Guǎng** 東話看得懂中文書，說 **Pǔ** 通話的人去 **Xiānggǎng** *(Hong Kong)* 玩，_____ 也看得懂街上寫的字了。

Part II. True or false   Read the paragraph again, and decide whether each of the following statements is true (T) or false (F).

a. (　) 在美國的中國 **chéng** 裏常常會聽到 **Guǎng** 東話。

b. (　) **Guǎng** 東話的 **shēngdiào** 比 **Pǔ** 通話多。

c. (　) **Guǎng** 東話和 **Pǔ** 通話之間的差別，在語法上比在發音上大得多。

d. (　) **Guǎng** 東話有很多 **Gǔ** 漢語所用的 **cíhuì**。

e. (　) 這兩個語言說出來不一樣，寫出來也完全不一樣。

Part III. Think and write   你 **cāi cāi** 看，說 **Guǎng** 東話的人如果要學中文，會有甚麼難 **chu**，哪方 **miàn** 特別容易？（如果你有說 **Guǎng** 東話的朋友，就去問問他們。）Your response should be at least 120 characters in length.

_____

_____

_____

_____

6.   American English vs. British English I

Using the context as your guide, as well as your knowledge of American English and British English, choose the most appropriate word in each group to complete this paragraph.

_____（a. 在 b. 對 c. 從）很多學英語的人來說，美式英語和英式英語都是英語。_____（a. 實際上 b. 說到 c. 另外）這兩個語言 _____（a. **hù** 相 b. 等於 c. 之間）還是有一些不同。最 **zhǔ** 要的差別就是 _____（a. 發音 b. 文字 c. 語法）。所以有人說，美國人到英國去旅行，也 _____（a. 不一定 b. 一定 c. **kǒng** 怕）完全聽得懂他們說的話。聽不懂有的時候也是因為一些 _____（a. 語法 b. **cíhuì** c. 語音）上的差別。比方說，"elevator" 在英式英語裏 _____（a. 叫做 b. 分成 c. 看作）"lift"。也就是說，_____（a. **xìngkuī** b. 的 **què** c. **jíshǐ**）你看到 "lift"，如果你不知道這個字的意思，你還是不知道那就是 "電 **tī**"。另外，美式英語和英式英語在文字的寫法上也有一點不一樣。美式英語的 "color"，英式英語 _____（a. 寫成 b. 寫好 c. 寫到）"colour"，多了一個 "u"，_____（a. 但是 b. 而 c. 也就是說）"theater" 和 "center" 在英國成了 "theatre" 和 "centre"。

7.   American English vs. British English II

Answer the following questions in Mandarin, based on your opinions and experience. You can consult outside sources to help you find the information you need to answer some of these questions. Your Chinese teacher may have you work on these questions in small groups and report your findings to the class.

a. 除了 "elevator/lift" 以外，請你說說美式英語和英式英語裏頭幾個不一樣的 **cíhuì**。

b. 除了 "color/colour" 和 "theater/theatre" 以外，你還能想到哪些 **cíhuì** 在美式英語和英式英語裏頭的寫法不一樣？請寫出兩個。

c. 你比較喜歡美式英語還是英式英語，為甚麼？

d. 你說的是哪一個，美式英語還是英式英語？你聽得懂另外一個嗎？

e. 除了美國和英國以外，還有哪些國家的人也說英語？

f. 有的時候因為說的英語不同，兩個人之間也會 **hù** 相聽不懂。請你講一個發生在你自己身上的事情。

8.　Form a cohesive paragraph

Rewrite these sentences, putting them in the correct order to form a cohesive paragraph about a difference between Putonghua and Beijing dialect.

a. 在 **Pǔ** 通話裏沒有那麼多的 "**er**"。

b. 有很多人以為北京話就是 **Pǔ** 通話，實際上北京話跟 **Pǔ** 通話不一樣。

c. 我覺得 "聽懂" 比 "好聽" 重要得多，所以請你跟我說 **Pǔ** 通話，別說北京話。

d. 北京人說話有很多 "**er**" 的 **shēng** 音。

e. 對我們外國學生來說，如果你說得很快，而且有很多 "**er**" 的 **shēng** 音，就很難聽懂。

f. 有的人覺得 "**er**" 的 **shēng** 音很好聽。

9.　An objective view

The paragraph below, from Part C of the Lesson 30 Dialogue, illustrates a way to present your opinion about some topic and to support your opinion with facts.

Part I.　Examine this paragraph. Identify <u>the topic, the narrator's opinion, information that supports the narrator's opinion</u>, and <u>the conclusion</u>. What is the purpose of the last sentence in the paragraph?

說到簡體字和 **fán** 體字，各有各的好 **chu**。很難說哪個比較好。比方說，寫簡體字筆 **huà** 少、省時間、可是很多人認為 **fán** 體字比較漂亮也容易認。 想學哪個，完全看你自己的 **xū** 要。現在中國大 **lù** 用簡體字，而台灣用 **fán** 體字。中國的漢字有幾千年的 **lìshǐ**，對附近的國家影 **xiǎng** 也很大。

Part II.   Using the same structure as in the paragraph in Part I, write about two of the following topics. Your goal is not to persuade your listener one way or the other, but to offer a neutral presentation, stating the facts of both sides. When you offer examples to support both sides, you can use the following expressions to introduce and connect your statements: 而且、再說、另外…. Your essays should each be at least 100 characters in length.

Suggested topics

a. 學中文 vs. 學西 **bānyá** 文 *(Spanish)*

b. 自己做午飯 vs. 在學校餐廳吃午飯

c. 上大學的時候住 **sùshè** vs. 住家裏

d. 放假的時候從學校坐飛機回家 vs. 開車回家

e. 帶朋友去 **guàng** 名 **shèng gǔjì** vs. 帶朋友去 **guàng** 街買打折的東西

f. 買 **ruǎnwò** 的火車票 vs. 買 **yìngwò** 的火車票

g. 旅行的時候帶一個好的照相機 vs. 帶一個可以照相的手機

h. 朋友生日的時候送 **lǐwù** vs. 送紅包或者 **lǐqùan** *(gift certificate)*

i. Your choice of topic: _____

First topic: _____

說到 _____, 各有各的 _____。很難說哪

個比較好。比方說, _____

_____, 可是 _____

_____。想選哪個, 完全 _____

_____。

_____

_____。

Second topic: _____

說到 _____, 各有各的_____。很難說哪

個比較好。比方說, _____

_____, 可是 _____

_____。想選哪個, 完全 _____

_____。

_____

_____。

Lesson 31 Workbook

 Listening and speaking

Structure drills

(audio online)

1. Because of this (Use and Structure note 31.1)

You will hear a noun phrase followed by a verb phrase stating that an action cannot be done. Restate the information with **yóu** 於 *due to, because of,* saying that due to the noun phrase, the action cannot be done, as in the example.

Example:
You will hear: 喝酒，不能開車
You will say: **Yóu** 於喝酒的關係，我不能開車。
Click "R" to hear the correct response: **Yóu** 於喝酒的關係，我不能開車。

(a)   (b)   (c)   (d)   (e)   (f)   (g)   (h)   (i)   (j)

2. Be interested in, Part I (Use and Structure note 31.3)

You will hear a pronoun, name, or noun phrase referring to a person or people, followed by a noun phrase or action. Restate the information by saying that the person is interested in the noun phrase or action, as in the example.

Example:
You will hear: 大為，中國文化
You will say: 大為對中國文化感興趣。
Click "R" to hear the correct response: 大為對中國文化感興趣。

(a)   (b)   (c)   (d)   (e)   (f)   (g)   (h)   (i)   (j)

3.   Be interested in, Part II (Use and Structure note 31.3)

You will hear a noun or noun phrase referring to people, followed by a noun phrase, verb phrase, or clause. Restate the information, saying that the subject is <u>not</u> interested in the noun phrase, verb phrase, or clause, as in the example.

Example:

You will hear: 我，你的考試成 **jì**
You will say: 我對你的考試成 **jì** 不感興趣。
Click "R" to hear the correct response: 我對你的考試成 **jì** 不感興趣。

(a)   (b)   (c)   (d)   (e)   (f)   (g)   (h)

4.   Something that concerns this (Use and Structure note 31.4)

You will hear a statement about an object that someone likes, or the object of some action. Restate the information using the structure <u>跟 NP₁ 有關的 NP₂</u>, as in the example. An English translation of the example is provided to help you to understand the structure.

Example:

You will hear: 我喜歡看經濟的書。 *I like to read economics books*
You will say: 我喜歡看跟經濟有關的書。 *I like to read books concerning economics.*
You will hear the correct response: 我喜歡看跟經濟有關的書。 *I like to read books concerning economics.*

(a)   (b)   (c)   (d)   (e)   (f)   (g)   (h)

5.   For one thing…and for another thing (Use and Structure note 31.5)

You will hear a situation followed by two things to consider about it. Restate the information with <u>一方面…另一方面…</u>, as in the example.

Example:

You will hear: 選甚麼 **zhuān** 業，要想到自己的興趣和畢業以後找工作。
You will say: 選甚麼 **zhuān** 業，一方面要想到自己的興趣，另一方面要想到畢業以後找工作。
Click "R" to hear the correct response: 選甚麼 **zhuān** 業，一方面要想到自己的興趣，另一方面要想到畢業以後找工作。

(a)   (b)   (c)   (d)   (e)   (f)   (g)   (h)   (i)   (j)

6.   Not only…but also… (Use and Structure note 31.6)

You will hear a situation followed by two things that must be done concerning the situation. Restate the information, using <u>既 VP₁ 也 VP₂</u> to present the things that must be done, as in the example.

Example:
You will hear: 選甚麼 **zhuān** 業，要想到自己的興趣和畢業以後找工作。
You will say: 選甚麼 **zhuān** 業，既要想到自己的興趣，也要想到畢業以後找工作。
Click "R" to hear the correct response: 選甚麼 **zhuān** 業，既要想到自己的興趣，也要想到畢業以後找工作。

(a)   (b)   (c)   (d)   (e)   (f)   (g)   (h)   (i)   (j)

Listening for information

1.   Job search

You will hear five students talking about the kind of jobs they are applying for. Based on **(CD2: 79)** their statements, fill out the form, including the type of job and the location where they want to work.

student	type of job	location
#1		
#2		
#3		
#4		
#5		

2.   Job application

Malilan has applied for a job in Suzhou. She called the company to follow up on her applica- **(CD2: 80)** tion. Listen to her phone conversation with the assistant manager of the company, and check the items in the list that have been received, completed, or decided upon.

items	completed
application letter	
recommendation letters	
résumé	
grade report	
Chinese oral test	
interview date	

3.   Message from a friend

(CD2: 81) You will hear a phone message from Bili. Listen to his message and write an email in response to his questions.

> Your email response to Bili's message:

4.   Writing an application letter

(CD2: 82) Teacher Zhang is telling the students how to write a good job application letter. Listen to her instructions, and write the four points of her instructions in English.

a.

b.

c.

d.

5.   Work experience in China

(CD2: 83) Teacher Pang invites Jenny, who is working in China, to give a talk to the students in her Chinese class. Listen to her talk and write down the work and living experiences in China that she mentions.

working	living

6.   A conversation

You are having a job interview with Miss Pan at CK International, a business firm. Listen (CD2: 84) to her questions and answer them in Mandarin.

a.

b.

c.

d.

e.

f.

7.   Interview experience

You will hear Jiaming describing her interview with a company last Tuesday, followed by (CD2: 85–86) five questions in Mandarin. Answer the questions in Mandarin, based on the information that Jiaming provides.

a.

b.

c.

d.

e.

8.   Dialogue I

You will hear two friends chatting about their jobs in China. Choose the correct answer for (CD2: 87) each question, based on their conversation.

a. What kind of company does the woman work for?
   1) a newspaper
   2) a TV station
   3) a business firm
   4) a research center

b. What's the woman's job responsibility in China?
   1) She reports economic news on TV.
   2) She analyzes economic policy.
   3) She writes articles on economics.
   4) She collects critical economic news.

c. What is the man's job responsibility in China?
1) He is an expert at bringing US companies to China to invest.
2) He is a contact person between the USA and a Chinese company.
3) He is a consultant helping to establish trading companies in China.
4) He is an adviser on how to promote US products.

d. What will the man do after next month?
1) He will switch to a better-paid job.
2) He will work for a US company.
3) He will advance his Chinese writing skills.
4) He will study international relations.

9. Dialogue II

(CD2: 88) Shanmu is asking his teacher to write a letter of recommendation. Choose a correct answer for each question, based on their conversation.

a. What does Teacher He particularly need to explain in the recommendation letter?
1) Shanmu's academic achievement
2) Shanmu's communication skills
3) Shanmu's Chinese proficiency
4) Shanmu's work experience

b. Why has Juanjuan not been to the USA yet?
1) Juanjuan and Shanmu just met.
2) Juanjuan cannot obtain a visa.
3) It is expensive to travel to the USA.
4) She does not have time.

c. What will Juanjuan do in the USA?
1) travel
2) work
3) study
4) visit friends

d. What will Shanmu do right after arriving in the USA?
1) start working
2) visit the company
3) find a place to live
4) rest for several days

Reading and writing

Focus on Chinese characters

1.   Number of strokes

Indicate the number of strokes used in writing each of the following characters.

a. 畢 _____   f. 短 _____

b. 望 _____   g. 面 _____

c. 安 _____   h. 希 _____

d. 紙 _____   i. 處 _____

e. 願 _____   j. 被 _____

2.   Which character?

Circle the character in each line that corresponds to the meaning on the left.

a. **xū (xūyào** *need*)   需   雷

b. **xìn** *letter*   信   這

c. **shēn (shēnqǐng** *apply*)   申   車

d. **lì (lìshǐ** *history*)   屬   歷

e. **gǎn (gǎn xìngqu** *interested in*)   咸   感

f. **bèi** *by*   被   披

g. **duǎn** *short*   知   短

h. **xī (xīwàng** *hope*)   齐   希

i. **bì (bìyè** *graduate*)   毘   畢

j. **chù (chángchu** *strength*)   處   虎

k. **yuàn (yuànyì** *willing*)   願   廁

l. **miàn** *side, face*   而   面

3.   First strokes

Write the first two strokes of each of the following characters.

a. 感 ____   f. 紙 ____

b. 畢 ____   g. 申 ____

c. 需 ____   h. 望 ____

d. 廣 ____   i. 處 ____

e. 安 ____   j. 希 ____

4.   Missing strokes

Complete each character by writing in the missing strokes.

a.   衤   **bèi** *by*

b.   曰   **bì** (**bìyè** *graduate*)

c.   虍   **chù** (**chángchu** *strength*)

d.    午   **duǎn** *short*

e.   亠   **jiāo** (**jiāotōng** *communication*)

f.    �   **lì** (**jiǎnlì** *résumé,* **lìshǐ** *history*)

g.   曰   **shēn** (**shēnqǐng** *apply*)

h.   亻   **xìn** *letter*

i.    厈   **yuàn** (**yuànyì** *willing*)

j.   幺   **zhǐ** *paper*

5.   Total strokes

Rewrite this list of characters, arranging the characters in terms of their total number of strokes. Begin your list with the character with the fewest strokes.

望	需	紙	感	面	短	被	歷	廣	畢	安	願	交	申	信	希	處

6. Radicals

Here is a list of characters that we have learned through this lesson. Rewrite each character in the row next to its radical. Use this as an opportunity to review these characters. If you do not know the pronunciation or meaning of a character on the list, look it up and practice it.

廣	雪	借	宿	預	望	顏	安	線	應	宜
帶	客	意	需	實	價	思	紙	希	像	練
知	寒	便	服	健	願	底	紹	短	信	床

月	
亻	
雨	
心	
巾	
糹	
矢	
广	
宀	

7. Character sleuth: Look for the phonetic

Group the characters below in terms of their rhymes or near-rhymes. Write the characters that rhyme with each other in the column on the right. Write the "phonetic," the shared part of each character, in the column on the left. There are at least eleven sets of characters that rhyme or partially rhyme and share a phonetic component.

廣	末	女	活	交	忙	錯	玩	該	黃
爸	餃	五	聽	右	孩	票	客	較	味
遠	漂	忘	妹	爬	把	廳	口	如	重
園	各	校	語	望	話	醋	懂	完	標

phonetic	characters that rhyme or almost rhyme and share a phonetic component

8. Scrambled sentences

Rewrite these phrases as sentences, putting the words in the correct order to match the English translations.

a. 事 / 不 / 件 / 請 / 千萬 / 把 / 這 / 他 / 你 / 告訴 / 要

Please absolutely do not tell him about this matter.

b. 一定 / 興趣 / 興趣 / 不 / 對 / 你 / 感 / 感 / 你 / 的 / 人

People you are interested in are not always interested in you.

c. 流行 / 這 / 鞋 / 既 / 式樣 / 便宜 / 也 / 雙

This pair of shoes is not only cheap, the style is also in fashion.

d. 為 / **shàn** 於 / 工作 / 人 / 介紹 / 她

She is good at finding (introducing) jobs for people.

9. Dictionary skills

Following the instructions in Lesson 17 of the Textbook, look up these characters in a Chinese dictionary and provide the requested information.

a. 留
   pronunciation:
   meaning:
   one two-character word or phrase in which it occurs:

b. 封
   pronunciation:
   meaning:
   one two-character word or phrase in which it occurs:

c. 祝

    pronunciation:

    meaning:

    one two-character word or phrase in which it occurs:

10.   Find the incorrect characters

Xiao Zhang has written this letter to Xiao Ye, but he has written ten characters incorrectly. Circle his mistakes and write the correct characters in the answer sheet below. Then, translate the paragraph into English.

> 我馬上就比業了。很多同學早九希忘能畢業了，可是我很怕。從小的時候到現再，我一真都在上學。上學的時後，我爸爸媽媽給我錢。學生的生活，對我來說，再習慣不過了。畢業就要白己找工作，不能讓爸爸媽媽給我錢，可是我從來沒有找過工作，也從來沒有工作過。一想道在報紙上找有關工作的廣告，寫間歷、申青信和請老師幫我寫 **tuījiàn** 信等等，我就很緊張。我要是一直可以上學就好了。

a. ____   b. ____   c. ____   d. ____   e. ____

f. ____   g. ____   h. ____   i. ____   j. ____

English:

11.   Reading for the main ideas I

The following paragraph contains a few characters that we have not yet learned, but you should be able to "read around them" and understand the main points of the passage. Read the paragraph for the main ideas and respond to the requests and questions that follow in English.

> 大為的英文名字是 David。老師給他的中文名字是 "大為"。開始的時候，他很不喜歡。他覺得他的中文名字跟英文名字差不多。老師告訴他為甚麼給他這個名字以後，他不但很喜歡他的名字，而且還常常跟別人講他名字的意思。中國人給小孩子名字的時候很注意名字的意思。"大為" 並不是英文 "David" 的聲音，"大為" 是 "大有作為"。"大有作為" 的意思是不管做甚麼都可以做得很好，很有成績。老師希望他將來能大有作為。現在大為就要畢業了。他希望能在中國工作一段時間。他在申請工作，希望能在中國大有作為。

a. State the main topic of this paragraph in <u>one</u> word.

b. State the two main pieces of information that the author provides about this word.

c. What is the connection that the author wants the reader to make about these two pieces of information?

12.   Reading for the main ideas II

Read the following paragraph for the main ideas, and then respond to the requests and questions that follow in English.

> 工作和興趣既有關係，也沒有關係。當然，如果你找到一個你有興趣的工作，你願意做的工作，你一定可以做好。但是在經濟不好的時候，工作不多，能找到工作就很不錯了。因為你需要錢，所以不管你對這個工作有興趣還是沒興趣，你都得做。開始的時候，你可能沒有興趣，很可能慢慢兒地就有興趣了。

a. State the topic of this paragraph in two or three words.

b. The author says that this topic poses a paradox. What is the paradox?

c. What do economic conditions have to do with this topic?

Focus on structure

1.   Due to this (Use and Structure note 31.1)

Here is a set of reasons and results. Express each relationship in a complete Mandarin sentence, using the structure **yóu** 於 (NP) 的關係 or **yóu** 於 S₁, S₂.

a. the weather   →   the party will be indoors (開會 *hold a party*)

b. bad grades (academic record)   →   he decided not to apply to college this year

c. her insufficient experience   →   the company wasn't willing to hire her

d. history   →   way of writing in Taiwan and mainland China is different

2.   Expressing interest (Use and Structure note 31.3)

Here are a few things that Dawei has become interested in while he has been studying in China. Use the structure 對 (NP) 感興趣 to say that he is interested in each of these things.

a. Chinese history   →

b. international trade   →

c. Sino–American (中美) relations →

d. Chinese dialects   →

3.   Something that concerns this (Use and Structure note 31.4)

Here is what Dawei has been doing to follow up on his interests. Translate these sentences into Mandarin, using the structure 跟 NP₁ 有關的 NP₂.

a. Because he is interested in Chinese history, he reads a lot of books having to do with Chinese history.

b. Because he is interested in international trade, he is applying to companies that involve trade.

c. Because he is interested in Sino–American relations, he has taken a lot of courses that have to do with China.

d. Because he is interested in Chinese dialects, he has also taken a few courses that concern Chinese language.

4. For one thing..., and for another thing (Use and Structure note 31.5)

Translate these sentences to English.

a. 找工作，一方面要自己 **nǔlì**，另一方面要有朋友幫助。

b. 我這次考得不好，一方面是因為我準備得不夠，另一方面考試的 **què** 很難。

c. 我下星期去上海，一方面是去旅遊，另一方面是去看一個老同學。

d. 我想 **chèn** 今年夏天到上海去工作。一方面看看朋友，另一方面多了 **jiě** 一下上海現在的情 **kuàng**。

5. Not only...but also (Use and Structure note 31.6)

Dawei is preparing for a job interview tomorrow by making a list of things that he is good at. Express each of these in Mandarin, using the structure 既 VP₁ 也 VP₂.

a. can speak English and can also speak Chinese

b. conscientious and hardworking and willing to help others

c. have study abroad experience and have work experience

d. like to work with others and like to work on my own

6. What are they good at? (Use and Structure note 31.8)

Translate the following sentences into English.

a. 王先生 **shàn** 於用最簡單的 **tiáoliào** 做出色、香、味都有的菜。

b. 你這麼 **shàn** 於學習語言，**jiāng** 來一定要找跟外語有關的工作。

c. 他不 **shàn** 於跟不認識的人說話，所以剛認識他的人，都以為他不願意跟別人交往。

d. 真正 **cōng** 明的學生很 **shàn** 於安 **pái** 時間，該學習的時候學習，該玩兒的時候玩兒。

e. What are you good at? Write one sentence in Mandarin, stating what you are good at.

7.   By all means don't do that! (Use and Structure note 31.9)

Complete these sentences in Mandarin by adding an action that you absolutely shouldn't do, and then translate them into English.

a. 你在外國旅遊的時候，千萬 _____。
   English:

b. 面談的時候，千萬 _____。
   English:

c. 朋友請你吃飯的時候，千萬 _____。
   English:

d. 考試的時候，千萬 _____。
   English:

e. 介紹你自己的時候，千萬 _____。
   English:

8.   Scrambled sentences

Rewrite these phrases as sentences, putting the words in the correct order to match the English translations.

a. 既 / 也 / 經 **yàn** / 經 **yàn** / 大學生 / 大 **bù** 分的 / 工作 / 生活 / 沒有 / 沒有

   Most college students don't have work experience and don't have life experience.

b. 經 **yàn** / 信心 / 所 / 的 / 不 / 工作 / 而 / 自己的 / 是 / 是 / 你 / 需要 / 對

   What you need is not work experience but confidence in yourself.

c. 都 / 大為 / 跟 / 對 / 感興趣 / 所有 / **mào** 易 / 的 / 工作 / 跟 / 有關

   Dawei is interested in all jobs that have something to do with trade.

d. 忙 / 都 / **yóu** 於 / **liánxì** / 少 / 很 / 我們 / 很 / 最近

   Because everyone is very busy, we haven't been in touch very often in recent times.

9. Translate into English

Translate these sentences into English.

a. **Yóu** 於現在的經濟情 **kuàng**，剛剛畢業的大學生很難找到工作。

b. 在跟別人交往的時候，要看別人的長處，不要只 **zhù** 意短處。

c. 大為對所有跟 **mào** 易有關的工作都感興趣。

d. 要學好中文，一方面要認真學習、做功課，另一方面要多練習說，不要怕說錯。

e. 我的同屋很 **qí** 怪，既不願意幫助別人，也不願意別人幫助他。

f. 在上大學的時候，一方面要多跟別人交往，多認識人，另一方面要 **nǔlì dú** 書，不要把時間都花在跟別人交往上。

g. 只有在中國住一 **duàn** 時間，才能真正了 **jiě** 中國的文化。

10. Translate into Mandarin

Translate these sentences into Mandarin, using the phrase or structure indicated in parentheses.

a. Because of being too nervous and not having confidence in myself, my first job interview was very bad (very not good). (**yóu** 於)

b. Several US universities (colleges) make students know (recognize) both simplified characters and traditional characters. (既…也)

c. My roommate is very good at studying languages. He can speak the languages of many different types of countries. (**shàn** 於)

d. On the web you can often see the expression (way of speaking) "contact us" (**liánxì** 我們). Actually, this is not correct. They ought to say "跟我們 **liánxì**". (實際上)

e. Companies that hire students who are studying abroad help them take their student visas and exchange them for (convert them to) work visas. (換成)

f. You can't use a credit card at that restaurant. When/If you go there to eat lunch, by all means don't forget to take a little cash. (千萬)

g. I take my lunch to school every day now. It both saves money and is convenient. (既…也)

Focus on communication

1.   Dialogue comprehension

Study the Lesson 31 Narrative and Dialogue. Then, read the following statements and indicate whether they are true (T) or false (F).

a. (　) 畢業生還沒有放假就開始找工作了。

b. (　) 申請以前，公 **sī** 一定會安 **pái** 你去面談。

c. (　) **Liú** 學生如果沒有工作 **qiānzhèng** 就不能在中國工作。

d. (　) 大為已經有十幾個面談了，但是他只喜歡三個。

e. (　) 大為申請的工作都跟 **mào** 易有關。

f. (　) 大為想請友文吃飯，因為他已經找到工作了。

g. (　) 大為找老師說話，因為他想請老師給他寫 **tuījiàn** 信。

h. (　) 面談的時候一定要對自己有信心。既不能緊張，也別忘了說 **qīngchu** 你的長處。

i. (　) 面談的時候，工作經 **yàn** 不是最重要的。讓他們了 **jiě** 你的長處更重要。

j. (　) 大為的長處是語言。還有，中西文化他都了 **jiě**。

k. (　) **Mào** 易公 **sī** 喜歡工作認真、願意幫助別人的人。

l. (　) 跟老師說話以前，大為對自己不太有信心。

2.   What do you say?

What do you say in each of the following situations? Type your answers, using characters where we have learned them, and email them to your Chinese teacher.

a. Tomorrow is a holiday. You need to post a sign in Chinese on the door of the school cafeteria that says: "Due to the holiday, the cafeteria is closed today."

b. You work in the Human Resources office. Call a potential candidate to notify her that you'd like to arrange an interview and ask if she's available next Thursday at 10:00 a.m.

c. Politely ask your Chinese teacher to write you a recommendation letter. Explain to her that you want to apply for jobs related to Chinese language.

d. You are at a job fair. Present your application and résumé and tell potential employers that you are interested in their company. Tell them your major and ask them to contact you if they have openings (jobs) related to your major.

e. Ask your friend to prepare you for a job interview tomorrow.

f. Your younger sister is getting ready for her piano recital. Tell her to never ever get nervous and tell her that you have confidence in her.

g. Your friend is heading for a road test to get his driver's license. Wish him good luck and tell him you'll be waiting for his good news.

h. You are currently on a student visa. Ask your potential employer if they would sponsor (help you change into) a work visa if they hire you.

i. As an interviewer, ask the candidate to tell you his/her strengths and weaknesses.

j. Explain to the candidates that the company is looking for someone who is hardworking and has good people skills.

3. Complete the mini-dialogues

Use the structure in parentheses to complete each mini-dialogue.

a. A: 你最近怎麼不去那家餐館吃飯了？

B: _____。（一方面…另一方面…）

b. A: 選 **zhuān** 業最要緊的是甚麼？

B: _____。（對…感興趣）

c. A: 明天是小張的生日，我想給他買個 **lǐwù**，你覺得他會喜歡甚麼？

B: 買甚麼都可以，可是 _____。（千萬）

d. A: 他們說的是甚麼語言？我怎麼一點也聽不懂？

B: _____，難怪你聽不懂。（既…也…）

e. A: 你想找哪方面的工作？

B: _____。（跟…有關）

4. Complete and translate

Using the context as your guide, choose the correct expression to complete each sentence, and then translate the sentence into English.

a. **Yóu** 於 _____，願意買房子的人越來越少。
   1) 房子越做越漂亮
   2) 經濟一直很 **zāogāo**
   3) 人越來越多

English:

b. 只有 _____ 才能省一點錢。

   1) 如果你不開車

   2) 你沒有車

   3) 少開車，多坐公共汽車或者地鐵

English:

c. A: 找工作越來越難，是不是？

   B: 是的。對我來說，一方面我沒有工作經 **yàn**，另一方面，_____，所以，很多公 **sī** 對我不感興趣。

   1) 我的中文不夠好

   2) 雖然我對自己有信心

   3) 如果我能有幾 **fēng** 比較強的 **tuījiàn** 信

English:

d. A: _____。

   B: 千萬別緊張，放 **sōng** 一點兒。

   1) 我昨天把十幾 **fēng** 申請信發出去了

   2) 時間過得真快，我們下個星期就要畢業了

   3) 明天晚上我要跟我男朋友的父母吃飯，這是我第一次見到他們

English:

e. A: 下個星期我有個面談。

   B: **Zhù** 你好運！_____。

   1) 千萬 **jì** 住，穿漂亮一點

   2) 他們一定很了 **jiě** 你

   3) 我等你的好 **xiāoxi**

English:

5.   Form a cohesive paragraph

Rewrite these sentences, putting them in the correct order to form a cohesive paragraph about preparing for a job interview.

a. 謝謝他們給你這個機會。

b. 回 **dá** (*reply to*) 問題的時候，要想好了以後再說。

c. 找工作的時候，面談非常重要。

d. 你可以去網上了 **jiě**，也可以問你的老師和朋友。

e. 面談以後，最好給跟你面談的人寫一 **fēng** 信。

f. 去面談以前要認真地準備。

g. 在面談的時候讓他們多知道你的長處，讓他們覺得你就是他們需要的人。

h. 另外，你要了 **jiě** 他們需要甚麼樣的人。

i. 不要沒有完全想好就開始說。

j. 你對 **gù** 人的公 **sī** 了 **jiě** 得越多越好。

_____

_____

_____

_____

_____

6. Job interview

This is a job interview at a Chinese trading company. Read the questions in Part I and find the matching answers in Part II.

Part I. Questions

a. (   ) 你的長處是甚麼？短處呢？

b. (   ) 你為甚麼來申請這個工作？

c. (   ) 有很多申請的人工作經 **yàn** 比你多，說說看我們為甚麼要 **gù** 用你？

d. (   ) 如果我們決定 **gù** 用你，你有甚麼問題要問我？

e. (   ) 如果你被 **gù** 用了，你打算做這個工作做多久？

Part II. Answers   Here are answers to the interview questions in Part I. Translate each answer into English. Then match it with the corresponding question, writing the answer letter before the corresponding question in Part I.

A) 我的 **zhuān** 業是經濟，而且我大學選了不少跟國際 **mào** 易有關的課。另外，我一直對中美關係很感興趣。兩年以前我就發現了你們公 **sī**。對你們所做的我一直很感興趣。

English: _____

_____

_____

_____

B) 做了幾年，有經 **yàn** 以後，我想回學校學習，希望以後能再回公 **sī** 做更多的事情。

English: _____

_____

C) 雖然我剛畢業，但是我工作起來既 **nǔlì**，又認真。我大學的老師都說我學甚麼都學得又快又好。另外，從大學開始，每年 **shǔ** 假，我都在我父親的公 **sī** 幫忙，這也算是有關的工作經 **yàn** 吧。

English: _____

_____

_____

_____

D) 我學中文已經學了七年了，對中西文化都很了 **jiě**，這是我比別人好的地方。而且我 **shàn** 於跟別人交往，又喜歡幫助別人。我最大的問題是我甚麼都想做好，所以，有的時候會讓自己太緊張。

English: _____

_____

_____

_____

E) 我想知道這個工作需要不需要常常到別的國家。我很願意學習新的東西，所以，如果有旅行的機會，就太好了。

English: _____

_____

_____

_____

7.   What's your answer?

Imagine yourself in the same job interview as in Exercise 6. Write down your answer for each question. You can assign the job title yourself so that you can be more specific about your answer; for example, a research assistant in the Department of East Asian Studies, etc.

Job title: _____

a. 你的長處是甚麼？短處呢？

_____

_____

_____

_____

b. 你為甚麼來申請這個工作？

_____

_____

_____

_____

c. 有很多申請的人工作經 **yàn** 比你多，說說看我們為甚麼要 **gù** 用你？

_____

_____

_____

_____

d. 如果我們決定 **gù** 用你，你有甚麼問題要問我？

_____

_____

_____

_____

e. 如果你被 **gù** 用了，你打算做這個工作做多久？

_____

_____

_____

_____

Lesson 32 Workbook

 Listening and speaking

(audio online)

Structure drills

1. When it comes to this (Use and Structure note 22.1)

You will hear a statement. Rephrase the statement, turning the direct object into the topic with the phrase 在 NP 上, as in the example.

Example:
You will hear: 老師很照顧我們的生活。
You will say: 在生活上，老師很照顧我們。
Click "R" to hear the correct response: 在生活上，老師很照顧我們。

(a)　　(b)　　(c)　　(d)　　(e)　　(f)

2. It makes me feel this way (Use and Structure note 21.8)

You will hear a sentence saying that someone feels a certain way because of some situation. Restate the information using 讓, saying that the situation makes the person feel a certain way, as in the example.

Example:
You will hear: 我很不高興因為他沒來。
You will say: 他沒來讓我很不高興。
Click "R" to hear the correct response: 他沒來讓我很不高興。

(a)　　(b)　　(c)　　(d)　　(e)　　(f)

3.   Giving thanks to someone (Use and Structure note 32.3)

You will hear a verb phrase indicating thanks to someone. Use that verb phrase in a sentence, saying that you give thanks to that person, as in the example.

Example:

You will hear: 感謝老師
You will say: 我 **xiàng** 老師表 **shì** 感謝。
Click "R" to hear the correct response: 我 **xiàng** 老師表 **shì** 感謝。

(a)   (b)   (c)   (d)   (e)   (f)   (g)   (h)

4.   It is time (Use and Structure note 16.3)

You will hear a statement saying what someone must do. Restate the sentence, saying that it is time for someone to do that action, as in the example.

Example:

You will hear: 我們應該說再見了。
You will say: 是我們說再見的時候了。
Click "R" to hear the correct response: 是我們說再見的時候了。

(a)   (b)   (c)   (d)   (e)   (f)   (g)

Listening for information

1.   Formal speech

(CD2: 91–92) You will hear two short formal speeches, A and B. Provide information about the speaker, audience, and purpose of each speech in English in the following form.

speech A	
speaker	
audience	
purpose	
speech B	
speaker	
audience	
purpose	

2. Jieke's birthday

It is Jieke's birthday today. Listen to what he says and answer the questions that follow in (CD2: 93–94)
Mandarin.

a.

b.

c.

d.

e.

f.

3. An outing

You will hear a phone message from Kaili, who is studying abroad in Taiwan. She suggests (CD2: 95)
taking the **Jiéyùn** (*Rapid Transit*) for an outing. Listen to her message and fill in the main
points of her message in English.

meeting place and time	
destination	
lunch	
activity after lunch	
how to contact her	

4. Thank-you speech

Listen to Dawei's thank-you speech, and complete the following list in English, providing (CD2: 96)
his reasons for thanking each of the people on the list.

person	reason
Teacher Wang	
classmates	
roommate	

5.   A conversation

(CD2: 97)   A classmate of yours is asking you about the usage and meaning of the new words and expressions in Lesson 32. Answer her questions in Mandarin.

a.

b.

c.

d.

e.

f.

6.   Wang Lian's courses

(CD2: 98)   Wang Lian is commenting on the courses that she has taken this semester. Summarize her comments for each course in English.

course	comments
culture	
economics	
history	
literature	

7.   Dialogue

(CD2: 99)   Listen to this conversation between two friends about the coming weekend. Choose the correct answer for each question, based on the conversation.

a. Why did the man call?
  1) to invite the woman to the lake
  2) to tell the woman about the fish that he bought
  3) to remind the woman of the Sunday event
  4) to ask the woman for a favor

b. What is the man worrying about?
  1) Friday's homework
  2) the lake being too far away
  3) the test next Monday
  4) his upcoming trip

c. What will they do on Sunday?
 1) call each other
 2) review Chinese
 3) visit an aquarium
 4) meet for a chat

d. What will the man do on Saturday?
 1) come back from the lake
 2) call the woman
 3) check the internet for information about the lake
 4) send an email to the woman

 # Reading and writing

Focus on Chinese characters

1. Number of strokes

Indicate the number of strokes used in writing each of the following characters.

a. 留 _____   f. 愛 _____

b. 顧 _____   g. 首 _____

c. 結 _____   h. 嚴 _____

d. 封 _____   i. 解 _____

e. 其 _____   j. 表 _____

2. Which character?

Circle the character in each line that corresponds to the meaning on the left.

a. **huán** *return*   還   環

b. **tǎo** (**tǎojià huánjià** *bargain back and forth*)   付   討

c. **shǒu** (**shǒuxiān** *first*)   首   宜

d. **shù** (**jiéshù** *conclude*)   束   本

e. **jié** (**jiéshù** *conclude*)   結   給

f. **shǐ** (**lìshǐ** *history*)   史   吏

g. **yán** *strict*   嚴   敢

h. **gù** (**zhàogù** *care for, take care of*)   顧   顧

i. **fēng** (**yī fēng xìn** *a letter*)   刲   封

j. **biǎo** *form*   表   衣

3. First strokes

Write the first two strokes of each of the following characters.

a. 留 _____   f. 討 _____

b. 解 _____   g. 顧 _____

c. 其 _____   h. 束 _____

d. 愛 _____   i. 封 _____

e. 禮 _____   j. 參 _____

4. Missing strokes

Complete each character by writing in the missing strokes.

a.   ⺈   **jiě** (**liǎojiě** *understand*)

b.   幺   **jié** (**jiéshù** *conclude*)

c.   二   **biǎo** *form*

d.   尸   **gù** (**zhàogù** *care for, take care of*)

e.   宀   **shù** (**jiéshù** *conclude*)

f.   爫   **ài** *love*

g.   吅   **yán** *strict*

h.   冂   **shǐ** (**lìshǐ** *history*)

i.   乚   **liú** *remain*

j.   丷   **shǒu** (**shǒuxiān** *first*)

5. Total strokes

Rewrite this list of characters, arranging the characters in terms of their total number of strokes. Begin your list with the character with the fewest strokes.

愛	表	封	顧	還	結	解	留	其	史	首	束	討	嚴	參	禮

6. Radicals

Here is a list of characters that we have learned through this lesson. Rewrite each character in the row next to its radical. Use this as an opportunity to review these characters. If you do not know the pronunciation or meaning of a character on the list, look it up and practice it.

連　封　男　顧　意　椅　遠　感　想　紙　機
束　本　運　各　講　結　題　語　對　留　線
給　台　史　預　還　計　練　顏　極　紹　標

口	
辶	
木	
心	
頁	
糸	
寸	
田	
言	

7. Character sleuth: Look for the phonetic

Group the characters below in terms of their rhymes or near-rhymes. Write the characters that rhyme with each other in the column on the right. Write the "phonetic," the shared part of each character, in the column on the left. There are at least eleven sets of characters that rhyme or partially rhyme and share a phonetic component among these characters.

廣　王　星　姓　請　較　間　其　五
孩　情　語　期　校　往　廳　餃　忘
青　聽　各　交　黃　客　望　該　簡

phonetic	characters that rhyme or almost rhyme and share a phonetic component

8.   Scrambled sentences

Rewrite these words and phrases as sentences, putting the words in the correct order to match the English translations.

a. 的 / 是 / 來 / 道 / 你們 / 遠 / 而 / 客人

You are the guests who have come from afar.

b. 短處 / 長處 / 住 / **jí** 體 / 也 / 在 / 有 / 有 / 裏 / 宿舍

Living in a group dormitory has advantages and disadvantages.

c. 畢業 / 起點 / **zhōng** 點 / 只 / 大學 / 不 / 是 / 是

College graduation is not the end point, it is only a starting point.

d. 感謝 / **dài** 表 / 朋友們 / **zhōng** 心 / 請 / 我 / 你 / **xiàng** / 的 / 表 **shì** / 的

Please represent me in giving my heartfelt thanks to your friends.

9. Dictionary skills

Following the instructions in Lesson 17 of the Textbook, look up these characters in a Chinese dictionary and provide the requested information.

a. 途

  pronunciation:
  meaning:
  one two-character word or phrase in which it occurs:

b. 向

  pronunciation:
  meaning:
  one two-character word or phrase in which it occurs:

c. 郵

  pronunciation:
  meaning:
  one two-character word or phrase in which it occurs:

10. Find the incorrect characters

Xiao Zhang has written this email to one of his friends back home, but he has written ten characters incorrectly. Circle his mistakes and write the correct characters in the answer sheet below. Then, translate the paragraph into English.

我在北京已經助了兩年了。剛來的時後，我對北京所有的東西都不西慣。我聽不懂北京人說的話，不習慣吃中國反，更不喜歡北京的天汽。先在我不但可以聽懂北京話，而且非常喜歡北京話。我們學的 **Pǔ** 同話裏邊沒有很多 "兒" 的 **shēng** 音，但是北京話裏有很多。慢慢兒地，在我說的漢語裏邊也有很多 "兒" 的 **shēng** 音了。另外，我現在非長喜歡吃中國飯。中國的地方很大。每個地方的飯都不一樣。個種風味都有自己的味到，讓你吃了還想吃。最後是北京的天氣。我現在也慢慢地習慣了。由於天氣的 **biàn** 化，人們穿不同的衣服、吃不同的東西、做不同的運動。這不是讓我們的生活更有意思嗎？

a. ____   b. ____   c. ____   d. ____   e. ____

f. ____   g. ____   h. ____   i. ____   j. ____

English:

```
┌─────────────────────────────────────────────────────────────┐
│                                                             │
│                                                             │
│                                                             │
│                                                             │
│                                                             │
│                                                             │
│                                                             │
│                                                             │
│                                                             │
│                                                             │
└─────────────────────────────────────────────────────────────┘
```

11. Reading for the main ideas I

The following paragraph contains a few characters that we have not yet learned, but you should be able to "read around them" and understand the main points of the passage. Read the paragraph for the main ideas, and then respond to the requests and questions that follow in English.

> 其實要了解一個國家的文化，最好的辦法就是去學習那個國家的語言。首先，人們每天不管做甚麼都要用語言。人們的想法、說法、和做法都是通過語言來表示的。其次，語言在變化。新的東西、新的想法會有新的詞匯來表示。最後，語言有很久很久的歷史。人們的傳統和習慣都可從語言中找到。通過學習語言來學習文化再好不過了。

a. State the main topic of this paragraph in English in one word.

b. The author says that you can use the topic for some purpose. What is the purpose?

c. Give an example of some specific thing that you can understand by means of this topic.

12. Reading for the main ideas II

This speech includes a few characters that you have not yet learned, but you should be able to "read around them" and understand its overall meaning. Read the speech, and then respond to the questions that follow in English.

> 同學們，你們好，
>
> 你們兩年的在中國留學的生活就要結束了。回過頭來看看，你們在各方面的進步都是非常大的。從一句中文不會說，到今天成了半個地道的北京人，你們不但學了中文，更重要的是了解了中國的文化和歷史，看到了中國今天的變化。學習語言不是一年兩年的事情，是一輩子的事情。你們的中文還會進步，中國在各方面也會進步。希望你們常回來看看。
>
> 再見

a. Who is the audience for this speech?

b. What does the speech let us know about the speaker? Where is the speaker from?

c. What does the speaker believe to be the primary thing that the audience has learned?

Focus on structure

1. **Prepositional phrase + verb phrase (Use and Structure notes 28.9, 31.3, 32.3, and elsewhere)**

In Mandarin, most prepositional phrases precede the verb phrase. Once you have mastered that rule, you still have to decide which preposition to use. Here are four prepositions that we have learned in this course. Complete each sentence by adding the appropriate preposition, and then translate your sentences into English.

給 *for, to*	**xiàng** *toward* (*direction, like* 往)	對 *to, toward*	為 *on behalf of*

a. 學生應該 ＿＿＿ 老師表 **shì** 感謝。
   English:

b. 我們 ＿＿＿ 中國的了解剛剛開始。
   English:

c. 我昨天晚上 ＿＿＿ 朋友打電話了。
   English:

d. 父母 ＿＿＿ 自己的孩子很 **jiāo'ào**。
   English:

e. 孩子出國的時候父母當然很 ＿＿＿ 他們 **dān** 心。
   English:

f. 我常常請她 ＿＿＿ 我們講 **gù** 事。
   English:

g. 他說他 ＿＿＿ 圖書館走。
   English:

h. 老師 ＿＿＿ 我們介紹中國的情 **kuàng**。
   English:

i. 他們 ＿＿＿ 經濟有興趣。
   English:

j. 你不要 ＿＿＿ 考試那麼緊張。
   English:

k. 我很感謝老師 ＿＿＿ 我們嚴 **gé** 要 **qiú**。
   English:

l. 他 ＿＿＿ 我們走過來了。
   English:

2. Translate into English

Translate these sentences from Mandarin into English. Be sure to identify the key structures and any noun description clauses as you prepare your translations.

a. 我父母讓我 **dài** 表他們來接你們。

b. 我認為，學習一種語言首先要學好發音，其次才是語法。如果別人聽不懂你在說甚麼，語法再好也沒有用。

c. 我最需要感謝的是我的中國同屋。他教會了我很多在課本上學不到的東西。

d. 我跟我的同屋，在學習上 **hù** 相幫助，在生活上 **hù** 相照顧。

e. 雖然小葉每次考試都考得很好，但是她從來都不為她的好成 **jì** 而 **jiāo'ào**。

f. "New words" 的中文意思是 "生 **cí**"。"**Cí**" 就是 "**cíhuì**" 的意思。"生" 是 "**mò** 生"，你不認識，不知道的。"生 **cí**" 早就有了，不是新的，只是你不認識。

3.   Translate into Mandarin

Translate these sentences into Mandarin, using the structure or phrase in parentheses.

a. We're just about to graduate and leave China. The thing I am most nervous about is that I have too many things and I won't be able to carry them away. (NP 多)

b. I just arrived in Taipei a few days ago. I am a stranger to all the places and things. (對 NP 很 **mò** 生)

c. Nowadays everyone uses email. Who is going to spend a lot of money making a long-distance phone call? (打 … 電話)

d. When it comes to respecting one's teachers, American students and Chinese students are very different. This is a difference in culture. (在 … 上)

e. These last two years they have given a lot of help and guidance. (NP₁ 和 NP₂)

1.   Dialogue comprehension

Study the Lesson 32 Narrative and Dialogue. Then, read the following statements and indicate whether they are true (T) or false (F).

a. ( ) 大為被選為留學生的 **dài** 表在畢業 **diǎn** 禮上講話，因為別人都不好意思去。

b. ( ) 大為覺得兩年的時間過得太快了。

c. ( ) 大為和他的同學請老師們吃飯，表 **shì** 他們 **zhōng** 心的感謝。

d. ( ) 大為的中文老師們不但教中文，而且還照顧學生的生活。

e. ( ) 大為會用中文討價還價，都是老師教他的。

f. ( ) 大為的中國朋友和同屋帶他們去 **guàng** 北京的地鐵和酒吧。

g. ( ) 這幾天很多畢業留學生的父母都到中國來了。

h. ( ) 大為認為，通過他們這些在中國學習的留學生，他們的家人也更了解中國。

i. ( ) 大為認為，畢業以後，他們就跟中國沒有關係了。

2.   What do you say?

What do you say in each of the following situations? Type your answers, using characters where we have learned them, and email them to your Chinese teacher.

a. You are writing to your Chinese teacher. Tell her time flies and you didn't realize it's been five years since you graduated.

b. You are an elementary-school principal. On behalf of the teachers and students (師生), thank a company that donated (送) computers to your school.

c. Tell your mom not to worry. You won't go alone to an unfamiliar place at night.

d. You introduce your roommate to your parents. Tell them how your roommate takes care of you in your daily life and teaches you how to bargain in Chinese.

e. You are the valedictorian at your graduation. Finish your speech by telling everyone that graduation is a beginning as well as an ending. Wish everyone good luck and don't forget your dearest school and respected teachers.

f. Tell your parents to relax. Your new boss (老 **bǎn**) has high demands on you all but has taught you a lot. You think working with him *opens a lot of doors for you* (gives you a lot of good opportunities).

g. You are at a farewell party for your favorite and most respected supervisor at work. Thank him for teaching you so much and for taking care of you when you first started at the company. Tell him that you will never forget him (for your whole life).

h. You are at your little sister's school play. After the show, tell her you are proud of her.

3.   Proverbs, fixed expressions, and literary expressions

Match each expression with the appropriate context.

A. **bìng** 從口 **rù**	B. 四 **jì** 如春	C. 生 **mìng** 在於 運動	D. 行行出 **zhuàng** 元
E. 願者上 **gōu**	F. 嚴師出高 **tú**	G. 一言為定	H. 學會 **Pǔ** 通話，走 **biàn** 天下都不怕
I. 遠道而來	J. 年年有 **yú**	K. **gōng** 喜發 **cái**	L. **guāngyin sìjiàn**

a. 畢業以後你想做甚麼就做甚麼，我覺得，＿＿＿＿＿＿，大家不一定都要當 **yī** 生。最重要的是你對自己的工作有興趣，能做好。

b. 年夜飯裏頭一定會有一 **pán** 魚，表 **shì** ＿＿＿＿＿＿。

c. 這個地方 ＿＿＿＿＿＿，難怪甚麼時候都有很多人來這兒旅遊。

d. 常聽別人說，＿＿＿＿＿＿，所以你會說中文，去中國一定沒有問題。

e. A: 星期六比較好。我星期天有事，不方便。

   B: 那就 _____，我們下個星期六見吧。

f. 你就別生氣了。是你自己決定要買那件衣服的，_____，買回來以後發現衣服不 **héshì**，這不是服務員的錯。

g. 我早就告訴過你，吃飯以前一定要先洗手，你沒有聽過 _____ 嗎？

h. 我知道這個老師要 **qiú** 嚴、功課多、考試又特別難，但是 _____，你上他的課，一定能學到很多。

i. 過新年的時候大家看到朋友的時候，都會 **hù** 相說：_____。

j. _____，沒想到才幾年不見，同學們的 **biàn** 化都這麼大，有的有孩子了，有的留學回來了，有的自己有一個大公 **sī** 了。

k. 你們 _____，我當然要請你們吃飯，再帶你們到附近的名 **shèng gǔjì** 去走走。

l. _____，所以我從現在開始打算天天去健身房，好好 **duànliàn** 一下身體。

4. Formal speeches on various occasions

Based on the scenarios, fill in the blanks to complete these formal speeches.

a. Scenario: A brand new bookstore, 三文書店, is opening today. The owner welcomes all the customers to their new store.

   Qīn 愛的 _____，大家好。_____ 大家來三文書店...

b. Scenario: At a speech contest, a student, 方以家, begins his speech by greeting the teachers and students off stage.

   各位 _____，各位 _____，大家好。我 _____。今天我所要講的是：中國現 **dài** 經濟的 **biàn** 化。

c. Scenario: At a Chinese karaoke contest, the MC first welcomes all teachers, parents, and students on behalf of all of the students. Then he introduces the ten participants (people who participate in the contest) today.

   Qīn 愛的 _____、_____ 和 _____，你們好。_____，我 _____ 全體同學 _____ 你們來。現在讓我 _____

   _____。

d. Scenario: At the same Chinese karaoke contest, one participant, 葉友文, introduces herself and says that she is going to sing 月 **liàng** *(moon)* **dài** 表我的心. It is her favorite song. She sincerely hopes everyone will like it.

   _____

   _____

   _____

Culture note: "月 **liàng dài** 表我的心" 可能是中國流行音樂裏最有名的歌。如果你有興趣，可以去 YouTube 找一找。很多離開家 **xiāng** 的中國人特別喜歡這首歌。

e. Scenario: At a high-school graduation, the class valedictorian opens his speech by saying how time flies and their school life is coming to an end. He thanks the teachers on behalf of all of the graduates and begins his speech. Lastly, he wishes everyone a new start (no matter) whether they are going to attend college or begin work.

_____，沒想到四年的學校生活 _____。在這裏首先我

要 _____。...最後，我 **zhù** 各位

畢業生 _____，都有一個新的開始。

f. Scenario: At a high-school graduation, a teacher gives a farewell speech. She talks about how the first day of school seems like yesterday, and she can't believe they are leaving now. She wishes everyone good luck, hopes they stay interested in everything after they enter college, tells them to have confidence in themselves, and, most importantly, asks them not to forget their beloved school.

..._____ 好像是昨天的事，怎麼這麼快你們

_____? ...最後，**zhù** 你們 _____。希望你們上大學以

後，_____，更重要的

是，千萬 _____

_____。

g. Scenario: At an awards ceremony, the winner thanks his parents, saying "without them, I wouldn't be standing here today."

_____

_____

_____

5. Giving a speech

Read the speeches in Exercise 4 again. Pick two scenarios that you like the most, and write a speech of your own. Your speech should be at least 120 characters in length.

Scenario one: _____

Your speech: _____

_____

_____

_____

_____

_____

Scenario two: _____

Your speech: _____

_____

_____

_____

_____

6.   Farewell letter

Using the speech in Lesson 32 as your model, write a letter to either all your classmates or to your teacher, thanking them and telling them how they have impacted your life in the past few years. Use the following procedure as you prepare your letter.

Part I. Brainstorming

a. Select the audience for your letter, either your classmates (   ) or your teacher (   ).

b. Make a list of ways that they have impacted your life and the things they have done for you.

c. Rewrite your list, organizing it so that it states each item in the order in which you want to present it in your speech.

d. Outline your letter so that it includes three parts. Use the following words to introduce each part: 首先, 其次, 最後.

e. Think about how to introduce and connect the information in each part of the letter. Use words such as 另外 and 還有 to do this.

Part II. Write your letter.   The opening and closing are provided for you. Your letter should be at least 150 characters in length.

Qīn 愛的＿＿＿＿＿＿＿＿：

我們馬上就要畢業了。首先＿＿＿＿＿＿＿＿＿＿＿＿＿＿＿＿＿＿＿＿＿＿＿＿＿

＿＿

＿＿

＿＿

＿＿

＿＿

＿＿

＿＿

＿＿

＿＿

＿＿

＿＿＿＿＿＿＿＿＿＿＿＿＿＿＿＿＿

Zhù ＿＿＿＿＿＿＿＿＿＿＿

你的 ＿＿＿＿＿＿＿ (friend, student)

＿＿＿＿＿＿＿＿＿＿＿ (your name)

Audio track listing

CD 1: Lesson 17–Lesson 25

	Lesson 17	
Track 1	L 17 Narrative	0:56
Track 2	L 17 Dialogue parts A & B	0:53
Track 3	L 17 Listening for information 1	0:36
Track 4	L 17 Listening for information 2	0:17
Track 5	L 17 Listening for information 3	0:30
Track 6	L 17 Listening for information 4	0:31
Track 7	L 17 Listening for information 5	0:22
Track 8	L 17 Listening for information 6: Narrative & questions	1:22
Track 9	L 17 Listening for information 7	0:29
Track 10	L 17 Listening for information 8	0:21
	Lesson 18	
Track 11	L 18 Narrative	0:51
Track 12	L 18 Dialogue parts A & B	1:03
Track 13	L 18 Listening for information 1	0:33
Track 14	L 18 Listening for information 2	0:31
Track 15	L 18 Listening for information 3	0:46
Track 16	L 18 Listening for information 4	0:39
Track 17	L 18 Listening for information 5	0:26
Track 18	L 18 Listening for information 6	0:46
Track 19	L 18 Listening for information 7: Narrative & questions	1:24
Track 20	L 18 Listening for information 8	0:58
Track 21	L 18 Listening for information 9	1:06
	Lesson 19	
Track 22	L 19 Narrative & dialogue part A	0:48
Track 23	L 19 Dialogue parts B & C	0:47
Track 24	L 19 Listening for information 1	0:25
Track 25	L 19 Listening for information 2	0:34
Track 26	L 19 Listening for information 3	0:30

Track 27	L 19 Listening for information 4	0:26
Track 28	L 19 Listening for information 5	0:21
Track 29	L 19 Listening for information 6	0:29
Track 30	L 19 Listening for information 7: Narrative & questions	1:12
Track 31	L 19 Listening for information 8	0:47
Track 32	L 19 Listening for information 9	0:48
	Lesson 20	
Track 33	L 20 Narrative	0:38
Track 34	L 20 Dialogue part A	0:41
Track 35	L 20 Dialogue parts B & C	1:00
Track 36	L 20 Listening for information 1	0:26
Track 37	L 20 Listening for information 2	0:39
Track 38	L 20 Listening for information 3: Narrative & questions	1:15
Track 39	L 20 Listening for information 4	1:42
Track 40	L 20 Listening for information 5	0:34
Track 41	L 20 Listening for information 6: Narrative & questions	0:58
Track 42	L 20 Listening for information 7	0:42
Track 43	L 20 Listening for information 8	0:35
	Lesson 21	
Track 44	L 21 Narrative	0:37
Track 45	L 21 Dialogue part A	0:44
Track 46	L 21 Dialogue parts B & C	1:23
Track 47	L 21 Listening for information 1	0:42
Track 48	L 21 Listening for information 2	0:31
Track 49	L 21 Listening for information 3: Narrative & questions	1:01
Track 50	L 21 Listening for information 4	0:28
Track 51	L 21 Listening for information 5	0:46
Track 52	L 21 Listening for information 6	0:38
Track 53	L 21 Listening for information 7.1	0:38
Track 54	L 21 Listening for information 7.2	0:35
Track 55	L 21 Listening for information 8	1:39
	Lesson 22	
Track 56	L 22 Narrative	0:46
Track 57	L 22 Dialogue parts A & B	0:55
Track 58	L 22 Listening for information 1	0:44
Track 59	L 22 Listening for information 2	1:21
Track 60	L 22 Listening for information 3	0:25
Track 61	L 22 Listening for information 4	0:50
Track 62	L 22 Listening for information 5	0:21

Track 63	L 22 Listening for information 6	0:28
Track 64	L 22 Listening for information 7	0:39
Track 65	L 22 Listening for information 8	1:04
Track 66	L 22 Listening for information 9	1:35
	Lesson 23	
Track 67	L 23 Narrative	0:37
Track 68	L 23 Dialogue parts A & B	1:47
Track 69	L 23 Listening for information 1	0:28
Track 70	L 23 Listening for information 2	0:52
Track 71	L 23 Listening for information 3	0:22
Track 72	L 23 Listening for information 4	0:32
Track 73	L 23 Listening for information 5	0:25
Track 74	L 23 Listening for information 6	0:59
Track 75	L 23 Listening for information 7	0:36
Track 76	L 23 Listening for information 8	0:46
Track 77	L 23 Listening for information 9	1:03
	Lesson 24	
Track 78	L 24 Narrative	0:37
Track 79	L 24 Dialogue parts A & B	1:09
Track 80	L 24 Dialogue parts C & D	1:15
Track 81	L 24 Listening for information 1	0:33
Track 82	L 24 Listening for information 2	0:13
Track 83	L 24 Listening for information 3	0:35
Track 84	L 24 Listening for information 4	0:25
Track 85	L 24 Listening for information 5	0:44
Track 86	L 24 Listening for information 6	0:53
Track 87	L 24 Listening for information 7	0:29
Track 88	L 24 Listening for information 8	0:59
Track 89	L 24 Listening for information 9	1:03
	Lesson 25	
Track 90	L 25 Narrative	1:35
Track 91	L 25 Dialogue parts A & B	2:03
Track 92	L 25 Listening for information 1	0:34
Track 93	L 25 Listening for information 2	0:26
Track 94	L 25 Listening for information 3	0:12
Track 95	L 25 Listening for information 4	0:32
Track 96	L 25 Listening for information 5	0:29
Track 97	L 25 Listening for information 6	0:41
Track 98	L 25 Listening for information 7	0:57

CD 2: Lesson 25 (continued) – Lesson 32

	Lesson 25 (continued)	
Track 1	L 25 Listening for information 8	1:31
	Lesson 26	
Track 2	L 26 Narrative	1:35
Track 3	L 26 Dialogue part A	1:05
Track 4	L 26 Dialogue part B	0:34
Track 5	L 26 Listening for information 1	0:26
Track 6	L 26 Listening for information 2	0:26
Track 7	L 26 Listening for information 3	0:37
Track 8	L 26 Listening for information 4	0:28
Track 9	L 26 Listening for information 5	0:17
Track 10	L 26 Listening for information 6: Narrative	0:34
Track 11	L 26 Listening for information 6: Questions	0:18
Track 12	L 26 Listening for information 7	0:17
Track 13	L 26 Listening for information 8	0:43
Track 14	L 26 Listening for information 9	1:05
	Lesson 27	0:18
Track 15	L 27 Narrative	1:35
Track 16	L 27 Dialogue part A	0:37
Track 17	L 27 Dialogue part B	2:03
Track 18	L 27 Listening for information 1	0:26
Track 19	L 27 Listening for information 2	0:31
Track 20	L 27 Listening for information 3: Narrative	0:52
Track 21	L 27 Listening for information 3: Questions	0:12
Track 22	L 27 Listening for information 4: Recipe	0:35
Track 23	L 27 Listening for information 4: Questions	0:24
Track 24	L 27 Listening for information 5	0:44
Track 25	L 27 Listening for information 6	0:31
Track 26	L 27 Listening for information 7: Narrative	0:34
Track 27	L 27 Listening for information 7: Questions	0:22
Track 28	L 27 Listening for information 8	0:42
Track 29	L 27 Listening for information 9	0:50
Track 30	L 27 Listening for information 10	1:06
	Lesson 28	
Track 31	L 28 Narrative	0:50
Track 32	L 28 Dialogue parts A & B	1:23
Track 33	L 28 Dialogue part C	1:21

Track 34	L 28 Listening for information 1	0:32
Track 35	L 28 Listening for information 2	0:34
Track 36	L 28 Listening for information 3	0:49
Track 37	L 28 Listening for information 4	0:29
Track 38	L 28 Listening for information 5	0:49
Track 39	L 28 Listening for information 6: Announcement	0:38
Track 40	L 28 Listening for information 6: Questions	0:24
Track 41	L 28 Listening for information 7: Narrative	0:41
Track 42	L 28 Listening for information 7: Questions	0:27
Track 43	L 28 Listening for information 8	0:39
Track 44	L 28 Listening for information 9: Announcement	0:55
Track 45	L 28 Listening for information 9: Questions	0:30
Track 46	L 28 Listening for information 10	0:38
	Lesson 29	
Track 47	L 29 Narrative	0:53
Track 48	L 29 Dialogue parts A & B	1:19
Track 49	L 29 Dialogue part C	1:13
Track 50	L 29 Dialogue parts D & E	0:56
Track 51	L 29 Listening for information 1	0:25
Track 52	L 29 Listening for information 2	0:23
Track 53	L 29 Listening for information 3	0:24
Track 54	L 29 Listening for information 4: Narrative	0:37
Track 55	L 29 Listening for information 4: Questions	0:24
Track 56	L 29 Listening for information 5	0:18
Track 57	L 29 Listening for information 6	0:31
Track 58	L 29 Listening for information 7	0:31
Track 59	L 29 Listening for information 8	0:39
Track 60	L 29 Listening for information 9	0:53
Track 61	L 29 Listening for information 10	0:50
	Lesson 30	
Track 62	L 30 Narrative	1:26
Track 63	L 30 Dialogue parts A & B	1:37
Track 64	L 30 Dialogue parts C & D	1:19
Track 65	L 30 Listening for information 1	0:43
Track 66	L 30 Listening for information 2	0:43
Track 67	L 30 Listening for information 3: Conversation	0:47
Track 68	L 30 Listening for information 3: Questions	0:24
Track 69	L 30 Listening for information 4.1	0:13
Track 70	L 30 Listening for information 4.2	0:16

Track 71	L 30 Listening for information 4.3	0:19
Track 72	L 30 Listening for information 5	0:23
Track 73	L 30 Listening for information 6	0:36
Track 74	L 30 Listening for information 7	0:46
Track 75	L 30 Listening for information 8	0:49
Track 76	L 30 Listening for information 9	0:57
	Lesson 31	
Track 77	L 31 Narrative	1:01
Track 78	L 31 Dialogue parts A & B	1:45
Track 79	L 31 Listening for information 1	0:56
Track 80	L 31 Listening for information 2	0:48
Track 81	L 31 Listening for information 3	0:34
Track 82	L 31 Listening for information 4	0:40
Track 83	L 31 Listening for information 5	0:58
Track 84	L 31 Listening for information 6	0:30
Track 85	L 31 Listening for information 7: Interview	0:50
Track 86	L 31 Listening for information 7: Questions	0:23
Track 87	L 31 Listening for information 8	1:06
Track 88	L 31 Listening for information 9	1:14
	Lesson 32	
Track 89	L 32 Narrative	0:36
Track 90	L 32 The speech	1:35
Track 91	L 32 Listening for information 1: Speech A	0:25
Track 92	L 32 Listening for information 1: Speech B	0:20
Track 93	L 32 Listening for information 2: Narrative	0:37
Track 94	L 32 Listening for information 2: Questions	0:28
Track 95	L 32 Listening for information 3	0:45
Track 96	L 32 Listening for information 4	0:49
Track 97	L 32 Listening for information 5	0:33
Track 98	L 32 Listening for information 6	1:11
Track 99	L 32 Listening for information 7	1:26